Spirit Journeys

Blessings
Marcia & Steve

*Step into the world of restless souls
who walk this earth in search of completion.
Meet wandering spirits
of the comatose and terminally ill
who wrestle with decisions about life and death.
Discover why some people seem to attract ghosts,
how to help loved ones move peacefully
beyond this physical plane,
and what you can do today to help yourself
experience more insight, joy, and peace.*

*Spirit Journeys brings you an opportunity
to learn about healing, within this life and beyond,
through the firsthand accounts of earthbound spirits
who courageously share their personal stories.
Their lessons and ours intermingle
as we journey together,
learning from one another
about the power of forgiveness,
the freedom to love,
and our enduring connection with Spirit.*

SPIRIT JOURNEYS

Freeing the Soul in this Life and Beyond

Steven Rogat & Marcia Rogat

CREATIVE THOUGHT PRESS
Chapel Hill, North Carolina
USA

Spirit Journeys: Freeing the Soul in this Life and Beyond
© 2002 Marcia L. Rogat and Steven E. Rogat

All rights reserved. No part of this book may be reproduced or used in any form or by any means—graphic, electronic, or mechanical, including photocopying, mimeographing, taping, or information storage and retrieval systems—without express permission from the author, except by a reviewer who wishes to quote brief passages related to a review written for inclusion in a magazine, newspaper, journal, or other broadcast. See "About the Authors" at the end of the text to contact the authors for more information.

Printed in the United States of America.

First printing, 2002
Creative Thought Press
P.O. Box 2791, Chapel Hill, NC 27515, USA

Cover design by Nick Zelinger
NZ Graphics, 1445 S. Quail Ct., Lakewood, CO 80232, USA
znick4@qwest.net

Book design and composition by Lorraine B. Elder
MetroGnome, Inc., 2400 Trinity Farms Rd., Raleigh, NC 27607, USA
www.metrognome.com

Special thanks to

Aysha Griffin
Editorial Consultant, Sante Fe, NM
aysha@cybermesa.com, www.constructivechanges.com

Genece Hamby, Blue Sage Group, 1524 Kudrow Lane, Morrisville, NC 27650, USA
www.bluesagegroup.com, www.genecehamby.com

Library of Congress Preassigned Card Number: 2002-091263
ISBN: 0-9672206-2-9

*This book is dedicated to
our ancestors.
May they walk in beauty.*

Contents

	Introduction	1
PART I	**Awakening to Spirit**	**5**
	1. Spirit Is Everywhere	6
	2. Steve's Story	11
	3. Spirit Channeling	15
PART II	**House Ghosts**	**19**
	4. Preparing the Way	20
	The Lost Hunter	*20*
	5. Clarifying the Intent	25
	Taking In Strays	*25*
	Just Trying to Help	*33*
	6. Holding On	38
	The Imperial Hotel	*38*
	"Unethical Research"	*39*
	A Big Production	*41*
	7. Letting Go	43
	A Sheep in Wolf's Clothing	*44*

Gold Fever	49
A Case of Mistaken Identity	62
8. Honoring Choices	**73**
The Gardener	73
The Ghost Nanny	78
9. Lasting Impressions	**87**
The Wedding Gown	89
10. Moving Forward	**95**
Soldiers Looking for a Fight	95
Just Following Orders	102
Divination in the Dormitory	109
Loyal Pets	114
Is My Husband Missing or Dead?	116

Part III Communication with the Living and the Dying — 121

11. The Dream Body	**122**
The Angry Husband	122
The Rejected Healer	133
12. Fond Farewells	**138**
Al and Edna	139
A Shared Journey	142
Goodbye, Aunt Joyce	144
13. Choosing a Direction	**149**
Sleeping Beauty	149
What's Your Decision, Joseph?	156

Part IV Personal Ghosts 163

14. Getting Involved 164
Where's the Party? 168
The Overprotective Husband 175

15. Empower Yourself 184
The Family Curse 184
The Medicine Man's Hex 195

16. Family Patterns 205
Parent and Child 205
Unborn Child and Parent 215
Ancestors and Descendants 218

17. Boundaries 220
My Space Is My Own 222

Part V Journey's End 231

18. Completion 232
Maintaining Healthy Boundaries 233
Communication 234
Forgiveness of Self and Others 235
Let Go and Let God 236

19. Together in Spirit 238

Appendices 241

A. An Overview: Elements of Completion 242
House Ghosts 242
Personal Ghosts 244
The Dying 245

B.	The Healer and Client in Trance	246
	The Healer in Trance	*246*
	The Client in Trance	*246*
	Approaches to Trance	*247*
C.	Guidelines for Clearings	248
D.	Questions and Answers	250
	About the Authors	254

Introduction

This book is about life. It is about you and me and our connection with one another. It speaks of our individual pathways toward awareness and our collective yearning to recognize and celebrate our spiritual nature. And most profoundly, it is about the healing of souls who, through their own experiences, teach us how to move through life and death with trust, reassurance, and faith.

For twenty years, now, I have participated in ghost clearings with my husband, Steven. We have been called to homes, schools, ancient battlegrounds, new office buildings, and rugged forests. I soon learned that the legendary "haunted" house with creaking floors and flickering candles was not the only home to earthbound souls. These spirits could be around us just about anywhere, anytime. Neither did a ghost's appearance coincide with a person's belief in their existence. People of varying philosophies—skeptics, priests, scientists, and scholars—often did their best to explain paranormal activity in just about any other way before they reluctantly admitted that there might be a ghost in their midst.

I also discovered that every ghost has a story. Upon learning how to observe, listen to, and make contact with earthbound souls, I realized that each one had something to share. Their interactions with people, choice of locations, and level of energy were directly related to strong feelings that dominated their perceptions and intent. As their stories unfolded, so did their emotional turmoil and confusion. Allowing compassion to overcome my fear, I joined Steven on a path meant to help these troubled souls, a path that, in turn, yielded unexpected insights and profound healing in our own life.

Recognizing that we have been blessed by our work with earthbound souls, Steven and I decided to write a book that would share many of the lessons about hope, forgiveness, communication, and love. We began by recalling our conversations with ghosts, writing down the words, images, and feelings to the best of our memory. We then realized how intertwined their stories were with the people surrounding them, making it important to include the background and personality of the people experiencing the ghostly activity.

Next, we wanted readers to have some clear direction about how to apply lessons and insights from these stories to their own lives. We have all experienced the frustration of knowing what to do but not knowing how to do it! Thus, we outlined steps showing how everyone can, if they so choose, pursue paths that help themselves and others move through life and death with a quieter mind and a more peaceful heart.

Finally, we wanted this book to give comprehensive directions to those of you who may feel called upon to guide earthbound souls toward a more restful place in Spirit. To help you communicate with ghosts and participate in their healing, we have included specific techniques within the stories, plus appendices at the end of the book, offering complete and concise steps for practitioners. At the end of many sections you will also find a list of "Points to Remember," designed to condense the most important information for quick reference.

The result of our cumulative experiences is a book that brings you a joyous and uplifting affirmation of life! Whether we are helping loved ones make the transition beyond this physical realm, searching for peace with those who have already passed on, or seeking guidance along our own path in today's busy life, *Spirit Journeys* offers encouragement, support, and direction. With commitment and compassion, we can learn how to free ourselves and others to live and love more fully right now. It is never too late, nor too early, to celebrate our soul's journey toward more life!

This introduction would not be complete without some comment on the experience of writing a book with one's spouse, for that in itself was a journey into new territory for our relationship. Steven and I began working on the text separately, passing our finished pages back and forth for suggestions, comments, and additions. We were very gentle in our feedback to one another, wanting always to be encouraging and supportive. But as the pages grew in number and the revisions began flying at lightening speed, there was no more time for diplomacy! We reached a critical point about six weeks into the project where we mutually agreed not to take personally any feedback from the other about our writing, no matter how bluntly stated. We had to be willing to share, in total honesty, without apologies or excuses. We had to let go of underlying fears of being hurt or of hurting the other. We had to affirm our trust in each other, the strength of our relationship, and the certainty of our common goal.

What followed was pure magic. With our focus clearly set on creating the best possible results, carrying out that intent became greater than any need to protect our individual egos. The writing came more easily, the revisions came more smoothly, and the joint venture became more fun! ("Yuck," "That sucks!", and "Start over!" really can be expressed with love and laughter!) Today, as Steven and I look over the finished work, neither of us can remember exactly who wrote what; the book truly became an independent creation with a life of its own, belonging to neither of us, yet conceived by both. It has been a process we look forward to continuing throughout our future writing endeavors.

A final word of thanks is due to all who have ever participated with us in ghost clearings. While Steven is a clairvoyant and trance medium, able to share with others the voices and feelings of the spirit world, everyone else present plays a subtler but equally important role. They bring to the group their personal energy, their faith in Spirit, and their absolute trust in the healing process. My heartfelt appreciation goes to all those friends, students, and clients who contributed their support to the healing outcome of each story presented. And now you, too, bring yourself into this circle of healing as we all participate in the experience of community and the joy of awareness. I welcome you and send you blessings on your journey.

Marcia Rogat

Part I

Awakening to Spirit

Chapter 1

Spirit Is Everywhere

"What were you doing, Emily?" we ask our three-year-old after witnessing a strange sidestepping dance she has just done on the stairs. We follow the gaze of her bright, innocent eyes as she looks back at the empty staircase. "I had to step around that man. He wouldn't move."

She runs off to play before we even have a chance to ask, "What man? What did he look like?"

A distraught woman comes for counseling. "My mother has been in a coma for two months now. She's been terminally ill for such a long time, and it's just so hard to watch her like this. They said she'd pass on weeks ago. Sometimes I feel her spirit around me. I know she's not in her body but, then, where is she? I wish I could do something to help her."

"Every time I go into the living room, I feel like I'm being watched by someone or something," a friend confides. "I can't even relax in my own house anymore! Am I crazy?"

The young college coed laughs nervously, her voice shaky at the other end of the telephone line. "The other day I felt my boyfriend playfully tugging on my hair while I sat at the kitchen table studying. But, when I said something and turned around, the room was empty! It was really spooky!"

"I awoke in the middle of the night and stared at the foot of my bed." The middle-aged businessman cleared his throat and continued, "I could swear I saw my father. He passed on a year ago, but there he was, just standing there, trying to say something...."

Spirits. Wandering the earth, they visit with us, interact with us, and sometimes create turmoil around us. Who are they, and what are they doing here? Are we at the mercy of their whims, or can we do something useful to help both them and ourselves? Throughout these pages we endeavor to share with you a journey of our own experience into their world, giving you the opportunity to meet earthbound souls who have honored us with their teaching and their trust. In our work over the past twenty years, we have witnessed great healing, been blessed by surprising insights, and been touched by the power of infinite love. By sharing these stories, we hope that you, too, may better understand the world of spirit.

Encountering the many and varied personalities in this book, you will discover that individual souls have much to teach us as they labor to complete their earthly concerns. Regardless of characteristics that distinguish them—race, religion, gender, ethnicity, or personal beliefs about life and death—each soul's journey leads to a similar conclusion as they free themselves to move from life on earth to life beyond earth. In telling these stories of helping the terminally ill, the comatose, the living, and the dead, we hope to open your eyes and heart to the many different pathways that let us move through life with joy and awareness. You will feel the love these souls learn to give themselves and others before, during, and after death. You will feel the strength of forgiveness and the discovery of faith as they go on toward more life.

Although most of the souls introduced in this book have captured our attention during or after their death, the powerful insights they offer are meant to help us throughout life. At birth we step into the tangible dimensions of time and space, where learning is ever present. Our interactions with other people, our surroundings, our body, and our emotions all provide the opportunity to release our fears and open ourselves to greater awareness. We then have the potential to pass through life—and death—more conscious of our enduring connection to Spirit.

By reaching a level of completion with others, with ourselves, and with our bodies throughout our lifetime, we are not only more at peace on a daily basis, but we are more easily able to release the physical realm when it is time to go. The souls we've encountered in the spirit world have helped us gain an understanding of what this "completion" means. Details of their stories differ greatly, but they share a common theme of universal love available to every one of us. Learning to love and appreciate ourselves in the present, we find the safety to explore anything left incomplete from the past. With intent and forgiveness, past interactions can then be reviewed and completed. In a loving state of completion with past and present, we can leap with trust and confidence into the future. When our love is stronger than our fear, we are free to pass through life and death more fully, lovingly, and completely.

To maintain a state of peaceful completion with past and present is one of life's greatest challenges. Strong feelings—such as anger, guilt, desperation, or grief—can become a central focus, blocking all perceptions of anything beyond our immediate distress. These emotions signal a state of incompleteness. Unresolved conflicts, unfinished business, or uncommunicated thoughts and feelings have a way of tugging at our attention, narrowing our field of vision.

A person's body may die and physical existence may cease, but one's spirit may still feel incomplete with affairs on the earth plane. Pulled by strong emotions, such a soul tends to hold on to its embodied past. Concentrating on what is yet undone, he or she hovers near the physical plane seeking resolution. This soul may become an earthbound spirit, unable to discern a path to free itself from the physical realm.

The same possibility holds true for the soul who is approaching death without awareness and completion. The individual spirit may find itself disoriented, stuck, unsure whether to hold on to earthly existence or to pass on to Spirit. This could be the terminally ill grandparent who phases in and out of consciousness for weeks, or the patient in a coma who neither reawakens nor dies. Straddling the line between separate worlds of life and death, confused about how to complete earthly concerns, the soul may hover for days, weeks, or years in its uncertainty.

It is in such a state of incompletion that skillful, loving intervention may assist these souls in moving toward completion in the healing Light of Spirit.

Two distinct types of earthbound spirits have emerged in our work: *house ghosts* and *personal ghosts*. A house ghost may merely be lost, or may busily be trying to put together the pieces that will allow it to feel complete. These souls, who die in a state of incompletion, linger in or near the physical location where their life ended, where there is a personal connection, or where they think they need to finish some business. You may meet such a spirit one day as the ghost in your attic... or on your stairs. Other entities, known as personal ghosts, are not tied strongly to a specific locale but, instead, to the energy of a living person. Leaving the attic and attaching themselves to individuals, these earthbound spirits try to play out the drama of incompletion with their host. Driven by a desire for awareness and love, they strive to feel complete in one form or another. The unique circumstances leading to these personal attachments are as diverse as the people involved. You will meet both personal ghosts and house ghosts within these pages, and you will discover how they were finally able to address their concerns, attain a desired state of completion, and rest in peace.

Living our lives day-to-day in a state of completion is an ongoing process. Every moment of life brings unanticipated experiences, feelings, and interactions. How we respond to them and what we do with them is up to us. We can consciously choose to become more aware, to act more lovingly on our feelings, and to accept help from others along the way. In this book we gladly share the insights offered in our work with earthbound spirits. Perhaps one of their stories will speak to you. Perhaps you will be inspired with the courage and the willingness to forgive and love yourself and others more. Perhaps you will become one who reaches into the mists to help earthbound souls experience the gift of completion.

In reading this text, some of you may wonder whether or not you have a ghost around you. Many people, at various intervals throughout life, do have spirits around them for short periods of time. This is a result of our natural connection with one another. Yet relatively few people attract ghosts for an extended period in which the ghosts actually create problems in their daily lives. You may find that dreams, visions, and deeper awareness surface during your reading, calling your attention to personal issues or past emotional upsets that may still be "haunting" you. But this does not mean you have attracted a ghost. Instead, it means you are more consciously creating an opportunity to heal.

Should you experience an increased sensitivity to unresolved issues affecting your life, we encourage you to approach these new insights with openness and faith. Knowing that you are surrounded by Love and Light, you can affirm your safety and your trust in Spirit. You can lovingly accept, complete, and release that which comes to your attention during your own journey on this Earth.

Most of the spirit journeys recounted in this book are told from the perspective of those who are either preparing to leave or have already left their body. They share the confusion and sadness, the love and joy, and the lessons involved along the way. Much of the information received from these souls was obtained while in trance, an altered state of consciousness allowing us to communicate outside the physical realm. The conversations are recorded to the best of our memory with the intention of preserving both the process of helping and the dawning of awareness. Names and places have been changed to protect the privacy of those people who wish to remain anonymous, and artistic license has been taken to put some of the stories into a more comprehensible framework. The souls involved, however, have spoken for themselves. Following is our story… and theirs.

Chapter 2

Steve's Story

My brother, sister, and I are playing in the yard. Mom is in the house. It's confusing because she's home early, but I shrug it off. After all, I'm just a kid, only eight years old. Playing is more important than worrying about her schedule.

A car pulls up. Our Rabbi gets out and calls to us. "I need to talk with you kids," he says solemnly. "Larry, Steven, Arline, let's go in."

Rabbi Silverstein and the three of us are all seated around the kitchen table. It's hard to focus on his words. He's talking about *something*, but I'm distracted by Mom. She's sitting in the bedroom crying.

"Steve." It's the Rabbi's voice again. "This is important. As I was saying, your Dad got sick today…."

Sick? The look on my face says it all—confusion, wonder, questioning.

"He got very sick. He won't be getting better. And, I'm sorry to say, he won't be coming back home. I'm sure he would want to, but he can't…."

Sick? Not coming home? I've been sick lots of times. I've been hurt lots of times, but I always get better. I get sick at school, and I come home. I get sick at home, and I stay home. Of course he's coming home. The Rabbi must not know what he's talking about. Daddy always comes home.

Larry and Arline start crying and, leaving the table, run in to see Mom. I look at the Rabbi, my mind still swimming with questions. *Of course he'll be home. What's everyone crying about?*

He misinterprets my silence as shock. "It's all right to be sad, Steve. It's okay to cry. Your Mom needs you now." *All right to be sad? About what?*

As I run into the bedroom, my confusion, insecurity, and uncertainty escalate. I start to cry. After all, everyone else is. Between tears, Mom is saying things, looking at my brother and me. "I'll need your help a lot for awhile. We're alone now. You're the men of the family now."

It wasn't until some weeks later that I thought maybe the Rabbi was right, that Dad wouldn't be coming home. "That's what death is," I was told. "You go away and don't come back." But as a kid, there's always hope.

I didn't really feel close to my dad. I loved him, of course, but I knew I wasn't his favorite child. And even though I never seemed to meet his expectations, I still wanted him back. If he came back, everyone wouldn't be so sad. Things would be like they used to be. Grandma wouldn't have to live with us. She and Mom would stop arguing and yelling at each other.

Before Dad left, we were going to get a new car. He had also promised us a boat. I wanted him back badly. Now we couldn't afford to keep living in the house we grew up in. We had to say goodbye to close friends, to being comfortable, to feeling secure. Dad would fix everything, if only he'd come home.

I don't remember truly grieving over my dad's passing until many years later, at the age of twenty-four. My relationships were shaky, my living situation was always in transition, and monetary stability was just a dream. On top of that, I was continuously sick or injured. Putting it bluntly, my life was falling apart. I thought I was dying. No matter what I did, whom I was with, or where I went, it just didn't work. It wouldn't work.

Psychotherapy wasn't helping very much, and meditation was only a temporary oasis. Feeling desperate, I sought out a Trance Channel and Spiritual Healer. Joining a group of other people in his healing class was, to me, a last resort. I didn't wish to struggle my way through life anymore. Something had to change. Something was missing. I didn't know what it was, but I needed it back.

Lying in the center of the healing circle during class one night, I open myself up. I surrender and become receptive to whatever Spirit has in store for me, to whatever healing the group can offer.

The teacher, Myron, is at my head. There are students all around me, some gently touching my legs, my arms, a few sitting to the side just watching, one gently holding her hand over my heart.

"I'm picking up a man," one person says.

"Yes, me too," another student chimes in.

"Sadness, loss, anger."

"Who is the man, Steve?" That's Myron, keeping things on track. "Who is he, Steve?"

"My father." Sadness starts washing over me. I'm lying on the floor, yet I feel like I'm falling down a big hole, disoriented, at a loss to describe the deluge of feelings.

"Where is he now, Steve?"

Before I can even think of an answer, I blurt out, "Here. He's right here." There's a cloud hanging over me, a weight pressing me down. I can't breathe. I can't move. I see Dad. He's with me. He's always been with me.

"Yes, we see him," another student replies.

"You're safe, Steve," Myron says reassuringly. "All of us here can keep you safe. We're doing the healing now, Steve. Just breathe, relax. Feel Spirit all around you." The weight starts to lift. I can breathe again. I see him. *Dad! Why did you wait so long to let me see you?* For the first time since his death I cry for his passing. *Why did you leave us? It was hard, real hard.*

"I see a woman, too," Betty says softly, so as not to disturb me too much.

Between tears, I manage a few words. "That's my mom. I left her a year ago to move out here. My sister can't really take care of her. My brother won't. And I don't want to, either." *Dad, even now I wish you would go back home, so I could finally leave, so I could feel good about having my own life. So YOU could take care of Mom.*

The tears are in full force now.

From one person, "Steve, you have to let him go now. Steve, he's been dead a long time."

From Myron, "Your mom can take care of herself now. She's not your responsibility anymore." *Who's he talking to, my Dad or me? I guess it doesn't* matter. I sense my Dad's sadness. I feel his loss and know that, for his own reasons, he had to leave when he did. He couldn't come back. And all the wishing in the world today can't change the past.

The sadness starts to pass. I understand. *It's all right, Dad. I just have to have faith that other people can take care of themselves. They have their lessons, and I have mine.*

Jim, another student, adds his sentiment. "You don't have to feel guilty about living your own life, Steve. Explore, enjoy, live. It's what your mom sincerely wishes for you. It's what your dad wishes for you, too."

Then the teacher again. "It's time, Steve. It's time to let go of your dad. It's time to send him to the Light. Release him to the Light." I can feel it. The weight's been lifted. My body has a new sense of strength. Myron puts my thoughts into words, continuing to guide me. "I forgive you for leaving, Dad. I forgive myself for holding on to you all these years. I love you. I bless you. I release you. Mom will heal. So will Larry and Arline if they haven't already. Go to the Light, Dad. I can take it from here. Goodbye."

"Let's all push him to the Light," Myron directs the class. There's a moment of silence. A couple of people are crying. The rest are breathing deeply, praying, murmuring, blessing my dad and me. *He's apologizing for having to go, and he thanks me for understanding. He starts to grow smaller. He's drifting away, going into the Light, thanking and blessing me. He looks up and the Light shines on his face, getting brighter and brighter until there's nothing left but the Light.*

I open my eyes to a new world. It seems brighter. Everything seems clearer. I didn't notice it before, but there's a gentle breeze blowing on my face. Some of those present are looking at me with love. Some are looking up at the ceiling with eyes full of awe and wonder. The Light is just fading now. And it leaves behind it the fresh scent of lilac.

"No, it's rose," another person argues.

"Lilac."

"More like honeysuckle."

"I distinctly smell orange blossoms."

I smile as I squeeze the person's hand holding mine. "It's life. And it smells so sweet."

Chapter 3

Spirit Channeling

Having experienced tremendous healing by releasing a spirit I had been holding on to, I became interested in helping others the way I had been helped. I wanted others to experience what I had—the wonder of life… and of death, a healing of the soul. If we can touch Spirit, the all encompassing, loving divine force within our lives, we can open to other realities. We can see the great plans in store for all of us. We are all connected, in life, as in death. Love and forgiveness heal anything, everything. And I wanted to share it with others.

I wanted to reach out immediately and heal the world. Then reality gradually hit—time and training would be needed to develop the intuitive abilities necessary to do the work. I practiced being able to get impressions from a person's energy. Realizing I could not trust myself to perceive everything, I began to rely on Spirit to guide me. To feel the right path to take, to say the right words at the right time, to connect with the deepest part of a person's soul, I needed to rely on Guidance more.

Getting my mind out of the way so energy and information could come through as purely as possible, I started going into deeper and deeper trances while working with people. Sometimes I would do hands-on healing. Sometimes a consultation or psychic reading to focus on life lessons would offer quicker, easier, more loving ways of learning those lessons. Yet, always, I would remind myself to get out of the way and let Guidance through. I was learning to trust Spirit.

My first experience, in 1980, of truly going into a trance deeply enough to let Guidance speak through me was at a holistic fair. It was rather surprising and, at that time, I hadn't even considered becoming a trance medium. With a clear intent to be helpful in whatever way Spirit wished, though, I surrendered to the experience. There's a time for everything.

I was sitting with a client, talking. A chill, a tremendous energy, shot down my spine. "Hold on a minute," I said aloud. "One of your Guides wants to speak with you. I've never done this before, but here we go…"

I prayed, relaxed, and let go. Opening my mouth to speak, I realized it was not my voice speaking. It was that of the client's Spirit teacher speaking through me. The words weren't mine. The voice wasn't mine. I felt the differing energies, the distinct personality of another being within me. It was as if my own awareness stood to the side, witnessing the process.

The trance only lasted for a few minutes, but it upset me greatly. Even though it was a voluntary possession, it was a possession nonetheless. My physical body was being used by an outside entity. It shook me up, and I wasn't sure I wanted to relinquish that much control.

I continued to do healing and psychic work over the course of several months without another trance experience. But then came the day I found myself at a loss for words while working with a new client. I called on Guidance for additional help and fell abruptly into a deep trance, channeling words that were not mine. This time, I was even more upset. When it had only happened once, I could accept it as a fluke, an isolated, freak occurrence. However, with the second event, I realized that if I were to keep doing my work, the trances would probably become a part of that work. If I were truly willing to trust and surrender to Spirit, I would need to get past the limitations of my fear. To me, this was a major life change, and I sure wasn't ready to commit to it yet.

I took a sabbatical. I canceled classes, stopped taking clients, and moved to a cabin in the mountains. Shortly thereafter, I had a vivid dream-vision of channeling one of my guides to a group of people. I then made the commitment to willingly explore trance work. Months later, after arduous personal preparations that included cleansing diets and fasts, energy exercises, inner dialogue work, and meditation, I had a duplicate dream-vision. It was time for me to reenter the world.

I started a class. It was a small group with only six people, but it felt safe. The class was also free of charge since they were to be my guinea pigs. I made the commitment to do trance every week. This was the first time I would consciously plan to and choose to go into deep trance. I was nervous but determined to create the opening and leave the results up to Spirit. The first week was unsuccessful; I couldn't get my mind out of the way. The second attempt was slightly more fulfilling. A dead person—a ghost—who happened to be in the area, wanted to speak. Being committed to trance, I let him. It was fun. It was strange, but unfulfilling. After a few minutes we said our good-byes and he went on his way. I learned that I needed to raise my energies even higher. I needed to focus my intention more on the Higher Spirit realms in order to get past the lower realms containing earthbound spirits. I wanted to help and to heal, not entertain and amuse.

The third class was met with more success, bringing through a Spirit Teacher of one of the students. *"Now we're getting somewhere,"* I thought to myself. *"But I want to contact one of my own Guides, the one from my dream visions."* The following session brought him through. His name was Michael (not the Archangel, he assured me, because he didn't want it getting to my head). His energy felt clean, pure, and even familiar in some ways. I trusted him. He has, in one form or another, been with me to this day.

I share this story of my beginnings to let you know that the words and messages in my work with ghosts are not totally mine. With the intent of raising my energy and bringing Spirit through me, Michael, or another of my Guides, is an integral part of the healing. The conversations with people, be they students, clients or Earthbound Spirits, are a mixture of energies—Spirit's and mine.

To contact a soul on a level outside of everyday consciousness, I enter a trance state. Getting impressions, sometimes I respond to them from my knowledge base, speaking as "Steven." Yet, at other times, Spirit comes through. Some sessions have entailed channeling the ghost through me, allowing him or her to use my body to speak, while Marcia or one of my students counsels the spirit onward. However, many clearings involve the energy of myself and my Guides speaking to the entity directly, while the client or group participants support the work being done. I hold down all sides of the conversation, verbally, visually, and empathically, while sending the soul onward. Spirit connects all of us, and the threads of energy miraculously weave a pathway for communication and healing.

Part II

House Ghosts

Chapter 4

Preparing the Way

Creating a sacred space in which to work is an important first step when helping earthbound souls to gain awareness. We begin by choosing a time that is comfortable for everyone involved, include only those participants who have a clear intention of promoting healing in a loving way, and always ask Spirit to guide us in our endeavors. The following story illustrates how gently and easily a clearing can meet the needs of everyone present.

The Lost Hunter

We couldn't have asked for a more beautiful country setting, sharing an isolated mountain home with friends. The clear air and cold water streams were both healing and invigorating. One of our house mates, Peggy, especially loved the quiet solitude of mountain life. The rest of us would go off to work in town, and Peggy would have the large, two-story house to herself. She could dance, play music, and write poetry to her heart's content with nothing but the occasional interruption of a squirrel's chatter. One frosty October day, however, Peggy discovered that she wasn't entirely alone.

It was mid afternoon, and I was returning home early after running errands in the city. While I was walking from my car to the house, Peggy came running off the front porch toward me. She was breathing hard, her face pale. She was a strong, independent woman who was not given easily to fearful imagination, so I knew something must be wrong.

"There's somebody in there!" she said in a hoarse whisper. "I was in the dining room rearranging some books on the cinder block shelves we made last night. I had the music down low, and I thought I heard someone upstairs. I figured it was one of you guys home early, so no big deal. When I looked outside, though, nobody's car was here. Just my imagination, I thought. It was quiet for a while, and then I heard footsteps right over my head! I switched off the stereo just in time to hear an upstairs door slam shut!"

Gasping for breath, Peggy went on to tell me how she had heard the footsteps again, noticed the closet door's distinctive squeak, and decided to go upstairs to see who was home.

"I went up, and nobody was there!" Peggy explained. "I looked through both bedrooms and was just heading back downstairs when I heard the closet door squeak again. I poked my head into the bedroom just in time to see the door being drawn closed. Somebody's hiding up there, Steve!" Peggy was close to hysterical tears. I reached out to take hold of her shaking hands as we walked back to the porch together.

"Slow down, Peggy. We can handle this," I said with as much reassurance as I could muster. "I'll take a look around while you just wait outside."

"Be careful, Steve!"

"Thanks. I have a feeling I'll be fine. Just let me go take a look."

Already suspicious that this was no body of flesh and blood occupying our house, I took a deep breath and entered. After a thorough search of the downstairs, I went to the upper bedrooms. In the room with the squeaky closet door, the air suddenly felt denser, heavier. Tingles on the back of my neck and a brief waft of stale lavender confirmed my sense of a female spirit. I looked in the closet anyway, already knowing I would find no intruder there. But, I knew I was being watched. To the air around me I announced, "We'll talk later this evening."

That night, while our house mates were busy elsewhere, Peggy and I settled down for a serious chat with the mysterious woman. We would do our best to help her move on to the Light.

Sitting face to face, holding hands, Peggy and I close our eyes and I begin to pray. "Mother-Father God, Infinite Power of the Universe, White Light of the Lord, White Light of our Higher Self, White Light of the Christ, we ask that you join us here, that you watch over what we do so that it may be for the Highest Good. We ask that any Karma that be released be taken into the Light and transmuted for the Highest good. Any Divas, Angels, Masters of Light or Personal Guides who wish to join us, please do so to add your love, your guidance and your support. Thy will be done."

I feel the calm reassurance of the familiar words awakening my heart. I continue with the next step. "We ask that any spirits present please let yourself be known." We sit in silence for only a few seconds when a sense of restlessness fills the space around us. A billowy presence takes shape at the same time I hear the name "Martha" in my head. She steps forward, her eyes nervously scanning to the left and to the right. An elderly woman, she wipes her thin, wrinkled hands on her apron and then gathers her layered skirts to move from one side of the room to the other. It appears to be the late 1800s. *"It's okay, Martha,"* I think to her. *"We're here to help you. Thank you for coming and talking with us."*

"I can't stay long. My husband will be home soon. Jonathan never stays out this long. He went hunting several days ago, just like always. Only he hasn't come back yet. Maybe he got a little turned around. Sometimes he gets confused these days, but he'll find his way home. I know he will."

Martha wrings her hands, pacing. *"I need to look for him. I know I can find him. I'll just walk beyond the old well and circle around the neighbor's pasture. I'm sure he'll make it home for dinner. He never did like to miss a good supper! He promised he'd be back. He promised!"*

I see what Martha's been doing. Day after day she makes her rounds, circling the neighboring ranches looking for Jonathan. She comes to the creek and stops, thinking, "I'd best not stray too far; maybe Jonathan has returned while I was out." She changes directions and follows the creek home.

I begin to speak aloud so that Peggy can listen. If she knows what's happening, she can add her emotional support to the proceedings. "Martha, wait awhile, sit a spell. I need to talk with you." I let my voice and my heart carry calmness and fullness to her. "You're dead, Martha. You passed on a long time ago."

Aghast, she starts to panic. *"But what if Jonathan comes back?"*

"Martha, relax. Listen. Jonathan passed on a long time ago as well." I sense her confusion as she struggles to digest this new information. "Dear Lady, you're both dead, and have been for quite some time! Jonathan is waiting for you in the Light. Jonathan got lost. He couldn't find his way home, and he went to the Light. Your days of searching are over. You don't need to look for him here any longer. You don't need to wait for him to come home. He's waiting in the Light for you, Martha. Just look up."

I mentally and spiritually call on Jonathan to come greet her. "Look up, Martha. You see him in the Light, don't you?"

A sigh of relief. Tears of joy. *"Yes. Yes, I do."*

"Goodbye, Martha, safe journeys. Reach out. Take his hand. Go ahead. Go into the Light. Everyone is welcome in the Light.…"

A shudder goes through my body. Opening my eyes, I see Peggy crying as well. Tears of sadness for a lost and lonely woman, tears of joy for a woman's yearning fulfilled.

We lived in that house for months afterward with no further visitations from Martha. She had apparently found her way to a new "home."

This house clearing is one of the easiest I have ever done. It took just five minutes to communicate with Martha and send her on. Peggy and I were able to get Martha's attention by first establishing a safe space. With the privacy, the invocation to Spirit, and our clear intent of helping, Martha came forward without hesitation, readily sharing her preoccupation with finding Jonathan.

After gaining an understanding of her turmoil, I let Martha know that her physical body was dead. What a surprise to her! This is not unusual when dealing with earthbound spirits. There is a shift in energy when a person passes on, and Martha, absorbed in her need to find Jonathan, used all of her available energy to focus on the one incomplete event in her life that overshadowed all others. Upon her death, she held one thought foremost in her mind: *"I must search the property for Jonathan. But I'd better not stray too far from home in case he returns. He will expect me to be here.…"* Carrying this thought with her to the other side, she used no energy to look at herself, to notice the changes in the household around her, nor to turn toward God, Guidance, or Spirit. She imprisoned herself in a closed loop of time, replaying the same distressing scene over and over without any recognition of past, present, or future. The intensity of her thoughts and emotions rendered her unaware.

Once we had Martha's attention and could help her focus on the passage of time, the death of Jonathan and herself, and the availability of a reunion in Spirit, she was ready to go. Her sorrow melted away, quickly replaced by the expanded awareness of love. Her soul reawakened to a realization of life beyond her most recent earthly existence. She was set free.

Points to Remember…

- ✧ Creating a sacred space in which to work is the initial step in any clearing. Invoking Spirit raises the level of loving energy, focuses the intent, and assures protection of everyone present.

- ✧ All participants in a clearing form a circle and hold hands throughout the process. This collective energy insures unity of purpose, empowerment, and safety.

- ✧ Earthbound spirits often do not realize they are dead and may react with surprise or confusion when informed.

- ✧ Some ghosts may inhabit a general area or neighborhood while others confine themselves to a particular house.

Chapter 5

Clarifying the Intent

We make an effort to ensure that everyone involved in a ghost clearing has the same intention of helping the spirit onward. However, genuine thoughts and feelings don't always become evident, even to the participants themselves, until the process is underway. Additionally, people often underestimate the spiritual connection we have with each other, not realizing the power our unspoken thoughts carry when communicating with earthbound souls.

Taking In Strays

Alicia had become a recent acquaintance of ours, introduced through mutual friends. She was a naturally caring and intuitive woman who, for years, happily provided astrological readings and spiritual insight informally to friends. Now she was studying for her degree in counseling and looked forward to applying her skills more broadly in a professional setting.

Cassie, Alicia's fourteen-year-old daughter, was a vibrant bundle of energy and joy. Bright and articulate, her flaming red hair and ready smile instantly captivated others. Like many teens, Cassie was beginning her search for some deeper meaning and understanding of life. With Alicia's guidance, Cassie was eagerly learning to read Tarot cards, get in touch with internal guidance, use positive thought, and look at personal responsibility as she grew toward Spirit. Alicia and Cassie spent many pleasant hours together talking about astrology, numerology, miracles, and healing.

Visiting with us one afternoon in our kitchen, Alicia told Marcia and me that Cassie thought they might have a ghost. Calm and unalarmed, Alicia explained that she herself had only experienced vague feelings of being watched, or of a slight breeze brushing the back of her neck once in awhile. One night she did hear plates rattling around in a kitchen cupboard. Cassie, on the other hand, had apparently befriended the ghost. She told Alicia about feeling a shy male presence in her downstairs bedroom, sensing his loneliness, and wanting to be kind to him. Although she hadn't really seen him, she thought she could tell whether or not he liked the music she played.

"So I guess he's been around for several weeks, Steve, mostly downstairs in Cassie's room and sometimes in the hall or kitchen. I was fine with him being there; I figured he'd move on when he was ready. But now he's got to go!"

"What happened?" Marcia asked.

"He scared Cassie. She came racing up the stairs two at a time yesterday afternoon. She'd been sitting on her bed doing homework when, out of the corner of her eye, she saw him. He moved from the foot of her bed around to the side and poked her in the ribs! She was really freaked out!"

Alicia laughed as she went on to recount how Cassie nervously imagined that he could watch her shower, dress, undress, sleep… But behind the laughter there was real concern for her daughter's sense of privacy and personal space.

"It's time to get him out of there. I don't need an hysterical fourteen year old on my hands!"

"We'd be happy to come over and do a clearing," I suggested.

"Great! And is it okay if Cassie joins us? She wants to be a part of everything, and I think she's mature enough to take it seriously. I don't want to discourage her interest in learning about these things."

"That would actually be good," I responded. "Now that she's ready to get rid of him, she could be a big help." We agreed to meet at her house the next morning.

Surrounded by mature trees on a quiet neighborhood street, Alicia's renovated turn-of-the-century home felt welcoming from the moment we parked out front. Flowering plants graced the foyer, while an overstuffed sofa and banquet-sized dining table seemed to beckon visitors to stay for a while.

Chapter 5   Clarifying the Intent

Taking our usual tour, Marcia and I found the main level bright and warm. In contrast, the lower floor felt stuffy and crowded in spite of its spaciousness.

Cassie proudly showed us her room, a teenage girl's world of clothes, music, poetry, and letters piled in an affectionate mess. It was cluttered but still livable. Opening the door to another room, I peered into the dimly lit space and jumped back with a start. Lying on a mattress along the floor, somebody was softly snoring with a blanket pulled up to his chin.

"Who's that?" I asked, turning to Alicia in surprise as I closed the door quietly.

"Oh, that's Luke, my nephew," she explained. "He was having a hard time getting along with his parents, so we brought him here to live with us until he gets his act together." She seemed hesitant to say anything else.

"Is that working out okay?" I inquired, pushing a little for her to share more.

"Well," she responded tentatively, "I guess it's okay, but not really. Luke's kind of angry with his parents and is taking his time growing up. He's only eighteen. We just felt that he needed some unconditional love outside of his parents' home, so we're putting him up." She took a deep breath, gathering her resolve, and continued. "He's still real angry but, since it's a temporary situation, we can put up with it a little while longer. He's only been here a couple of months."

"Mom always lets other kids stay here," chimed in Cassie. "Ever since my two older brothers grew up and moved out, we have plenty of room. And besides, I don't like sleeping in the basement all alone. Last year my best friend's older brother, Nick, stayed here after his parents kicked him out."

"We have a rule here though. They always have to work or go to school," Alicia interjected. "Luke is looking for a job right now, but he just hasn't found anything yet."

Alicia's commitment to helping these young men into adulthood impressed me. "That's nice of you to put people up like you do. Everyone needs a helping hand every now and then." Nodding, she acknowledged my support. *"She's really kind,"* I thought to myself, *"and I do hope she's taking care of herself in the process."*

"Okay," I said. "Let's finish taking a look around, and then we'll do the healing. Will Luke be getting up soon?"

"Oh, no," Alicia said with a laugh. "He'll sleep until at least noon. We never see him upstairs before one o'clock."

"Does he know about or sense the ghost?" asked Marcia. Alicia dismissed this with a wave of her hand, shaking her head side to side.

Gathered in the living room, Alicia, Cassie, Marcia, and I settled in a comfortable circle on the floor. "What will happen to the ghost?" asked Cassie. "Will he be okay?"

I assured her that we would be sending him on to the Light, to his loved ones who had passed on. I also shared my feelings that this would be for his own growth and healing, and in the best interest of everyone concerned.

"As long as you're sure he'll be okay…" Cassie said with some reluctance, "…then I'm ready to do this."

Touched by her caring attitude, I could still tell she wasn't entirely convinced that the ghost would be better off without her. Knowing Cassie's strong intuitive nature, though, I decided to proceed. Perhaps, in the clearing process itself, she would experience a firsthand sense of the powerful, loving energy awaiting this entity.

Holding hands, praying, inviting any entities to come forward, it takes only an instant before a slim, young man, obviously eager to have our company and attention, steps into my awareness. A tousle of red curls crowns his head, and I realize he could pass for Cassie's brother. Images of his life begin dancing before me: Mom and Dad separate, and "Stewart" goes back east with mom. But, being a teenager, he is definitely a handful. Mom doesn't know how to deal with him, doesn't really want him there at all. Without even a hug goodbye, she sends him to Dad out west, cutting off all contact with him.

Dad dies shortly thereafter, leaving his son to fend for himself. I see a lonely, confused, and sad boy wandering from family to family, looking for handouts from local strangers. He's hoping to find a family willing to take him in. Regretfully, he is killed in a horse and buggy accident before finding that family.

Stewart is not a particularly religious or spiritual person and, not really knowing his own family nor bonding with another one, he doesn't know where to go after being killed. He resorts to roaming the neighborhood, becoming a stray. "Here's a generous family," he thinks when he comes upon Alicia's home. "They'll take me in."

"Stewart," I speak clearly to get his attention, wanting to convince him that he can find a welcoming home in the Light. "You passed on a long time ago. Your parents did, too. They're in the Light, Stewart."

"*But,*" he cries plaintively. "*They didn't want me. They never wanted me. They…*"

"Stewart, that was a long time ago. They didn't know what to do, how to take care of you. Forgive them." Sensing his reluctance, I continue. "They're waiting for you, wanting your forgiveness, your understanding. They regret their lack of caring, their lack of courage. They sincerely want you now. Home is waiting for you."

His face lights up, emanating hope and anticipation. "*Goodbye then. Thank these fine people for taking me in and letting me stay.*" He turns away and appears to move on toward Spirit. With a deep breath, I bring my awareness back to the here and now.

Following the session, Cassie is uncharacteristically quiet. After some hurried farewells, Alicia sees us to the door, and Marcia and I head home.

"Do you really think he moved on?" Marcia asks as soon as we're alone.

"I *think* so. It was interesting, though. Stewart spent most of his time hanging around Cassie. She paid him the most attention and acknowledged his presence more than anyone else in the house. But he really identified with Alicia's nephew, Luke; an angry kid who also feels emotionally abandoned by his own parents. I don't know. I hope he moved on. I thought so, but I have my doubts."

"Yeah, me too," mused Marcia. "I don't know if Cassie was really serious about letting him go. And even Alicia didn't seem that sure, almost like she didn't want to send him on if Cassie didn't want to. And maybe we should have had Luke in on the clearing as well."

"Time will tell," I quipped. But I did have my doubts. It was almost too easy. Stewart agreed and moved on so quickly. Consequently, it was no surprise that, calling to check in with Alicia a week later, she reported that Stewart was still around.

"I guess it works sometimes, and other times it doesn't," she said flippantly. I could almost feel her shrug over the phone.

"Alicia," I began with all the gentleness and sincerity I could muster, "I really suspect that maybe Cassie wanted to keep him around. If all the people aren't behind sending a ghost onward, sometimes the clearing doesn't work. We could have another go at it, but it's real important that we're together on this."

"Yeah, I guess you're right," she answered rather hesitantly. "Give me some time to speak to Cassie, and I'll get back to you."

Three weeks passed before I heard from Alicia again. "Steve, I talked with Cassie, and she didn't want him to leave. She said she was still worried about him. I reminded her about what you said, that it would be for the better. And she says she trusts you now. She's ready to let him go."

"Okay, then," I respond automatically. "It sounds like she really means it this time. We can set this up for next week sometime." I wait for Alicia to say something, but the silence stretches onward. "Alicia, you there?"

"Yeah, I'm here." She sounds disappointed or possibly just tired. "Maybe we should hold off on this one for awhile." I hear her take a deep breath and continue, "I think I might know another reason why he didn't move on. Towards the end of the clearing when we were all saying goodbye to him and sending him into the Light, I sent him a kind of thought. I didn't really mean to. And I didn't really think he would hear me. But I told him he would be welcome if he ever again needed a place to stay. Cassie told me she did the same thing, telling him he could come back anytime."

"Darn!" I don't always control my frustration as much as I want to. "Well, since I've already been there and he and I have talked, I could probably contact him without even coming over. I can finish the job from here, but you guys have to be behind me all the way."

It was at that point that Alicia gave up all pretenses and told me to wait awhile before doing anything more. For now, Stewart was welcome at her home, and they would call when they were ready to send him onward. No amount of persuasion on my part could convince her that it would be better to do this sooner rather than later. So I gave up.

"Well, if you feel that's best, Alicia. When you're ready to claim your house again and ready to get rid of the strays, just call me. I'll be here. In the meantime, though, I don't want things to get worse. I don't want Stewart to become invasive. I trust you to take care of yourself and your family in the process. Just call me when you're ready."

Almost a year later, I bumped into Alicia at a local bookstore. Upon seeing me, a big grin came over her face. She seemed rather pleased with herself when she related that they finally got sick of their nephew. "Luke wasn't keeping his agreements to find a job. He wanted to get into fighting with us and was verbally abusive to Cassie. I finally decided that the best thing I could do for him and for us was to quit taking care of him, so I kicked him out. And guess what?" She added with satisfaction, "Within a few days, Cassie and I both realized that the ghost had disappeared, too! I guess all it took was for me to stop taking in strays!"

I thanked her for sharing all that had happened, and I reveled for a moment in the tingle of excitement I feel when someone "gets it." Alicia and her daughter were well on their way to learning about responsibility toward one's self and others.

"And thank you, Steve," she added as she turned to go. "Thanks for understanding that this was just a process I needed to go through. You pushed just hard enough to make me think about things, but you never tried to force me to do something I wasn't ready for. I appreciate that! Let's keep in touch."

Waving goodbye, I got another little tingle. *I guess maybe I'm "getting it," too.*

This experience with Alicia, Cassie, and Stewart highlights the importance of intent when doing any sort of spirit expulsion. Everyone present at this clearing did not have the same intention of helping the ghost move to the Light. Cassie and Alicia had their own reasons and needs at the time for offering Stewart an alternative choice to stay. However subtle their thoughts or however loving their reasons, neither of them was really ready to have Stewart go. Consequently, he accepted their offer and stuck around.

In retrospect, this served as a gentle reminder to me about my role and responsibilities. I was reminded to take a little more time to clarify with clients the nature of their intent, the personal needs and connections they may feel with a ghost, and the current events in their life which may impact our clearing work. Most earthbound spirits are here due to strong emotional needs of their own, and if we entice them to avoid completion, their emotional urges and habits may well overpower their trust and faith in the Light.

In addition, this clearing exemplifies how the circumstances, lessons, and emotions a family may be going through can attract a ghost. Unlike Martha (in the previous story) who remained on the property because it was the location where she thought she needed to be, Stewart had been drawn to this particular household because the dynamics within the family welcomed him. Alicia had opened her doors to several stray youngsters who were angry and sad about their own home situations. Cassie, following in her mother's pattern, had done the same. With loving hearts and good intentions, both mother and daughter strove to provide a safe, nurturing environment for growth.

Alicia and Cassie, however, were still learning about setting limits and claiming their own space. They needed to commit to not allowing others to misuse or abuse their kindness. Both of them needed to acknowledge others' mistreatment toward them. Ultimately, they got to the point of exercising their own personal power and reclaimed their space with love toward themselves and others. Once the pattern was broken and the lesson learned, Stewart naturally felt less welcome. The family, meanwhile, naturally felt freer to let him go. Having previously been made aware of his option to go toward the Light, we can only trust Stewart made that choice.

As for me, I am grateful for the lessons about patience and the reminder to honor the personal journey of others. My place is not to force my will on another. Once again I thank Spirit for guidance as I continue to learn how to help, to heal, and to love.

Points to Remember…

- ⬥ Like attracts like. A ghost may be attracted to a specific home because of the family atmosphere.
- ⬥ Sometimes the people living in a home that attracts a ghost have as much to learn as the disembodied spirit.
- ⬥ Honoring the personal journey of others is a lesson healers are often reminded of when, seeking to help, they encounter resistance.

Just Trying to Help

It's a lazy Sunday afternoon. The sun, shining through the windows, leaves great rectangles of yellow light on the floor. A slight breeze tickles the wind chimes hanging by the door. I am busy doing nothing when the telephone's intrusive ringing interrupts me. Sluggishly I get up to answer it, putting on my best professional voice.

The woman on the other end is timid and hesitant. "Excuse me. I don't even know if I've got the right number. Are you the ghost guy?" Apologetically, she continues. "I hate to bother you on the weekend, but the bookstore gave me your name and number. They said you do ghost stuff."

"Yes, I do. And yes, you have the right number. But you're one up on me. I don't even know your name yet."

"Oh, sorry. My name's Joanne. And you're going to think I'm crazy." I smile at this familiar phrase. "But I think I have a ghost. I didn't know what to do except to call someone."

I assure her that she sounds reasonably sane, and I urge her to share more. Selfishly, I am hoping I won't have to hear a big, long story. After all, it's Sunday. Maybe we can make an appointment for later in the week, and I can get back to doing nothing today.

Joanne explains that she had moved into this one bedroom, garden level apartment a couple of months ago. "I live in a fairly old building that's been remodeled. About four weeks ago, I came home and found the front door open slightly. I mean, I freaked! I thought someone was inside or that I'd been robbed. So I went and got a neighbor to come in with me and look around. Everything was normal. Nothing had been disturbed, so I just figured I forgot to close the door tightly when I left for work.

"Then, in the… hold on a second."

She comes back a few seconds later and continues. "I was watching TV one night. I'm sure I closed and locked the door completely, but there it was again, open a couple of inches. I closed it tightly and locked it again. It felt a little weird, but I put a chair in front of the knob to make sure it stayed closed. I did that whenever I went to sleep for a few nights. It made me a whole lot less nervous."

"I don't blame you. It is, after all, your space," I assure her.

"Yeah," she says quickly, brushing off my comment. "But that's not the half of it. I put the chair in front of the door at night when I slept, but during the day I just left it alone. Nothing happened for several days, and the door was always locked when I came home from work. But then…hold on again. I'm sorry.

"Well, that's weird," she says when she returns. "Every now and then, for the last two weeks, the door would unlock itself and open while I was home. Just once every few days. That's why I decided to call you. But it's just done it twice in the last few minutes! There it goes again! This is freaky."

I hear the nervousness in her voice, the confusion and bewilderment quickly turning to fear. "Wait a second, Joanne. There's nothing to be afraid of. I just need to clarify a couple of things. Have there been any other strange things happening around the house? Any other unexplained events or odd feelings?"

"No. Just the door. That's weird enough for me!" she says with a self-conscious laugh.

"Well, I think we can sort this out pretty quickly. Since you haven't been hurt, or even touched, the ghost is probably just an annoyance, not intending to harm you nor anyone else. And, based on what's been happening the last few minutes, the ghost is probably there right now. It's listening to our conversation and letting its presence be known. Tell it to stick around for a minute. We want to talk to it."

"I can't…" she starts to respond.

"Just do it, Joanne. It's no big deal." If I can get her to help me, I have the feeling we can take care of the whole situation right now. I don't want her to slide into fear or embarrassment. "Hey, you've been living with this thing for a while already. What's a few words more or less?"

"OK," she says with determination. "Do I say the words out loud?"

"Either way, but saying them out loud can help you feel more certain and more powerful. It also helps you focus your thoughts. Just ask the ghost if it'll stay for a few minutes so we can talk."

I hear her speak the words. She seems pleased with herself, more relaxed.

"Okay, Joanne, I have an idea. The ghost is there now and obviously wants to communicate. I'm not there but, if you're willing to help, we can do this together over the phone. Let's just talk with it a bit. Okay?" After reassuring her of the simplicity and safety of what we are going to do, she agrees, even getting a bit excited.

"Joanne, close your eyes, and stay with me. Relax. We'll do a little prayer first and then I'll ask you to repeat what I say. Speak loudly, clearly, and from the heart. It's probably just a lost soul that needs our help."

Finishing the invocation to Spirit, I get a picture in my mind of a middle-aged woman wearing a freshly pressed cotton pinafore and sturdy shoes. A cloth satchel dangles from her shoulder. She looks like she is going to work. With her head slightly bent, I watch as she steps quickly up to a front entry and, turning around to look nervously about, she unlocks and opens the door. She does it again and again, following an almost mechanical routine… "I've got to let the children out, I've got to let them out," I hear her echoing over and over. A sense of powerlessness and sadness accompanies her actions. "I've got to let them out of there."

The ghost, Rachel, had been working as a nanny, taking care of two children being raised by their father. The impressions I'm getting aren't clear. Maybe she had worked in Joanne's building or was, perhaps, here for some other reason. *Ah, there it is. I'm seeing clearer pictures now.* When her employer was present, he often abused the children physically and emotionally. Rachel's compassion and love for the children were too great to allow her to stand by and watch them be hit or belittled. One day she spoke up and was immediately fired.

"I only made things worse," she repeats to herself over and over. "I couldn't do anything. I was so powerless!" Being a caring and devoted nanny, she blamed herself for having to leave them, carrying the burden throughout her life…and death. After death, Rachel returned to this location, carrying out what she felt most driven to do. Unable to rest, she repeatedly opens the door trying to "let the children out."

"Rachel, it's over. The children are long gone," I explain gently, appealing to her rational nature. I know that Rachel will not give up her routine unless she trusts that the children are okay. "They're grown up now. They did get out. They're safe. Their dad is long gone, if not dead. He is powerless to hurt them now! You did your very best. But there is nothing more for you to do here now."

I hear Joanne on the other end of the telephone repeating my words. "There are plenty of people waiting to thank you and love you. Look up to the Light, Rachel. There are people there who wish to help children, too. If you still need to help others, you can find better ways of doing so in the Light. Look up, Rachel. Search for loved ones in the Light. They are there. Call on them…Go on… Go to them…."

With a sigh of relief, she finally lets go of the doorknob. I watch her disappear into the world of Spirit.

A follow-up with Joanne two months later revealed no further incidents. The door, when closed and locked, stayed that way.

Joanne's ability to get past her fear, her eagerness to send the ghost onward, and her willingness to participate according to my directions allowed this clearing to go easily and smoothly. Although I would not usually anticipate carrying out a spirit expulsion over the telephone, both Joanne's capability and Rachel's gentleness made it seem safe and timely. With Spirit guiding us, Rachel was quickly able to let go of the desperation and guilt that kept her earthbound. She needed to know that the children were safe, that they had grown up and left home.

Rachel also needed the reassurance that she had done enough for them. Her guilt was unnecessary and unproductive. If she insisted on being useful, Spirit could help her find better ways to continue helping more children. Practical in nature, Rachel was satisfied and moved on. Joanne was satisfied, even rather impressed, with the discovery of her own strengths throughout the clearing.

I was also satisfied. I had let go of my fear of being interrupted on a precious lazy Sunday afternoon. This little excursion was a nudging reminder that "work" need not be hard nor intrusive to be productive. A few minutes had been well spent, with plenty of time left to do nothing.

Points to Remember…

- ✧ When all people, within the body as well as disembodied, wish to listen and cooperate, communication can be simple and expedient.

- ✧ Courage and loving intent make the clearing a rewarding experience for everyone involved.

- ✧ This work need not be hard nor intrusive to be productive.

Chapter 6

Holding On

We like to think that all souls, once released from the physical body, benefit by moving on toward the Light. Spirit offers great insight and experiences beyond our limited earthly comprehension. We are consistently amazed at the love we feel whenever a soul approaches the Light during a clearing. Admittedly, a part of us wants to follow these souls, to bask in the acceptance, forgiveness, and purity felt in such holy love. In spite of our eagerness to nudge others toward this awareness, considerations such as timing, individual circumstances, and clarity of intent enter into our decision to participate in any ghost clearing.

Following are three very different situations where earthbound spirits definitely were present. However, introducing these spirits to the Light did not seem the best option. With Spirit guiding us, we are reminded that our job is to overpower no one. We, too, have many lessons about trusting and respecting the choices of others, and there are times when we may serve best by walking away.

The Imperial Hotel

Few would be surprised were you to encounter a stately Madame roaming the corridors of the Imperial Hotel in Cripple Creek, Colorado. For years, guests at this hotel have caught her reflection in mirrors, seen her figure through clouded, second-floor window panes, and watched her float down the stairwell at night. She has been featured in advertisements, stories, and books catering to tourists as well as scholars.

Throughout my longtime residence in Colorado, people would invariably ask what I thought about this well-known female spirit. I, personally, have never attempted to contact her. Would I even try to do a ghost clearing? Probably not. First of all, the owners have never asked me to help remove her from the premises. Additionally, plenty of people are pleasantly intrigued with the notion that a nice, womanly ghost may be haunting the hotel. Her reputation has become a legend and a tourist attraction. Also, the Imperial Hotel is a very old establishment, built during Cripple Creek's rich past as a gold-mining capital. Recently, with the legalization of gambling in this small mountain town, the sleepy, run-down hotel has been elegantly restored. Amid vibrant red and gold velvet brocades, the lobby rings with slot machines and gaming tables noisily beckoning both crowds and their money. The Madame ghost, possibly a past owner or manager of the saloon, is probably thriving in her element once again.

Marcia and I did visit the new Imperial Hotel and Casino one Saturday afternoon. My impression upon entering the building was that this Madame was excited to be surrounded by the hustle and bustle. She was happy being there. Others were happy to have her there. The success, or even advisability, of doing a clearing is, at best, questionable.

"Unethical Research"

Research into the paranormal is always a challenge. Trying to scientifically validate that which occurs outside the limits of logical reasoning can be frustrating for all involved. Methods for gathering data rarely meet rigorous scientific standards, and people tend to perceive only that which supports their personal hypotheses. Thus, I had my reservations when invited to participate in a university research project.

Having a good reputation as a trance medium, researchers wanted me to go to a home, contact a ghost that the owners had encountered, and let this ghost speak through me in a channeled session. At the very least, if I could not channel this female entity, I would simply speak with her, allowing all to be recorded in a "lab-like" setting. I was expressly directed NOT to send this spirit onward. The university involved wished to perform continuing research at this site, and they wanted the status quo to remain constant.

This initial request rubbed me the wrong way: tape recordings, status quo, and no permission to improve the situation if possible. But then I realized that research and potential "proof" of life after death could be very valuable. Handled in the right way, the results could benefit many. Still, my concern surfaced for the spirit, possibly trapped in a painful emotional loop. After careful consideration, I informed the university that I would be willing to do one session with the ghost to get any information or historical references from her. Following this, I would send her on to the Light. The researchers were disappointed; they wanted more time and more encounters. Reconsidering, I agreed to do two sessions, but even this fell short of their expectations.

After several days of negotiations and soul-searching on my part, I finally agreed to meet with the ghost three or four times ONLY. I also wanted the scientists' reassurance that, after these sessions, I could counsel her onward with their support and acceptance.

My proposal was not good enough for the university. They wanted to keep the ghost around for as long as possible. They were not concerned about a possibly displaced and unhappy soul, nor that one being's misery might be prolonged unnecessarily. While it was possible that the spirit might agree to be helpful, I wouldn't know that until I met her. And I wouldn't agree to the researchers' agenda without her input. I felt backed into a corner, and I didn't like the options offered to me.

In the end, I was dismissed by the homeowner, being told that I was "a danger to research." So be it. Interesting, though, that their very fear that the ghost might choose to move onward only serves to confirm their acknowledgment of the power of free will—the very same free will they argued for me to ignore as unimportant in the name of research.

The situation left me unsettled. In search of a resolution for this earthbound spirit, I did some meditation and some prayers to Guidance. I was told to go ahead, contact her, and help her assess her choices. From the comfort and privacy of my living room, I journeyed to speak with a kind, elderly woman who had gotten sidetracked looking for her grandchildren. Now, however, she was ready to move on, with or without the homeowner's permission. My impression is that she stepped into the Light to rejoin Spirit. If she did, I hope the owner of the house wasn't too angry at her disappearance. If she didn't move on, I hope the researchers are happy with their work and that this gentle grandmother is not trapped in an unfulfilling relationship. We all have our choices.

Looking back, I acknowledge that perhaps my own limiting thoughts contributed to an unworkable situation. Maybe I was afraid of not being able to meet the expectations of scientists. Maybe I was afraid that I wouldn't channel information correctly. Maybe I was afraid I wouldn't be able to explain inconsistencies or contradictions in the ghost's story. Whatever the reasons, if the owner and/or researchers are reading this, to you I say, "Sorry. I did what I felt was ethical under the circumstances. I might do the same thing today if asked. Ghosts, after all, have feelings, too."

A Big Production

Another short involvement that didn't turn out as expected took place at a private residence nestled deep in a thick, pine forest far away from city limits. The four adults living in the house reported seeing a shimmering apparition, a cloud of smoke accompanied by a burnt smell in their living room, and strange dancing lights outside their home at night. Objects had floated through the air, and cupboard doors had been opened. The residents had even caught some of the phenomena on their Polaroid camera. When they called me to clear the house, I looked forward to meeting this active, if not somewhat mischievous, ghost or ghosts.

The clearing was scheduled for a Saturday morning in October. Additionally, I was told that camera crews would be there from a popular television show. They were to interview the residents, capture on film any nonordinary occurrences they could, and subsequently follow my work throughout the clearing. Having watched their TV show several times, I was confident that all would be handled respectfully and they would honor my intent to help the ghost move onward. Although this ghost seemed to have a flair for entertaining his audience, the residents had never experienced anything threatening or hurtful. I felt certain that with Marcia and a couple of students, we could handle the situation. We'd be ready for whatever presented itself.

Early in the morning on the designated Saturday, I was roused from bed with a phone call. It was the owner of the house. Three of the four residents had come down with the flu. He'd get in touch later to reschedule.

I didn't hear from the owner so, after a week, I called him back to inquire about scheduling the clearing. His answer was actually one I expected: "We've decided to put it off for a while, Steve, and see what happens." He had second thoughts about clearing the ghost. The possibility of television coverage and the activity of the ghost had generated a lot of excitement and attention that was hard to give up. Even getting sick on the day we were to do the clearing was, most likely, no coincidence. There was definitely resistance to "giving up the ghost." Although disappointed, I was not surprised.

In the following months, the owner of the home was interviewed on the radio several times, and his home was featured in a television documentary on paranormal activity. I was not contacted again and, to my knowledge, no attempt was made to clear the house. Eventually, I gave up interest and lost track of the situation. There was too much energy behind keeping the spirit present for me to attempt contacting him independently. However, I do hope that everyone is getting along superbly with one another. I must admit that, somehow, I have my doubts.

Points to Remember…

- ⟡ Deciding whether or not to do a clearing sometimes involves ethical decisions. Whose choices are we to honor: those of the homeowner, the ghost, or ourselves?
- ⟡ Everyone goes through the perfect experiences, learning lessons at the right time and in the right form.
- ⟡ Knowing when to retreat from a situation is as important as moving ahead with a clearing.

Chapter 7

Letting Go

Thus far, we have emphasized the importance of establishing a sacred space and clarifying intent prior to engaging in any sort of ghost clearing. All of the people involved are, ideally, focused on the same goal of lovingly helping earthbound spirits move onward. As you have seen, this is not something to take for granted. Nevertheless, this is sometimes the easier part of a clearing. More challenging may be the task of actually helping another soul discover a pathway toward completion.

Earthbound spirits can project fierce protectiveness, anger, and even rage during a clearing, along with desperation, hopelessness, and absolute despair. It is vital that, throughout our work with ghosts, we maintain a certainty that there is always an alternative to pain. Not knowing exactly what we will face prior to going into a clearing, we do know that we will give it our best to find a thread of love, hope, and forgiveness. We want to help a soul awaken, discover a resolution of the present circumstances he or she is experiencing, and move into the ever-welcoming Light.

Finding this pathway to completion can be a major challenge when counseling a ghost onward. However, the beauty and blessing of this challenge opens our own hearts as we empathize, understand, and become more cognizant of our own interactions. In the following stories, several souls take us with them on their journey toward awareness.

Part II House Ghosts

A Sheep in Wolf's Clothing

"No! You can't speak with her," screams the man. *"I won't let you."* Hot waves of anger pound at me. *"Leave us alone!"*

How did I end up here? I ask myself. *This is actually scary. He's one of the angriest ghosts I've ever met. I hope and trust that I'm up to the task.*

It started when I got a call from a fellow therapist reporting some definite, strange goings-on over the last few months in her healing center. People were getting sick in the old Victorian house that had been converted to office space two years earlier. Clients would come for counseling and leave more distraught than when they came. Others would come for body work and get sick with headaches and nausea while there, or they would find themselves exhausted for days afterward. A colon therapist had a client unexpectedly bleed during routine colon irrigation. Several people felt "weird" using one of the bathrooms. Four or five people reported being pushed down a staircase by an invisible someone or something. Herbal remedies and supplements were discovered missing from inside a locked room. I had promised that, as soon as I had time, I would get back in touch.

A few days later, I happened to be in the neighborhood and decided to drop by for more personal, firsthand information. The three-story house, with its array of health practitioners, looked bright and cheerful in freshly painted lavender hues. Because this was an impromptu visit, with my seven-year-old son, Joseph, with me, I decided to make it short and sweet. For safety's sake and my own comfort, I reached down and took Joseph's hand as we approached the front door. I wanted him right by my side, where I could see and hear him the whole time we would be in this house, because the entire situation was feeling very creepy. There was some definite ghost activity here.

Inside, the foyer was sunny and inviting with plants, stained glass, and the sweet scent of mild incense. When Joseph and I walked up the stairs from the first floor, however, I noticed my body suddenly feeling heavy and tired. On the second level, I entered the bathroom in which several people reported feeling uncomfortable. Opening myself to impressions, I had an intuitive flash of blood followed by an enormous wave of nausea. Looking down at Joseph, I saw his face turn pale. He stood very still and quiet until I tugged at his hand and we moved on. The narrower staircase up to the third floor began to feel uncomfortably dark and foreboding in spite of ample wall lamps shimmering with light. Standing in the hall, I shivered as anger closed in around us, smothering me with a distinct message that we were not welcome in this space. Joseph pulled at my sleeve, I nodded, and we cautiously picked our way back downstairs.

I left with a commitment to get back in touch and set up a time to do the work. I told Nancy, the manager of the center, that I needed time to gather several students and friends who would do the house cleansing with me. I would not do this one alone under ANY circumstances. The energy was too hot, too angry, and too strong to face on my own.

Nancy contacted me the following day saying there would be no shortage of support to help with the work. She herself, plus several therapists and friends were all interested in clearing the building. A week later Marcia and I arrived at the house around dusk (the best time to do such work, as the veil between worlds is thinning) and were surprised to find at least a dozen people there. They wished to participate, to add their energies, prayers, and blessings. Great! The more the merrier for this particularly active situation.

We started the work with the usual invocation to Spirit after gathering in a circle in one of the upper meeting rooms. We also did a little extra prayer and took some deep, centering breaths just to be sure we raised our energies sufficiently. And so we began....

I feel the Love and Light. The energy of the circle flows through me. Going into trance, I receive impressions of a sad and lonely woman—a ghost who has been through a lot of pain and anguish. I pick up the name Mary and invite her to come closer to share her story with us. Everything seems normal enough until...

"Go away now!" The anger slams at me as a man's energy fills the room with foreboding. Tensing up at this aggressive intrusion, I instinctively tighten my grasp of Marcia's hand. Then, remembering that no one will break the circle, I start to relax.

"Go on! Get out! You have no right to be here!" A tall, rangy man waves his arms in the air while screaming at me. *"No, you can't speak with her. I won't let you. Now leave us alone!"*

My head starts to throb. I might have a terrific headache after this is done. But wait. I do not have to be threatened by this. The loving energy and positive intent within this circle is great enough that I do NOT need to succumb. Trust. I trust in the power of Spirit.

"Wait a second!" I quickly interject, interrupting his tirade. "We're just here to talk." I speak aloud for the benefit of those around me and to focus my own thoughts more clearly. Surely the people in the circle must feel this anger. I explain to the group as best I can, without breaking the conversation, that I'm picking up a man, a very angry man. His name is Carl, and he wishes to protect Mary from us. He wishes to stop us from doing this clearing.

"Carl, we're not here to push ourselves on anyone. We'd like to talk with you, and we're not going anywhere until we do." I force myself to keep my voice low, steady, and filled with certainty. "The people in this building are not going anywhere. They belong here and bring a healing energy to this place. Let them...."

"You can't stay," he interrupts. *"This is my place, mine and Mary Lou's. And she's not speaking with anyone!"* Carl has lowered his volume, but his intent to stop us is still strong.

Pictures and feelings start rolling through my head: A young woman from long ago. A pregnancy that was not wanted. The bathroom and, specifically, the bathtub on the second floor. A self-induced abortion gone bad. Too much blood. Baby and mother both die. Too much pain, too much sadness. Tears stream from my eyes as I feel the sorrow and the loss.

I bring myself back to the present.

"Carl, listen! Whatever she did, it isn't your fault. You're not to blame."

"Yes I am! She knew I didn't want a baby. Times were hard enough already. She knew! She didn't even tell me she was pregnant. Things had calmed down after our last fight. I thought she forgave me. But when she wouldn't talk to me for awhile, I figured I'd leave her be until she cooled off. I just went up to my room for a couple of hours. And then to come downstairs and find her like that."

Carl's eyes reflect only anguish and despair now. "My beautiful Mary! Now we'll never be together again. Of course it was my fault. I should have been there for her. So dead, so lifeless, so alone, that she'd do this and not even tell me. I feel so ashamed. I know we had our bad times, but…"

"Carl!" I raise my voice in order to get his attention. I don't want him to drift off into a self-deprecating stupor. "Carl, listen. I know you wanted to be there for her. She loved you very much. She remembers now that you always came back after a disagreement. She knows that you did love her, and that you obviously still do."

I see him in my mind's eye shutting himself away in the third floor room—drinking liquor, not eating, not taking care of himself, not taking visitors, slowly killing himself. The self-blame that he carries demands he punish himself. I remember the director of the center telling me that the ghost problems started when they opened up that third-floor room to make it into another office space. The problems started when he could no longer be alone with grief.

"She knows you let yourself rot away after her death. She knows that you just let yourself die in mourning. She blames herself for that. She chose not to tell you she was pregnant, and she also blames herself for that. You need to go to her." I sense a change in Carl's demeanor, a longing to reach gently toward the woman he has loved. "You've paid enough for what you think you did, Carl. The people who now work in this house have not been badly hurt, and even the people you pushed on the stairs are well. They understand and forgive you. You don't have to keep people away from Mary Lou anymore."

I see him taking a deep breath, a sigh of relief. "Yes, Carl. It's true. Just talk with her," I continue urging him. "Get her to forgive herself. And as she goes on to the Light, you can go with her. Please, Carl. You won't go unless she does. She won't go until you do. You, Mary, and the baby are dead, Carl. It's been quite a while already. The mess has been cleaned up for a long time. The baby's spirit is still with Mary Lou. It's time to leave this place. It's time to go on to the Light where you can be together." I watch the wall of guilt and pain surrounding Carl begin to loosen, to let in glimmers of realization, to crumble as it is replaced by hope.

I change my focus. "Mary. Mary Lou. Carl is here. He's not angry anymore. He wants to talk."

"*I know that,*" comes her gentle voice from right outside the circle. "*I've been listening.*" Mary Lou raises her eyes to me. In them I see sadness replaced by a sparkle of awareness, and I know she is okay. She is already healing. "Thank you," she whispers. "*We'll just talk for a bit and then be on our way. Sorry for all the trouble we caused. Please tell them. Tell them all I'm sorry.*"

"Okay, Mary. I'll tell them. Bye, Carl. Thanks for helping out." I see mother, father, and baby draw together as all three spirits are slowly surrounded by the Light, gradually being enveloped within that energy. A slight breeze blows through the room carrying the smell of gardenias, the fresh smell in the air after a spring shower.

I open my eyes to a room full of Light. Some people are smiling. Others are wiping tears from their eyes. It's a new beginning for all of us.

This clearing had quite a twist to it. Carl blamed himself for what his wife had done. Mary Lou blamed herself for what she had done. Neither was willing to accept forgiveness. Both had condemned themselves to their personal hell, an afterlife of isolation and misery. Things at the house had been quiet when the healing center first opened its doors, and they remained quiet for a while afterward. Opening up the rooms on the third floor had disturbed Carl, setting off his tirade of anger and defense. His activity then awakened Mary Lou. That is when the phenomena first started.

Carl and Mary Lou were both active ghosts, but they did not communicate with one another. Each carried a shame so great, they denied themselves the love and support available from their partner. Nor did they realize that as they withdrew and punished themselves, they became unavailable to help the other person.

Carl and Mary Lou serve as good reminders of how we can allow guilt to immobilize us and blind us to all but our own misery. Far better and more useful to forgive ourselves and reach out toward a world which both welcomes and offers support.

A follow-up with Nancy, some months later, revealed that things had quieted down enormously throughout the house—no more pushing, unexplained thefts nor eerie feelings. Both clients and practitioners actually got well at the healing center! Every now and then someone would report hearing a baby giggling, but it could have been his "imagination."

Points to Remember…

- Safety and success in a clearing require keeping the healing energy at the highest possible level. Participants must be committed to keeping the circle intact.
- Sometimes the ghost is quiet until he or she is disturbed by a change in environment.
- Souls are forgiven for what they did or didn't do. There is always an alternative to pain.

Gold Fever

I have always admired Alex' connection to the earth. No matter where he traveled, he was conscious of the changing ripples of energy beneath his feet. He especially loved the Rocky Mountains of Colorado, those soaring, jagged peaks that seemed to pulsate with unleashed power. Standing on a ledge at 12,000 feet, cold mornings and clear air have a way of cutting through the distractions of city life, leaving one's soul naked before God. Alex liked that feeling…the meeting of earth and sky, body and Spirit, intent and energy. Thus, it was no surprise to me when Alex purchased two hundred acres west of Boulder, with mineral rights to an old gold mine. Gold prices were on the rise, and several mines in the area were back in business and turning a profit. If anyone could be successful in partnership with the earth, it would be Alex.

Under the vibrant blue skies of winter, I watched with amusement as Alex enthusiastically began preparations for reopening the old mine. Clearing overgrown access roads, purchasing timber for bracing tunnel walls, and filing paperwork to obtain permits were only the beginning of a long process.

By springtime, Alex's optimism was waning. He had felt completely certain about the mining operation, but numerous roadblocks seemed to rise out of nowhere to stand in his way. The legal papers he had spent hours filling out and handing over to the county had gotten mysteriously "lost." The clerk had no memory of ever seeing them, and Alex would have to begin the process all over again. Clearing the roads was more laborious than anticipated; timber was misdelivered and priced incorrectly; and getting reliable machinery became an unexpected challenge. To top it off, his car broke down on the way up the mountain.

Determined to pursue his dream, Alex forged ahead in spite of the challenges. Sounding confident and self-assured when he called me in May, he was ready to start digging. "But where should I start, Steve? The possibilities are endless!" His voice shook with excitement. "I can't understand why they closed the mine down! They didn't even scratch the surface in several areas."

I agreed to meet Alex at the property the following week to do some dowsing for gold. Most known for its use in locating underground water tables, dowsing can also be applied to locating lost objects, ley lines, and a variety of seemingly "hidden" items. Although not my particular specialty, I had experienced some former successes in finding a plane crash, buried cables, and a missing dog, so I figured there was no harm in trying!

With maps in hand, Alex greets me at the only cabin still standing on the property, a rickety shell of weathered planks held together by cobwebs and dust. His eagerness is contagious, and before long we are spreading out maps and orienting ourselves as we settle in for a good day's work. Alex recounts what he has discovered about the mine's history, pointing out each shaft drilled and tunnel bored. Like many sites, some digs end abruptly, many take unexpected turns, and others are recorded as merely becoming unprofitable. Alex was right; the possibilities are endless. My job would now be to narrow the choices and zero in on the most likely locations for striking a rich vein of gold.

I take out my pendulum, a simple quartz crystal hanging on a chain. It's my preferred tool for dowsing. Clearing my mind and affirming that all I do is for the Highest Good, I relax into a comfortable connection with my subconscious self. Then, focusing my thoughts on "gold," I hold the pendulum in my right hand while pointing at locations on the map with my left hand. The quartz starts swinging wildly! I relax again and give my pendulum directions, enabling impressions from the more subtle realms to be brought to my conscious, physical awareness. "Please give me a counterclockwise circle for negative findings," I instruct, "and a clockwise circle for positive gold concentrations."

"It's working, Steve! It's working!" Alex can hardly contain his excitement as the pendulum swings into a vigorous clockwise circle. I, too, am excited as I remind Alex to make notations on the map. We continue this for a couple of hours, dowsing, rechecking, comparing one site to another, discussing possibilities. Discounting some sites because of little or no response, Alex notes which tunnels may be worth exploring.

One particular shaft draws my attention. It doesn't seem to go far, but it's worth looking into. My pendulum starts its positive swing. I move my finger along the map pointing down the shaft. The pendulum's movements increase. "This could be a good one, Alex. It's definitely worth…Wait a second…." We watch as the pendulum first becomes erratic, then stops completely.

"Try it again," he almost yells at me. Getting caught up in the thrill of discovery, only to have this unexpected turn of events arise, is unnerving. "Try it again! See what happens!"

"Okay, okay. Just give me a minute," I say quietly. "Getting too excited won't accomplish anything."

I focus on that particular site and start over. The pendulum gives me the beginnings of a positive swing, increasing as I move down the shaft. Increasing, increasing, then it stops dead. "Hmm. That's odd. Let me meditate here for a sec and see if anything else becomes more apparent."

I focus on my breath, going into a deeper trance rather easily. After all, I've been in a light trance for a while already, so I'm primed. Slipping into a familiar breathing pattern, calling on the Light, I focus my attention outward. Breathing the Light in the top of my head and out my forehead, I project my consciousness toward the site in question. "It looks just like a hole in the ground, Alex. There's dirt sliding in from the sides, but that seems fairly normal considering the amount of time that's past. I am getting impressions of people working this hole a long time ago. They're taking out the dirt and sifting through it. There's a lot of excitement. They've found gold. They're going back to dig deeper!

"I'm going down. I want to see what happens next." I project my consciousness even further down the shaft. Wood braces are firmly in place. Dirt and rock have been taken out. Tools are scattered at the mouth. There's activity all around as men hustle to be the next miner to find rich ore. I start to descend. I want to go down just a little bit more… and then things go blank.

I come out of trance with a start. "Everything went blank all of a sudden. I'll try it again." The same thing happens, this time more quickly. "There's something odd here, Alex. I can only go so far, then things blank out. Let's try something else." An idea occurs to me. "Maybe we can get in another way. Let me have the map."

He looks at me askance. "Sure, but I don't know what you're up to. I really want to find out about that hole." Hesitantly, he hands me the map, scrutinizing me the whole time.

"I just want to see. Yes. Look at this tunnel." I point to another shaft starting a little distance away. "It starts over here, then angles toward the hole we're having trouble with. Then it just peters out and ends."

"You're right," he says, anticipation coming back into his voice. "Let's start to…"

The rest of what he says is lost to me as I regain the trance state. I'm going down the new tunnel. It goes down a bit, then levels off and turns. I can feel myself moving toward the first shaft. Getting closer, closer still. The tunnel starts to narrow. Feeling a little cramped, I slow down, but then I remember that I'm out of my body. *Nothing can hurt me physically down here,* I remind myself. Continuing with more confidence, I feel my excitement growing. *I'm an explorer looking for my fortune. This must be what it felt like to actually mine for gold! The adventure, the suspense, the thrill!*

Disappointment strikes hard as the tunnel abruptly ends.

Wait a minute! No problem! I can send my awareness through this wall of rock. I am still traveling without a body, and I can find out what's on the other side! I am slipping through the solid barrier of rock when a wave of dizziness strikes me. I take a deep breath, relax, focus, deepen the trance, and continue. Wham! The headache that hits me feels like I've just been bludgeoned with a hard object to the side of my head.

"Steve! Steve!" I can hear the concern in Alex's voice. "Steve, is everything okay?" I must have shown signs of distress because, as I open my eyes, I see Alex standing over me, eager to do something to help. A look of confusion is on his face. I can't blame him. I realize my eyes are squinting. My shoulders are hunched over. I'm leaning to one side. And if I look anything like I feel, then I must look like I've just been run over by a truck.

"Yes, I'm okay. Just ran into a bit of trouble down there." I relate my experience to him. "There's something fishy going on down there. It almost feels like there's something or someone preventing me from exploring that first tunnel. Let's take a break and then decide what to do next." A few gulps of cold water and some physical movement help to shake off the headache, but Alex and I both feel a gnawing curiosity about that particular shaft. We are eager to get some answers.

Looking over the map again, we decide to head uphill through aspen groves and Ponderosa pine to locate the actual opening in the earth. It's a beautiful afternoon in the Rocky Mountains, and there are plenty of worse ways to spend a day than hiking through this wild countryside. Twenty minutes later, Alex is pointing, "There it is! Just ahead and to the left!" I recheck the map and smile inwardly at this man's boundless energy.

The sun is shining. The birds are singing. There's a sweet-smelling breeze moving the air just enough to be comfortable. Alex and I climb across slippery tailings to approach the mouth of the old shaft, now looking like nothing more than a vague depression in the earth's surface. Stepping cautiously toward the lip to peer downward, I am gripped by a sudden jolt of fear. I experience a tightening in my stomach. Feeling dizzy, I start to teeter, to fall, then remember to jerk myself back upright. The headache is back, stronger than before. Alex looks at me quizzically. "You're starting to scare me, Steve. What's going on?"

"There may very well be a spirit nearby, one that's not so keen on us being here. I suspected it earlier, but now I'm almost sure. There's someone here who doesn't want us around." I survey the surroundings. The shaft has been partially filled in, possibly by accident, possibly on purpose. Broken tools are strewn around the ground. Corpses of rusting machinery lie stiff and abandoned.

"Let's go a little ways from here and talk," I whisper. "I need another short break." As we walk away, my headache starts to clear. By the time we're downhill about fifty feet, it clears completely.

"There's definitely some ghost activity here, Alex, and their desire to keep us away is very strong. I'd like to do what I can to help clear this up, but not today. We're both too tired for any serious investigation. I'd like to approach this when we're better prepared and rested. Also, the energy and support from some other people would be most welcome when we do get started again. I'd like to contact another psychic, or maybe a student, and come up at another time."

Alex's disappointment is obvious, but he understands. "Ghosts, huh? Well, I guess the gold's not going anywhere! I'd like to know that reopening the mine isn't going to hurt anyone, and it would be nice if any spirits hanging out here were on my side! It's been hard enough getting this operation moving. I don't need more obstacles standing in my way." We agree to meet again next Saturday to do a ghost clearing....

Joella, a friend and student of mine, is happy to be invited along. She has been learning to use her growing empathic abilities and is eager to participate in her first conscious encounter with ghosts. I'm glad she's with me. After the strong physical sensations I experienced the last time, I welcome her support.

Alex meets us outside the old cabin. "I went to the county seat to recheck historical records, but there was no additional information about any cave-ins or accidental deaths," Alex shares. "This shaft has a short record of excellent production and then, boom, it's as if it doesn't exist anymore."

Not surprised, I decide that some centering would be good before we get close to that shaft again. I don't need another headache! We would be doing the actual clearing work close to the mining site, but it would be best to approach with clarity. Seated in a tight circle on the ground, we call in the Light and pray that this work be for the Highest Good. We breathe. We relax. We heighten our perceptions and our energies. We focus our intent on healing and then set out for the mine shaft.

Arriving at the site, we wander around the perimeter for a few minutes. I don't feel anything, yet, except a profound gratitude for life, friends, Spirit, and this beautiful Colorado spring day. Everything is wonderful. Feeling safe and assured, I remind myself of our purpose here and open up my perceptions. Within moments, images of a young Native American boy float before me, and I am flushed with feelings of confusion and sadness. He looks up in surprise as a woman, his mother, steps in front of him. Her bold stance is one of defiance and protectiveness. I jump at the sound of an unexpected gun shot, then watch in horror as her body crumples to the ground.

I am jolted from this vision by a sudden moan seemingly right next to me. "Joella! What's wrong? Talk to me!" She is standing a few feet away, doubled over, holding her stomach. Her face registers shock and pain.

"I don't know what happened. I was walking along slowly, staying open to anything I might feel. And then it felt like someone just kicked me right in the gut. God, it hurt for a few seconds! I don't like it! Something violent happened here."

The color starts returning to her face as she talks. She's taking some slow deep breaths, relaxing, centering, and starting to stand upright once again. "I still really want to know what went on here, but I'd also just like to do the work and go."

"Well, if you're up to it. You look mostly recovered. Just take a few more deep breaths and release any energy that's not yours. Remember to ground yourself." As I watch, I am reminded of why I like to do ghost clearings with trained people like Joella. They're not so easily frightened and, if they do pick up unwanted energy, they can quickly let it go. I keep an eye on Joella as she continues breathing deeply, flushing any limitations or foreign energy down the grounding cord that connects her to the Earth. The energy will be taken away to be cleansed and renewed.

Joella now stands completely straight, eyes full of Light. "Ready?" I ask. She gives me a firm nod.

We call Alex over and explain the pictures I received along with the feelings Joella experienced. The three of us form our small circle once again. Joining hands, we are empowered, centered, and ready for anything. "Mother-Father God, we ask you to join us here…" The invocation continues. "We'd like to talk with whomever may be here, any spirits that may be inhabiting this place."

I see a Native American woman, her dark hair a mess of tangles and her face streaked with dirt. Wearing a simple, one-piece shift, her body shakes as she stands crying. I let her words, her feelings flow through me as I speak aloud. *"I couldn't save him. My son. I tried, but they just shot me. No questions, no bargaining. The Barbarians! I tried to make a trade for the things he stole, but they wouldn't listen. No harm was done. My boy. So proud. Just trying to prove himself. Is that so wrong? I tried…."* The words begin repeating themselves, and then the conversation is lost amidst the tears.

My awareness is filled with images of the boy. I watch the scene unfold as, alone, he silently creeps into the miners' camp. The workers are underground, and he takes this opportunity to examine their black cooking pots and long, silvery spoons. When he spies a shiny hunting knife on the ground, he tucks it into his breechcloth and hurriedly backs away from the site. Returning to his own campfire, he presents the knife to his father who is fascinated and proud.

One day the boy does not return home for the evening campfire. His mother follows his trail to the mining camp, becoming frantic in her search. When she hears his cries, she breaks into a run, stumbling into the midst of miners who have circled around her son. They don't understand her speech, and they grow impatient with her sign language. As she defiantly stands between the men and her boy, one miner raises his rifle and shoots her in the stomach.

I come out of trance slightly, focusing on my own energies again. I need to get back to the mother. "Please wait," I call to her as she floats in the periphery of my awareness. "We wish to talk with you. It was wrong to kill you. It was wrong for your son to be here in the first place, but children don't know any of that. They just try to grow up and do the best they can. And you couldn't do anything to stop this tragedy."

"Yes, I could have. I should have. If only he'd listened to me. I told him not to come down here again. These white men with their machines and their greed. They take our land, our deer, and then our people. They took my son. I tried to stop them. They took him anyway. I cannot return now to face my people, my husband. I can't!"

Anger rises in her voice as she continues. *"But I showed these white men. I broke their machines, kicked a little dirt around, and made them sick until they finally quit tearing up the earth and went away. I will not let them come back and hurt me anymore!"*

"You did a good job," I interject. "A real good job. But now it's over. Your son is waiting for you to be ready to leave. He would like to rejoin his ancestors, but he will not go without you."

"My son is here?" she asks with round eyes full of hope.

"Yes," I assure her. "Do you realize they killed him anyway, shortly after they shot you? He has been hiding, blaming himself for your death. The more anger and grief you carry, the more guilt and sadness he bears. He will not move from this place until you are ready to go, too."

She looks around for her son. Slowly, he uncurls from behind a large boulder. Keeping his head low, long dark hair falls over his face to cover his shame. The woman moves quickly toward him. Falling on her knees in front of him, she reaches gently to brush back strands of hair and to tip his chin so she can look into his eyes. The boy's thin, brown arms wrap around her neck, and she pulls him to her in a firm embrace.

Through tears of sadness and joy, I interrupt their reverie. "There is nothing more for you here," I assure her. "A new person has moved onto this land now, and he will not bring any harm to your son or your people. He seeks only to follow his own agreements with Mother Earth. He promises to respect the land. If he takes anything from the earth, he'll let the land heal when he is done. Is that okay? Tell me. Let me know. Can you finally let go of this place?"

"Yes," she sighs. I feel my own shoulders drop in relief. *"I can let go. I can take my son."*

"Then it's time to go to the Light...." Uh oh! I knew that was the wrong thing to say the second I said it. She tenses up. Confused. Thinking I was her friend, then calling on the white man's image of God. I hurry to correct my mistake. "Wait! You know where to go. Spirit is waiting for you. Your ancestors are waiting for you. They'll understand. There is no more blame. They know you did what you could. They know the boy was being curious and brave. You can return to your people WITH your son. Success is yours. They'll be proud."

Suspiciously, but with a modicum of trust, *"Yes. I'll get them to understand. I'll take him to his father."*

I call on her ancestors, the Ute. I sense them coming, but they stop a fair distance away. "What's wrong?" I ask her. "I thought you were going."

"They'll wait," she replies, a little condescendingly. *"They'll wait for me to finish down here. We need three days to mourn our passing. Three days to prepare. Then we'll go on. Our people understand this."*

She seems sincere. I feel a strong need to honor her traditions and her request. She and her son have already cut their cords with the land, letting go of any need to stick around and protect the earth. I'm confident they'll keep their agreement and move on. I nod my assent, watching as mother and son, hand in hand, disappear into the woods.

With the clearing finished, Alex, Joella, and I breathe more easily. We take a much-needed break, dispersing in our own separate directions for some time alone with nature, with Spirit, and with ourselves. I start heading off toward a small grove of trees, but Alex holds me up for a second. "Steve, let's discuss our other goal—gold! I know it seems trite after what we've just been through but, after all, an intuitive survey of the area was one of the original reasons for you being here."

"I'd be happy to come back at another time to do some in-depth work, Alex, but I really am not up for much concentration on that level right now. What I'd like…"

"Steve, don't misunderstand me. Most of the work is already done. I have enough to go on for quite a long time, and I'm really grateful. The only site we didn't get to was this one…because of the problems." He looks at me hopefully. "It'll just take a second…"

Chapter 7   Letting Go

I am amused rather than put off. The lure of gold is not something to be trifled with. "All right, I'll see what I can do. If it's easy enough, I can complete it. But if it becomes too much of a strain, or if I can't trust the information, I'll quit."

Alex bows his acquiescence as I stroll off to get into the mental space I'll need. I stop a short distance away, breathe, relax, and center again. I still have my reservations about doing this now, but I'll give it a shot. Taking my pendulum out of its bag once again, I talk to it. "Please give me a positive directional swing when I face the direction of the most easily accessible location of gold." I turn slowly in a circle. The pendulum is responding. I CAN do this work for a little while yet today. "Thank you," I say gently to my dowsing instrument as it gives me a direction to center on. "Now please give me a positive swing when I am over the location."

I hold my pendulum out in front of me, watching as it starts to swing. I walk in the direction indicated. The pendulum swings more freely, definitely more of a positive flow. I start getting excited. I.… Wait! There's a noise, an interruption.

It's Joella. She's coming straight toward me, hollering. "Steve, hold up a second, will you? Hold up. I need to talk with you. Are you dowsing right now?"

"Yeah…" I'm getting more than a little nervous here. "Why? Is there a problem? Did something happen?"

Joella stops in front of me and looks around as if to see whether or not someone may be listening to us. "Well, I figured that we just gave them three days to wrap things up. Are we keeping our agreement? Shouldn't we wait three days before doing any more work?"

Thud! I step back with a gasp as the quartz stone on my pendulum falls to the ground. The rock picked that precise moment to come unseated from its mounting. "Okay, Joella. Good idea. Thanks. I guess gold fever just hit me a little hard. But obviously," I gesture toward the crystal lying on the ground at our feet, "we're done for today." We both start laughing. I am thankful that the student has just taught the teacher to be more aware and more sensitive to others' feelings.

Walking back to let Alex know we're leaving, we're still joking about the whole situation. The atmosphere has lightened up tremendously, but I can't help noticing Joella looking around, looking behind us. Does she think a ghost might pop out of the bushes at us any second? I start to laugh until I realize that I am doing the same thing.

We pick up our step a bit. "Okay. Let's go. The sooner the better."

Alex and I did get together one more time to complete the dowsing and, yes, that particular shaft seemed to have several very promising veins. Although I never checked in with him after he began mining, I trust Alex. Whatever he's doing, I'm sure it's in partnership with Earth and Spirit.

Dowsing, scrying, clearing… this was an adventurous undertaking with many unexpected turns. I thought I was simply going to help a friend consider where to dig for gold, but it turned out to be so much more.

Dowsing with a pendulum to access "hidden" information can be mastered as a person learns how to ask appropriate questions and how to teach the dowsing instrument to give clear answers. I find my pendulum particularly cooperative when the information I'm seeking is not personal to me. When I am not invested in the outcome, my own hopes and feelings are not as likely to get in the way of honest revelations. The pendulum (some people dowse with wire rods or a Y-shaped stick) serves as the tool by which I can "read" the answers given as my subconscious, or lower self, connects with the energy of that which I seek. Because things were going so well with the maps and the pendulum at the mine, it was totally confusing to reach a sudden halt at one particular site. There were no personal expectations that Alex nor I could identify as interference. Thus, it was almost as if Spirit was saying, "Pay attention, Steve!"

Once my curiosity was piqued, I decided to project my consciousness beyond my body in order to travel down the mine shaft. This is known as scrying, and it is similar to what people may do when they gaze into a crystal ball to "see" events outside their immediate, physical perspective. Our awareness is able to transcend time and space when traveling without a body. Having no density, it can pass through walls, travel in tight places, or relocate instantaneously. Choosing to do this consciously has, for me, involved focus, trust, and plenty of practice. As always, I want Spirit guiding me. Before scrying, I clarify my intent, ask guidance to lead the way, and then trust that I will get whatever information is for the Highest Good of everyone concerned. In this case, I was given a big, fat headache! Once again, Spirit was saying, "Pay attention, Steve!"

Putting together the resistance I met in working with the pendulum, the headache I got when trying to penetrate the resistance, and all of the difficulties Alex had experienced while readying paperwork and equipment for mining, I suspected we were encountering a fairly powerful earthbound spirit. The energy and intensity of purpose this soul projected was not something I was eager to encounter again on my own. I was grateful that Joella and Alex wanted to participate in the clearing.

Joella is an empath. She feels the energy of others and gets much of her intuitive information by noticing the physical and emotional sensations that arise in her own body. Thus, she "felt" the gunshot wound in her stomach at the same time that I was "seeing" it happen. Anyone with strong empathic tendencies is also advised to learn how to notice and then let go of the energies they feel which are not theirs. None of us needs to walk around carrying the pain, sadness or anger of other people! Joella opened herself up beautifully to feeling the energies, but she needed a reminder to release them. Once reminded, she recovered very quickly.

The Native American woman we met in this clearing was so passionately focused on one intent—to keep the white men away—that the strength of her interference was especially powerful. Not only had she apparently shut down the mining of that particular shaft during the original excavation but, over a hundred years later, was still doing her best to intimidate outsiders. This was her struggle for completion. She saw herself unable to protect her son, unable to return to her people in disgrace, and unable to forgive herself for her inadequacies. What she could do, however, was wreak sufficient havoc to discourage others' progress. As she became aware of her son's presence and his need for her to forgive herself, she let go of the struggle. Acknowledging Alex's respect of the land, she focused on the welcoming circle of ancestors. This vigorous Ute woman could at last give up her earthbound fight and rejoin Spirit.

My own lessons throughout this clearing continued to the very end. When my pendulum fell apart, Joella was already several steps ahead of me, trying to remind me that I'd made an agreement to leave everyone and everything alone for three days. I had ignored my feelings and given in to Alex' earnest request for that one last tidbit of information. I thought I could complete then and there on my agreement with Alex. But timing and respect are important! There is no completion if the steps we take are in disregard of others. Looking at the quartz rock of my pendulum on the ground, I swear I could hear Spirit saying, "Pay attention, Steve!"

Points to Remember…

- ⟡ There is neither time nor space in Spirit.
- ⟡ Letting go of personal concerns and selfishness enables us to work most effectively.
- ⟡ Respecting the feelings and traditions of those we are trying to help increases their trust in the process.
- ⟡ Sometimes a departing soul takes up to three days to emotionally wrap up earthly concerns—three days to mourn his or her own passing.

A Case of Mistaken Identity

The following is a case study in which I first channeled a ghost. Technically, it could be called a séance. However, the associations with the word *séance* are limiting and inaccurate. They bring to mind people sitting around a shaking table while calling on the dead, candles levitating and being blown out, moans, and fakery. For this reason, I call my workplace a "healing circle."

We form the circle to heal the living and the dead. Although I've been doing this work for many years, I still wonder if I am actually communicating with the dead and if they are communicating with me. Is it real or imagined? The experiences seem real. I see, hear, feel, and sometimes become the spirit entity, but is it real? It is unsettling, exciting, sad, painful, loving, and wonderful, but is it real?

I can only fall back on the adage that the results of the work speak for themselves. Healing takes place for everyone involved. The initial focus is often upon the people who are first "bothered" by an apparent entity, or it is upon the property or physical location. Yet, as the circle expands to initiate a clearing, everyone, regardless of the role he or she takes—that of the homeowner, the people gathered to do the clearing, myself, the spirit entity—each one is drawn closer to the Light. Invariably, we are all, after the work is done, closer with Spirit, more certain of ourselves, more in touch with our hearts. Healing happens. That is real enough for me.

Thus, when a trusted colleague called to ask me if I would take on a new role in the healing circle, I was uncertain, unprepared, inexperienced, but determined to let the healing happen…

"Steven," Dianne starts the conversation. "I know you do channeling, and I've had a somewhat challenging request from my Spiritual Studies class."

Dianne is a professional psychic and teacher with a loyal and committed following. A woman of small stature in her mid fifties, she appears at first glance wispy and frail. Making judgments about her by merely looking at her, though, is illusory. Assertive, direct, outspoken, certain of her abilities, and sometimes demanding, she is full of power!

"We've been called to clear a house. Normally I would just do it myself, but I'd like to invite you."

"Great, Dianne! I'd love to participate in something like that. But I really haven't had much experience with…"

"Steve," she interrupts. "Don't get me wrong here. I'm not inviting you to participate. I'm asking you to lead the clearing with me, to channel the ghost if you can."

I start getting nervous. "I've studied about ghosts for years off and on. I've spoken with them at times. But I've only once channeled one. I usually focus on channeling what I think of as Higher Energies—guidance, angels, Spirit teachers, and so on. I don't know if…"

She interrupts once again. Dianne's real good at that. "You don't have to decide now. It's an emotionally charged situation, and we strongly suspect the entity in the house of violence toward a family member there. I'd like to do the clearing with you present, at least for support. I'd like to have your energy and input. And I'd love to see if you could channel the entity. I'd be there to safeguard the process and to send him or her onward.

"It just feels right to have you there," she continues. "You don't have to do anything that doesn't feel right. You don't have to channel the spirit. Just the willingness to do so if it feels right is enough. Please consider this seriously. This would be a wonderful opportunity for you."

"Ooh, she's good," I think. *"I know my experience in this area is limited, but I'm intrigued."* She's already cast the bait, set the hook, and is starting to reel me in. *"Should I make a run for it?"* Sensing my hesitation, she offers one more lure. "Steve, I've been guided to call you. I've already told my class that you do wonderful channeling, and they practically begged me to have you do the clearing. They also want you to be a guest lecturer in some of my classes. I practically promised them you'd do it."

Quickly, before she has a chance to continue, "Okay, Dianne. I'll do it! I'm hooked. I'll give it a go."

I met Dianne at the address she had given me. The house, approximately fifteen years old, was rather unremarkable—a split-ranch with a family room on the lower level, living area in the middle, and three bedrooms on the third floor. There was nothing lacking, yet nothing pretentious nor outstanding about the house. It was a typical, middle class home in a typical, middle class, suburban neighborhood.

Coffee and donuts awaited our arrival. The owner, Mrs. Vasquez, introduced herself and her fourteen-year-old son, Joseph. I was instantly drawn in by the warmth of her rich Spanish accent, her disarming smile, and her sincere acceptance of us into her home. We were family just coming by for a visit.

We gathered in the living room, Mrs. Vasquez, Joseph, Dianne, several students and I. Mr. Vasquez had planned to be there but was called away on business. Adopting a matter-of-fact tone, as if commenting on the weather, Mrs. Vasquez started relating her story. She needed to explain to the group exactly what had transpired and why she had called on us. We settled in patiently to listen.

About eight months ago, she and her husband were awakened by loud noises coming from their son's room. They jumped out of bed and ran to his room to find him huddled in the corner. Sitting on the floor several feet from his bed, he looked exhausted and confused. A bit bruised and shocked, he remembered nothing after going to sleep earlier that evening. He just woke up in his present position.

All three of them hesitantly agreed it was probably a sleepwalking incident. It was a plausible explanation and, after all, no one was really hurt, just shaken up a bit. They shrugged their shoulders, reassured themselves and went back to bed. Then it happened again a few nights later.

Joseph vaguely remembered a feeling of being lifted off his bed and then pushed across the room. "Oh, God," his parents thought. "The worst has actually happened. Seizures of some sort." Mrs. Vasquez explained that Joseph's birth had been traumatic and wrought with difficulties. Their son had come into this world with minor nerve damage to his left arm. To this day he had never gained full mobility of that arm and hand. After his birth they had feared additional complications would arise, and they were relieved when none surfaced. None, that is, until the events beginning eight months before. "No!" they thought. "It can't be, but it is. There IS nerve damage, maybe even brain damage. Now he's got seizures!"

Frantically, they made an appointment with the pediatrician and were promptly referred to a neurologist. Testing began but produced no conclusive results. "Wait and see," they were told. "We'll have to see what develops." That was fine with everyone since he hadn't had any additional seizures lately. So they waited.

A few weeks later, Joseph had another episode. However, this time he had seemed to sense someone standing over his bed before he was "thrown" across the room. "But," he said, "it could have been my imagination, maybe just a dream."

"Just a dream," they concluded. There hadn't been anyone else in the house. The dog had slept comfortably throughout the whole affair. What else could it possibly be, anyway?

Part II   House Ghosts

Time went on. Even a trial period of medication produced no results. Every few weeks the seizures would recur. At one point, Joseph told his parents that he had heard footsteps in the hall and seen a man standing in his doorway. Then things had gone blank until he awakened across the room, bruised and disoriented.

"So sad," his parents thought. "We were right to suspect seizures. The doctors even said that sometimes they could be preceded by audio and/or visual hallucinations." A vow was made to see a new doctor, again, for new tests, advice, and maybe even a new treatment. Maybe they would even see a psychiatrist. Maybe the whole problem WAS a result of some sleep disorder like someone had suggested.

They promised themselves to follow the medical and psychiatric routes more intensely, with more diversity and more avenues of exploration. Appointments were set. The ball was rolling. They would discover the cause of this medical dilemma.

And then one night they, too, heard the footsteps just before Joseph was "attacked." For "attack" was the only word they could use at that point to describe the situation. Once again Joseph was curled in the corner, a fresh bruise already swelling on his arm. "Impossible," they muttered to one another. "A ghost. We really don't believe in ghosts. But what other plausible explanation could there be?" Contacting a local metaphysical bookstore for advice, the parents were referred to Dianne.

So here we are. We have moved up to the bedroom where all the activity has taken place. It is here that we will sit to perform the clearing. Within the circle are Mrs. Vasquez and Joseph. Dianne is sitting to my right. She gives my hand a squeeze for reassurance. I respond in kind, hoping that at least I convey a minimum sense of certainty.

I have almost no experience with this, and I am extremely nervous. "I AM HERE." I hear the familiar voice of Guidance clearly within my head. "YOU HAVE COME HERE TO DO THIS. YOU ARE PROTECTED." I start to relax, my excitement and anticipation growing. The voice I hear is Michael, one of my Spirit guides. I'm immensely reassured. I've channeled him many times before and have grown to trust him.

"USE ME AS A FILTER," he continues. "I WILL CHANNEL THE BEING, AND YOU WILL CHANNEL ME. SPIRIT IS WITH YOU."

But Michael, what happens if I go too deep? This isn't the Higher energy that I'm used to channeling. I've been told to give myself over as much as possible. But this is…"

"Are we ready to begin?" asks Dianne, interrupting my silent conversation. She brings me back to the present situation.

"Mother-Father God, Infinite Power of the Universe…" I begin the invocation. "We ask that you join us here, that you watch over what we do…" Slowly I continue, leading the group through the process of creating the sacred space. Additional deep breathing, additional prayers. My breathing becomes fast. My hold on Dianne's hand tightens as I am filled with Spirit.

I feel Michael and then another presence. "Why have you come here?" A voice comes through me and I allow the words to come out of my mouth. "What are you doing?" I receive the image of a Latino male, mid fifties, dressed in work clothes. Dried dirt and sweat streak his face.

"Who is speaking now?" Dianne inquires. "We'd like to talk with you, but we need to know your name first. Mine is Dianne."

"I am Emanuel. I live here. I work here." I get a mental picture of him, a wife, and son working a mine many years ago.

"But Emanuel, you're dead. What type of work can you be doing here?" Dianne asks. "Other people live here now."

I stop breathing. I feel confusion, fear, the urge to run. Are these Emanuel's feelings or mine? Dianne interrupts my perplexity. "Emanuel! Talk with us. Whatever has happened, we're here to help."

"Please, Emanuel, be patient." I fill my inner voice with as much reassurance as I can muster, projecting my thoughts with genuine caring. *"Listen. It's safe."* Then, "I AM HERE." That's Michael, but I can't tell if he's speaking to me or to Emanuel.

"The mine." Emanuel seems to have made a decision to stay, to speak with Dianne. His words flow as I relax and surrender more of my physical body to him. "We're working the mine."

Dianne tries to keep him on track. "Emanuel. You're not working the mine now. You're here talking with us." But there's no interrupting him.

"It's dark and cold and dirty. We've put our lives into this hole. And for what? Oh, God, Dios mío, save us!" He is almost screaming now. I feel his anguish, his pain. I see a fire and the beginnings of a cave-in. It's all around me. I'm in the middle of it. There is no separation between Emanuel and myself. The smoke billows, the ground rumbles. "Look out!" Rocks start falling from the ceiling. We're trapped! Got to get out. Got to save my family. But then my son grabs my arm. What amazing strength for a boy of fifteen. He pushes me out the mouth of the cave.

"M'ijo! My son! No!" The cave collapses, burying my wife and my only son. "No!"

Dianne interrupts. She sounds frantic. Things are getting out of control. "Emanuel! It's safe now. That was a long time ago. You're here with us now! Steven, come back. Steven, let us know what's going on."

I take a deep, shuddering breath, tearing myself free of Emanuel. "I AM HERE. YOU'RE DOING FINE. RELAX. GO BACK. CONTINUE." There's Michael again.

"What the hell happened there, Michael?" I'm more than a little scared and in shock. *"You're supposed to run interference for me. I felt lost."* The adrenaline starts to subside, but I'm still feeling angry. *"Don't leave me again."*

"I WON'T. I AM HERE. THIS IS A GOOD EXPERIENCE FOR YOU. YOU ARE SAFE." Michael projects calmness, love, and Light to me and to Emanuel. *"Yeah, sure. Thanks,"* I respond sarcastically.

"Steven. Emanuel. Are you there?" Dianne pulls on my hand slightly.

"Yes. I am sorry." Emanuel returns. "There was an accident. A fire. The mine collapsed. It should have been me. I couldn't save them. I tried. But I couldn't. It was impossible. It should have been me." I am aware of tears streaking down my face, my body wracked in sorrow.

"Emanuel, please. That was long ago. You're dead now. And so are your son and wife. There's nothing you can do now." Dianne is firm and direct.

"Calm down Emanuel. We can go through this together. We're here for healing," I project to him silently.

Then Michael, "GOOD JOB, STEVEN. I AM HERE. IT IS SAFE. YOU'RE DOING WELL." A moment ago I was starved for Michael's reassurance. Now, however, it's almost a distraction. "AS IT SHOULD BE, STEVEN. CONTINUE."

"It should have been me. It's my fault. I dragged them out here with promises. So many promises. It should have been me in there. And now all is lost. Dios mío." The tears flow freely.

"Emanuel. All is NOT lost. Listen to me," Dianne commands. "You're wife and son are fine. They're dead, but they're waiting for you in Spirit."

Fear, unimaginable terror, courses through me. I stop breathing. I can feel my hand tightening painfully around Dianne's frail fingers. She squirms, then gasps because of the pain. "It's okay, Emanuel!" Dianne is almost screaming. "It's okay. Relax. I'm sorry. You don't have to do anything right now. Stay a while and talk with us."

The fear subsides. Sorrow returns. "I'm sorry. I can't go to them. I killed them. How can I live with myself? How can I face them? I killed them. I killed my son. M'ijo!"

Dianne distracts him. "Why have you come here, Emanuel? Why have you bothered this family? Why do you harm Joseph? He's done nothing."

Confusion, disorientation, then a silent memory. I am Emanuel. Caught in a relentless dream of sorrow, fear, and guilt, I try to push my son out of the way. I had been drifting aimlessly around this site. Then the Vasquez family moves in, Joseph reminding me so much of my own Pedro. Each time I relive the disaster, I try to push him out of the way. I peer at Joseph more closely now. He is not Pedro. I feel even more guilt, followed by embarrassment.

"Steven," Emanuel speaks to me in my head. "*Don't tell them. I am ashamed for mistaking Joseph for my own son. Don't tell them! I'll go. But please don't tell them that I was so foolish.*" Emanuel is pleading with me for help. "*Don't tell them.*"

I ask for guidance. I need to separate a bit from this loving, desperate entity. "*Michael. Help. Put the words in my mouth.*" Aloud now, Emanuel speaks the words that Guidance seems to provide both of us. "I come here. I see this boy. He reminds me so much of my own Pedro. I didn't mean to harm him. I just wanted to get his parents' attention. He is so special. He is connected with Spirit. So caring. So smart. And his parents ignore him, thinking him ordinary. Now they will not. He will continue his studies. He will grow to be strong."

"Emanuel," Dianne continues. "It's alright now. No great harm was done here. The family forgives you."

She must have given the Vasquezes encouragement for they, too, echo her sentiments. "That's right. I'm okay," Joseph says.

Then Mrs. Vasquez: "You're forgiven. We WILL spend more time with him. We will listen to him more. Thank you for helping."

Internally, again, I speak to Emanuel. *"They bought it! Our cover-up worked. And you HAVE helped them be more aware of Joseph's needs, even if you didn't know that's what you were doing."*

"Thank you, Steven. Gracias, Estefan." Emanuel is greatly relieved.

"I AM HERE." That's Michael again. "YOU'RE DOING WELL, BUT YOU'RE TIRING. IT'S TIME TO SEND HIM ONWARD."

"Emanuel, this is Dianne again. This family forgives you. Your own family has forgiven you for so long now. You are forgiven in Spirit. All is forgiven. They know you couldn't save them. They cherish the time they had with you. They shared your dream of fortune and a good life. They love you. The only thing they want right now is for you to join them in the Light."

Feelings of relief and peacefulness. "Gracias, Senora. Thank you all. Again, I am sorry. I'll go now. Vaya con Dios, Joseph." Contentment. A long time of wandering, of sorrow, and of guilt come to an end. I look up and see the Light. My son, my wife. They're up there, waiting, calling. I start to rise, feeling lighter and more diffuse.

Rising, expanding. Brighter, accepting, loving. The Light. My family. Tears of joy, of homecoming. I can see the Light. I can feel it. I'm going in, letting myself be surrounded. Drifting in forgiveness, in Love.

"Steven!" Dianne raises her voice. "Steven, come back now. Come back. It's not your time." She sounds upset. Gosh, she sure gets emotional sometimes.

Damn! That's right. I am Steven, not Emanuel. It's his time to go, not mine. But I don't want to come back! My body is down there. Rent to pay. Work to be done. A car to fix. Relationships to repair. Damn! "Good bye Emanuel. Bless you. Thank you, Michael. Thank you so much for this." *So it's NOT my time to go. Oh, well. At least I can bring some of this back with me. I will remember this as long as I live…and beyond.*

"It's okay." I take a deep breath as I relax and return to my body. "I'm back. Give me a second." I lightly squeeze Dianne's hand in reassurance. "Just a moment or so." I languish in the aftereffects. I still feel the Light, the expansiveness. I let my tears of overwhelming joy run freely.

I open my eyes and look around at the people gathered. Some have tears in their eyes. Others look at me with obvious confusion and bewilderment. *"Who are you? What did you do? How did you do that?"* they seem to be asking.

I shrug my shoulders. *"I don't know. I'm just glad to be alive."*

Channeling a ghost in a healing circle was a leap for me. To let another entity, besides Guidance and the familiar energy of Michael, actually use my body and my voice took a tremendous amount of trust and faith. Prior to this clearing, I would usually contact the ghost, carry on a private conversation on a different plane, and then convey the words and meaning to the group. In channeling the ghost, however, I feared I might somehow lose myself, lose touch with Guidance, lose touch with my body. I thought I might be overly dependent on Dianne to counsel the ghost and to bring me back safely. I feared a loss of control over the outcome.

All I knew going into this was that I had the explicit encouragement and reassurance of Michael, whom I trusted. Therefore, I trusted the situation and moved forward. As things turned out, Dianne was more anxious throughout than I was, perhaps because she did not realize that Michael was right there with me, and that I was conscious of all that went on.

In channeling Emanuel, I felt his emotions, his fears, almost as intensely as I imagine he did. Likewise, as I moved into the Light, I felt the tremendous outpouring of love and acceptance which is only recognizable to me as Spirit. It was awesome. Yet when back, I carried some of the awe and wonder with me. I was committed to living life more fully, with more awareness and appreciation.

Since then, I have felt freer to choose whether to channel the ghost directly to a group, while Marcia or another person counsels them onward, or to convey the story more indirectly while I counsel the spirit. Either way works. There is a time and a place for each. I let Guidance lead me.

Emanuel's experience and need for completion are self-explanatory. He replayed, in a dreamlike state, that split-second moment when his son did for him what he could not do for his son—save his life. Shame and anguish were his companions thereafter. Was it just coincidence that the family Emanuel interacted with had an only son who could use some extra attention from his parents? Was it any coincidence that Joseph, at age fifteen, was open to acknowledging ghosts and Spirit? In spite of Emanuel's humiliation at his mistaken identity of Joseph for Pedro, our hurried "cover-up" may have been truer to the mark than we knew. Perhaps Joseph did need the recognition and support for his strengths. God works in mysterious ways, and I tend to think that all is perfect. We receive the experiences necessary in order to grow.

Dianne and the Vasquez family, some time later, consented to an interview with a newspaper reporter writing an article about ghosts in the area. Their story was published in the Colorado Springs Sun in July, 1982. The feature article was, thankfully, respectful, and sincere, introducing many people to the awe and wonder of Spirit.

Seven years after the clearing, I encountered the Vasquez family. They told me Joseph had experienced no more "seizures" within that time. Mr. Vasquez, not having been there for the clearing, had been a little suspicious, but grateful. The doctors remained baffled. They discovered neither what caused the problem nor why it unexpectedly ended. As for the rest of us who were there, we know.

Points to Remember…

- ✧ As healers, we need to be open to receiving impressions, but remain emotionally separate!
- ✧ Prejudgments limit our awareness; what initially seems hostile may merely be misunderstood.

Chapter 8

Honoring Choices

🌿 Following are a couple of clearings in which things did not go exactly as planned. You decide whether or not they were successes or failures. Success and failure are, after all, a matter of perspective.

The Gardener

Holly, an energetic, young receptionist at a local health spa, had been living alone in a quaint little cottage situated on the rear grounds of a large estate. She enjoyed the privacy of having her own space, surrounded by expansive gardens and lush lawns, along with a sense of comfort and safety at being tucked behind the main house. After several months, however, her contentment began to wane. "Strange" things started happening.

At times Holly felt she was being watched but, when she turned around to look, no one was there. Occasionally she heard rustling in the shrubs outside the front window, but she assumed it must be an animal. Reading quietly inside one evening, Holly heard distinct scratching noises on the side of the house. Again she looked, found nothing, and decided it must be the bushes blowing against the cedar siding of the exterior wall. She shrugged it off and went back to her book.

After work one summer evening, Holly was outside pulling weeds among the peonies when she was startled by a shadow "dashing by" at the edge of her vision. The form disappeared before she had a good look at it, though, and Holly decided to ignore the impression. Logic was telling her nobody was there. She must be imagining things because reality is dense, solid, and stationary. Over the next two weeks, however, it happened again and again. Imagination or not, Holly decided to call me.

Several days had passed between Holly's first urgent phone call to me and our appointment at her house. As I turned off the car engine and admired the vibrant purple iris lining the driveway, she stepped outside to meet me.

"Glad you could make it, Steve. But I've got to tell you, I almost called you yesterday to cancel this visit." She seemed much calmer than when I had spoken with her by phone the previous week. Back then, she could hardly wait for me to come over.

"Oh? Why's that?" I asked, feigning ignorance. Although I had a pretty good idea why she might want to call this off, I needed to know if she simply doubted her perceptions or if she had become less willing to release the ghost. "We do have time to take care of this right now, don't we? You don't have any pressing appointments, do you?"

"No!" she sputtered, seeming a bit embarrassed. "It's just…I feel kind of foolish, but the problem seems to have disappeared. I mean, even if I have a ghost here, you might not find anything."

"Is that all?" I responded with a reassuring smile. "Don't tell me. Right after we talked last week, things got quiet. Over the past few days, everything seems to have returned to normal. No unusual noises, no shadows passing by windows, no one watching you."

Shock, then curiosity. "How did YOU know?" she asked.

"Well, lots of times ghosts are aware of what's going on," I explained. "They often know when a person calls someone to take care of the situation. If they don't want to move on or don't want to talk with me, they may go into hiding. I'm glad you didn't call it off."

"You mean it's not just my imagination?" Holly asked, seeking reassurance.

"Lots of people I've worked with have had real similar experiences. We make an appointment, things quiet down, and they call off our meeting thinking everything has resolved itself. Three days later the phenomena start up again, and they're back on the phone asking me to come immediately. I usually remember to tell people not to be surprised if things quiet down. I'm sorry I must have forgotten to mention it to you, but I'm really glad you didn't call off the clearing."

Feeling less self-conscious, Holly relaxed as we walked toward the cottage. Reassured that we were going to proceed, I deliberately opened up my intuitive senses, ready to perceive whatever might be present. Right away, I had a feeling of being watched, and those same eyes followed me into the small living quarters. "You're not alone, Holly," I shared. "I feel exactly what you reported. Somebody is watching us right now. He's being cautious and keeping some distance, but he's here. Let's settle in and get to work."

On a small wool rug in the main room, we sit facing each other, Holly's hands in mine. Closing our eyes and relaxing, we focus our intent. We call on the Light. Forming the circle, we run the energy, each of us breathing the Light in the left hand and out the right.

I see an older man now. He has suddenly appeared before us. The strong scent of sweet lilacs fills the room, indicating to me that he is a peaceful being. Yet, I feel impatience exuding from him, an urge to get on with things.

"Thank you for coming." I speak aloud in order to focus my thoughts and to include Holly. Still, I feel the impatience as he starts to waver from my vision. "Wait! We need to talk."

"I have nothing to talk about. I've got to go," he answers curtly.

"Where do you need to go? Please, this will just take a few minutes."

His image strengthens. The impatience subsides, only to be replaced by a resigned acceptance. *"How may I help you?"* he asks with a bit of humor. It's almost as if he's patronizing me.

"We're here to help YOU. Do you..."

"I don't need your help!" he interjects. *"I just want to get back to work."*

I follow his thoughts to the garden in front of the cottage and along the edges of the main house. He works there, peacefully tending the plants in silence and solitude.

"Wait! You know you're dead. You don't need to tend the garden anymore. There are loved ones waiting in the Light for..."

He interrupts again. *"I don't need to go there. I'm here to take care of the garden. That's my job. That's what I'm good at. The plants like me. We talk. I have all the loved ones I need right here."* I get a picture of the main house, a Buddhist monastery, a place of refuge and retreat. Monks stroll softly through the gardens and are comforted by this man's work. The plants flourish.

"This was your cottage, wasn't it?" I ask quietly. "You were the caretaker."

"I AM the caretaker!" he corrects me. *"And I've got work to do."*

"But what about the afterlife? Don't you have anywhere else to go? What about the Light? Haven't you paid your Karma? You deserve to get off the Wheel of Life…" He starts fading again, faster this time.

"Wait!" I seem to be saying that a lot. "This woman here with us has some things to say. This is her cottage now. She's living here and she's disturbed by some of the noises you make."

"But I've got to take care of the garden. There are things that need to be done."

"Yes," I reply gently, "but she helps take care of the garden, too. She helps to water and weed. She also trims the bushes. If she's bothered too much, she'll move. Then someone else might move in, someone who may not care for the plants as much as she does."

That piques his interest. I know it's a threat, but I need to get his attention for at least a while longer. He starts solidifying again. *"All right. I'm listening. But I'm not done here yet. I've still got work to do, and I'll know when it's time to stop."*

"That's fine," I reassure him. "All we ask is that you work on this part of the property when she's not home. You can work away from the cottage while she's here. And trust her to keep taking care of the place. She'll stay as long as she feels safe, as long as she can have her privacy. You understand how that feels, don't you?"

I see him taking a long, deep breath, visibly relaxing. *"Oh, is that all? I can do that. But what I'd also like is for her to ask at the main house for some help with the rest of the premises. They don't listen to me. I'd like to see more people helping and taking care of the place. It can be so beautiful, you know. Plants are good."*

"She promises to ask for more maintenance on the property, the lawns, and the gardens." I speak for Holly because she may still be hearing only my side of the conversation. "She just asks for peace, the same thing you want."

The word *peace* must be a trigger. I see him nodding in agreement as he starts to fade again. On his way out, he picks up a little hand shovel and starts bending over to tend to some young plants.

"Goodbye, whoever you are. You're doing a great job here. Others appreciate it. And when it's your time to let someone else take over, when it's your time to go on, you'll know."

"*I will*," he replies softly. He totally fades away, leaving just the slightest smell of sweet, moist Earth…and the delicate scent of lilacs.

Checking in with Holly several weeks later, she related some pleasant surprises. She had called the landlord and asked for more grounds maintenance. The response was immediate. A new company was hired to take care of the lawn. New shrubs and flowers were planted, including an abundance of lilac bushes. And Holly was offered a discount on the rent if she would take care of the gardens.

The past caretaker never bothered Holly again. She sometimes missed his presence, but she decided not to take undue chances by calling on him. Needless to say, the gardens throughout the property were beautiful.

Points to Remember…

- ✧ Sometimes the ghostly phenomena seem to disappear immediately after calling on someone to take care of the situation. The spirit goes into hiding.
- ✧ Occasionally a ghost is well aware of alternatives and chooses to stay. If there is no harm, we respect that choice.

The Ghost Nanny

"…Steve, this is Mary. You did a ghost clearing for a few friends of mine a while back." She sighed. "And I think I need your help."

"Sure, Mary. What can I do for you?"

"Well…" she continued with what seemed to be a forced cheerfulness. Underneath, I heard the tiredness in her voice. "My daughter, her baby, and I moved into this house a few months ago. I work a lot and am rarely at home. But my daughter, Sylvia, spends much of her time here alone with my granddaughter. I haven't noticed anything except maybe a chill in one room. And one time I think I saw a shadow or something. Well, anyway…" embarrassed to admit this, "I saw someone or something standing in a doorway. It disappeared immediately, so I never gave it another thought. But it seems Sylvia's been bothered by different things. And I found out only a few days ago."

As she talked, Mary got increasingly excited and upset. "Okay Mary. Slow it down a bit," I interjected, attempting to calm her. "Whatever it is, we can probably take care of it. Let's take it one step at a time. How active is the ghost?" I asked gently.

"Well, that's why I called," all the meekness gone from her voice. "Sylvia said she was pushed! She was just sitting in the living room, watching TV, and holding the baby. And something came up behind her and pushed her!"

I interrupted her before she could get into a frenzy. "That's a pretty active ghost, but…" She started to say something else, and I hurriedly cut her off. "Was she hurt in any way? Has anyone been hurt? Being touched by a ghost is pretty spooky but, really, it's not that uncommon. I want to know how hard it was. In what way was she pushed?"

Calmer, she responded a bit tentatively, "Well, actually, maybe it wasn't really being pushed as much as it was being poked. But she says it happened several times, and always in the living room. Now she's afraid of staying in there alone too long. And she's…we're both worried about the baby."

"Okay, Mary. I'm glad you called because now something can be done about it. But first, what else has happened besides the poking?"

"Just some footsteps upstairs a couple of times. And then what sounds like the kitchen cupboards opening and closing in the middle of the night...."

Being booked for the next couple of weeks, I told her I couldn't make it over there for a while. It didn't sound like an emergency to me, but there were things Sylvia could do in the meantime.

"Mary, tell Sylvia that if she gets excited the ghost will just get more active. The next time something happens, she should first take a deep breath and relax. Then, calmly facing the ghost, or its approximate location, she can forcefully, yet quietly, tell it to stop. You see, when the ghost is interacting with people, it is also open to receiving communications from whomever it is involved with. Basically, DON'T react with fear. Be assertive, and tell it to 'chill out.' Tell the ghost that someone will be there in a little while to talk with it. Tell him or her to stop and wait. Someone will be there soon."

"Okay, I guess we can do that," she assured me. "When can you come?"

"I can be there within two weeks. I'd like Sylvia to be there with us. Also, someone will need to be available to take care of the baby outside or, better yet, away from the house all together. We'll need a private space to work—no animals, no interruptions, no people coming and going.

"Gotcha!" she said excitedly.

"I'll come over with my wife and maybe a student or two. Since the ghost has actually touched someone, I prefer not to do the clearing alone. Hang in there. If something more extreme or threatening happens, call me. I'll get there sooner, or I'll call someone else I know who can get there quickly." We set a date and time for the clearing. "If I don't hear from you, we'll just see you in two weeks."

The old Victorian house Mary is renting seems rather unremarkable. There are many of them in this part of the country and, this one, white-washed from top to bottom, fades into the background against its colorful neighbors. As Marcia and I enter, I am instantly aware of a heavy feeling in the foyer, but I am not overly impressed with the intensity of the energy. It could be the psychic and emotional energies of the people living there, or it could be a ghost. We'll see.

Marcia looks at me and nods, letting me know she's felt it too. Upon entering the living room, however, we both abruptly stop. The heaviness has increased. There's a pervasive, musty odor like something stale or rotten. Again, Marcia and I look at one another.

As if on cue, Mary speaks up. "This is where we've had most of the problems." Sylvia is standing quietly in the corner, watching.

"Yes," I say, pointing to Marcia. "We both felt it when we came in. And I do sense a presence here. This is where we'll probably do the work, but I'd like to check out the rest of the house first."

The remainder of the first floor is uneventful. The heaviness and musty odor is concentrated in the living room. Even the basement seems clear. Upstairs, however, is a different story (no pun intended). Once upstairs, I feel lightness in my step. The whole floor looks brighter, more cheerful. I breathe more deeply and freely.

"Do you feel it too, Steve?" Marcia confirms my suspicions. "Totally different than downstairs. Let's go in here." She leads me into one particular bedroom. Spontaneously, we both look in the corner. "I thought I just saw a woman standing there," she hurriedly whispers to me, not wanting to alarm Mary or Sylvia. Additionally, we do not want to "spook" the ghost.

"Yes. I saw it too, but I can also feel her. This is a totally different energy than the one downstairs. There could be two different ghosts, one up here and one downstairs."

Leading the two women out of the room and back down to the main floor, Marcia and I share our perceptions. Sylvia, who has been mostly silent since we arrived, has trouble waiting until we're finished talking. She's getting more excited and restless with each passing moment.

"That explains it!" she blurts out. "I felt a couple of different things, too. When I was in the living room it was kind of weird. I felt afraid. But upstairs, even though I thought someone else might be up there, I felt kind of warm and safe."

"Well, Sylvia, we can still take care of things, even if there are two ghosts."

A sad look comes over her face. "Well, okay. But you're not going to hurt them or anything, are you?"

I try not to be too amused, as I have run into this before. "I understand your concern, but nobody will be hurt. My intent is not to harm, but to help send them on to a better place, to help them complete their journey. Everybody deserves heaven, or whatever it is that gives him or her peace. So let's get on with it...."

We form the circle, centering ourselves, doing an invocation, and stating our intent. I start to get impressions... A man, an angry man feeling left out, ignored. He presents himself and almost immediately starts to leave. "Wait," I say aloud, "We're not ignoring you now. Stay with us a while."

The images flow freely. A man, who gave up everything safe, everything secure, in his home back east to move Out West. He left behind his title, his family, and his inheritance. He told people he wanted to start a new life, a life of adventure and exploration. Some admired his bravery and courage while others called him foolish. "You'll be sorry, Daniel," his father said. But Daniel was resolute and determined.

Used to being an important man on the East Coast, Daniel moved west with pride and confidence. But pioneers at the foot of the Rocky Mountains didn't care about his fancy manners or his father's political power. These early western settlers had each struggled in their own way to leave the past behind and create a new dream. They laughed at Daniel's expectations of high regard. Undaunted, Daniel mingled with the wealthy and fell in love, opening his heart to the daughter of a successful land baron. They shared many happy afternoons strolling through the woods and stealing kisses in the garden. But in the end, she turned him away.

"I cannot support you marrying that pauper," her father had yelled. "It's high time for you to give up this childish infatuation and find a suitable match worthy of your station!" The young woman bowed to her father's wishes, eager to maintain her own social status. She told Daniel she never wanted to see him again.

Sadness washes over me, and then is gone. I notice tears on my cheeks. "Daniel, that's over now. That was...."

"*No, it isn't!*" The anger slaps me in the face, but I take a slow deep breath and continue.

"Daniel, you can't force someone to love you. And those people who would put money before love are to be pitied, not punished. Whoever she was, she is long dead, and so are you. You've been alone too long.

"Up in Spirit, there are no such judgments. Love and forgiveness come first. Both of your parents are up there. If you listen closely, you can hear them apologizing for the hardships they helped to create. They ask forgiveness for their lack of trust and support."

"But I never did get the family I wanted here. I don't want to give up on it. I never got to show my parents that I could make something of myself here." Daniel's determination is still strong.

I hurry to answer before he has a chance to dig in his heels. "It's NOT too late!" I find myself almost screaming. "It's never too late. You can start over again, but this time with the love and blessings you know you deserve. We all know you deserve it. Other family members are in the Light to help. Again, they ask your forgiveness, and they promise to do better in the future. They know they were selfish and unsupportive. They know you deserve their blessings, and they want to ask you to forgive them for their fears."

He starts to fade, and I feel encouraged that he is no longer putting his energy into being here. But there is one more thought I need to share. "Daniel, the people here in this house forgive you for any inconvenience you may have caused. They know now that you just wanted to be noticed, accepted. They also apologize for not understanding what it was you were going through. They know you meant no harm. They understand how painful it's been, and wish you peace." I hear Sylvia across the circle sniffling back tears. "It's time to go to the Light now, Daniel. Look up. Look for loved ones—not only family, but others as well. They're in the Light. Call on them. Go to them."

I feel a sigh of relief escape my lips as a weight is lifted off me. "Bye, Daniel. God bless."

After a moment or so, "…I now call on any other entities who may be inhabiting this house. Please make yourself present. If there is anyone else here, please…" My attention is called to the corner of the room where a bashful young woman appears. Hands folded in front of her white apron, she wears a floor-length black dress with delicate lace adorning the high collar and long sleeves. Staring at the floor, she approaches shyly. "Please, it's safe. We just want to talk," I encourage her.

I turn my attention to the group. I share my impressions with them, including them, and trusting that they will send a sense of safety and welcome as well. The woman comes a bit closer. Sadness washes over me. I stop breathing. Tears start to form.

"What is the sadness?"

"*I lost my child to the fever. All I want is my child. They wouldn't even let me help her.*" This woman, Sarah, speaks in a voice heavy with passion and distress. "*My baby, they wouldn't let me near her! All I wanted to do was help!*" I see the bedroom, the doctors. Sarah is there, crying. She moves in a frenzy around the room, wailing and complaining on the edge of hysteria. She stops to tug at a doctor's arm, pleading with him to save her child. Her distraction gets in the way of his work and, gently but firmly, he sends her out. Feeling frustrated and useless as she paces the kitchen, Sarah isn't even present when her baby passes on.

"*I just want to help,*" Sarah moans. "*I just want to be here. I CAN be of help.*"

Sarah's conviction is unwavering, and I realize that this may be a difficult situation to resolve. Aloud I say, "Sarah, your baby has passed on, and so have you. You're forgiven for not being able to help. They stopped you. We know you loved your daughter, and so does she. There was nothing you could do to…"

"*But I can!*" she interrupts. "*I can! I can be here. I love the baby here. She's like my own. And her mom needs my help.*"

"Sarah, listen. Sylvia is fine taking care of the baby. She's got her mom here to help, and she's doing better all the time. It's time for you to go on to the Light." As I finish the sentence, Sarah disappears, replaced by the Light. It seems strange, even suspicious, that she would disappear so fast. But she's gone. I try calling her back, but only halfheartedly because, if she actually did move on to the Light, I do not wish to disturb her. I decide that this is all I can do for now. I can live with the ambivalence. If Sarah reveals her presence again, I will come back at a later time.

I come out of trance and relate my impressions to Sylvia and Mary, telling them first about Daniel's transition and then about Sarah. When I share my misgivings and confusion about Sarah's process, Sylvia clears her throat.

"Okay," I think to myself, "here it comes. She's looking guilty about something."

"Uh, Steve, I forgot to tell you something. I don't know if I really wanted to get rid of Sarah. I told my mom what happened just a few days ago, but I guess I should tell you, too. The other day I left the baby upstairs on my bed just for a minute." Guilt fills her voice, "I mean, I thought she was asleep and she would be okay. When I went back upstairs—and I know I wasn't hallucinating—I saw her gently rising in midair from about halfway down to the floor. Maybe she fell or something, but she just floated up over the side, and back onto the bed."

"Sylvia, it really would have been helpful for me to know this ahead of time."

"But I forgot! I didn't mean to forget!"

Not intending to put her on the defensive, I drop the exasperation from my voice. "That's okay. I know it's been hectic lately. It's hard to keep up with everything. But I feel that when Sarah disappeared, she didn't go to the Light. She just hid from me because she wants to keep hanging around here, helping."

"Well, what's wrong with that?" Sylvia counters. "If it makes everyone happy, then there's nothing wrong with it. I feel good just knowing Daniel is gone. We're safe. Sarah HAS been helpful to me, and maybe she NEEDS to help. Sarah saved my daughter!"

I don't have a good response to that. Maybe the results are what everyone needs and wants. If everyone is happy, then it isn't my place to be more forceful. Who am I to say that Sylvia should let Sarah go, or that Sarah would be better off in the Light? I remember that we all have our lessons, and we'll all make it home to Spirit at the perfect time.

"I don't know," I acknowledge. "But if you really want Sarah to be here, and she wants it too, then we're not going to be able to send her on anyway. When the time comes that you feel you can take care of things yourself, when the time comes that it feels right to send her onward, you'll know."

Chapter 8   Honoring Choices

"At that time, you can just meditate, call in the Light, and see if you can send her on by yourself. When she and you are both ready, I trust you to give her that choice. Just remind her of what we said today. Thank her for her help, and let her know that she's complete now. She's helped enough. Let her know that there are other loved ones, maybe even her own daughter, waiting in the Light for her. You can say your good-byes then and gently nudge her into the Light."

"Thank you, Steve." Sylvia looks straight into my eyes. "I will. I promise I will. When we're both ready."

The preceding cases involving the gardener and the nanny are examples of free will—the soul's choice to remain on the earth plane, and the living person's choice to accept that soul's presence. They bring up an ethical dilemma. Are we to do what WE think is right, or do we respect other people's decisions? Even though I personally feel it is best to release the ghost, I also need to respect people's individual choices. Looking back on these clearings, I feel good that we did the most we thought possible and ethical at the time. In the case of the gardener, it was the ghost's expressed will to be left alone and to stay. He was aware of his choices and acknowledged that moving on to the Light was an option. He was loving and kind. In many ways, he was content. With Sylvia's ghost nanny, there was an agreement between the ghost and the tenant. It was unlikely that we could send Sarah onward because she had an invitation to stay. She had someone agreeing to share the house with her, giving her more energy to linger. Since there was no noticeable harm done to anyone, living or "dead," Marcia and I surrendered to the situation.

However, I hope that at some time or another after the attempted clearings, the ghosts will move on to the Light. Perhaps my own perception is biased, but I still feel that their journeys from this physical plane remain incomplete. I still have an urge to nudge them onward along a pathway toward Spirit, to a resting place where the Light lends perspective, peace, and infinite love. Maybe our contact with them during the attempted clearings will have, in some way, opened a door of awareness for them. At least now I can rest, knowing that I did my best to help them be conscious of their choices in the present and their options for the future.

Points to Remember…

- ✧ Throughout a clearing, everyone present has an impact upon the outcome.

- ✧ Surrender does not mean defeat; surrender means letting go with faith and trust.

Chapter 9

Lasting Impressions

People are full of emotional, mental, and psychic energy. Our love, joy, anger, and despair spill out from us regularly, extending toward space, objects, and people around us. Others can choose whether or not to join in our energy. They may share it and respond to it, or they may push it away, wanting no part in feeling our feelings.

Objects surrounding us, on the other hand, do not make a conscious choice about our energy. As we project our feelings, consciously or unconsciously, toward or into particular objects, those objects tend to absorb the emotional and psychic charge, hold onto it, and reflect it back outward. Thus, we become comfortable with our surroundings, our furniture, our wall hangings, and our favorite clothes. They feel like a part of us.

A house, for example, may be considered a big object. We often put a lot of energy into our home. On a physical level, we paint the walls, decorate the windows, plant flowers, and claim the house as our own. While we are doing this, the house also absorbs our emotional energy. Our caring, anger, love or sadness go into the same walls we are painting, and the whole house takes on an aura based on the energy we have projected. When we sell the house, and new owners move in, they bring a different energy. In the process of making the house theirs, they may remodel the kitchen, replace the carpet, fill the rooms with new furniture, and, in effect, put their energy into the house. If they do this with gusto and fervor, the previous energies quickly dissipate, and the house takes on a new feeling.

Similarly, smaller objects to which we become attached or carry in our possession for a long time absorb our energy. We may "love" a particular piece of jewelry, a favorite rocking chair or a trusty set of tools. Likewise, when we acquire objects from someone else, we make them ours by polishing old gems, refinishing antique furniture or thoroughly cleaning an heirloom picture frame. In doing so, we help erase the former imprint of energy and begin the process of imbuing it with our own.

Sometimes we consciously choose to cleanse or not to cleanse an object. When a favorite grandmother dies and we are left with her ivory pendant, we may cherish the feelings, memories, and love that emerge when we hold, look at or wear the piece. Or we may buy an old diamond ring from a pawn shop and want to cleanse it. We can do this by soaking it in spring water, letting it rest in sea salt overnight, or placing it on a sunny windowsill after scrubbing it. By focusing our energy and intent on cleansing the object, we can usually clear it of previous impressions.

There are also some rituals designed specifically to cleanse a physical space. Smudge is traditionally a mixture of sage, cedar, and sweetgrass. It may be loosely mixed or, more often, can be purchased as a tightly wrapped bundle of dried plants, called a smudge stick. Lighting the smudge and then blowing out the flame, the mixture smolders and emits an aromatic smoke that can be fanned to wash over objects. In clearing a house, we would bathe the corners of each room in smoke while focusing on a prayer of intent to cleanse and bless the space with positive thoughts. Frankincense and myrrh have the same purpose, as does Holy water blessed by a priest. Regardless of the technique used, however, it is the focus of attention, the intent, and the energy we put into the ritual, which results in cleansing the space.

There are times, however, when claiming and cleansing an article is not enough to clear it of past energies. Every once in awhile, an entity will have attached itself to an object. We have already met several ghosts who were attached to a particular house or property, but sometimes the object is much smaller and the ghost gets passed along unexpectedly.

The Wedding Gown

"Steve, your name was given to me by the bookstore. You've also done some work for a friend of mine." The woman on the phone spoke calmly and with an accent, maybe Middle Eastern. "I definitely think I have a ghost. Let me tell you what's been happening."

"Wait a second," I interrupted. "First, I'd love to know your name!" I know that once people finally reach me, they're anxious to spill out their story to someone who will understand. But I need a connection, a sense of who I'm dealing with.

"Sorry. My name is Nishma. It's just that I finally decided to call you, and it feels kind of weird."

"That's okay, Nishma. But I really do like to know who I'm talking to. Sorry if I interrupted. Go ahead."

Silence. I didn't mean to slow her down that much! So I jumped in with my usual questions.

"What type of house do you live in? And for how long?" And then the prickling sensation came. Starting at the base of my neck, little pins and needles of energy began crawling upward until I gave an involuntary shiver. For me, a sure sign of some ghostly activity. Now I was excited, too!

"What kinds of things have been happening? Have you had problems at other houses in which you've lived? Have there been any problems outside of your home? Have you…"

Now it was her turn to interrupt. "Steve, wait. You don't understand. It's not the house I'm worried about. It's a dress, a wedding gown."

"O-kaaay." I drawled while the impact of her words sunk in. A dress. This was bound to be an interesting story. "Tell me about the dress, Nishma. What's been happening?"

"Well, I bought it a few months ago. I've been engaged for almost a year, but Gordon and I haven't set an exact date yet for the wedding. Still, I'm real excited and I think about our upcoming marriage ceremony all the time. So I was out shopping one day, looking for a birthday present for my brother, and I saw this beautiful old wedding gown hanging in the window of a vintage clothing store. I mean, I wasn't looking for a wedding dress at all, but I just had to go in and see this gown!"

Full of lace trim, pearl beadwork, and a long silken train, the dress beckoned to her, "Take me, wear me, cherish me." Knowing only that she had to have the dress, Nishma bought it without even trying it on. Cradling it in her arms, she brought it home. "This is perfect!" she thought.

Over time, Nishma replaced some torn lace, restitched some beads, and had it cleaned. Satisfied that it looked finished, she misted it lightly with steam one evening and hung it over the bathtub to shed any wrinkles. Happily exhausted, she went to sleep assured that all was in readiness. She would be prepared for her wedding…whenever that was.

Then the problems started. "I woke up that night to noises coming from the bathroom. It sounded like cloth rustling, like when you rub against it," she explained. "And like things bouncing around in the tub, like buttons falling off or something." But when she got up and opened the door, all the noises disappeared. Upon inspection, there was nothing wrong with the dress. Nothing was out of place.

"I felt like a fool," she continued, "until the same thing happened the next night, and the next! Finally, I couldn't handle the lack of sleep and the weirdness of it all. So I made a space in a downstairs closet for the dress and put it in there, hoping to get the whole thing out of my mind." Days passed with Nishma only peeking in at the gown occasionally. But she missed it, had to see it more often, wanted to get excited about her own upcoming wedding.

She took the gown out of the closet and hung it in her bedroom "to air out." She left it out, needing to look at it, to touch it and take care of it. Trying it on almost every evening, she soon realized that it had become an obsession, but she couldn't stay away from it. It felt good being near it, yet at the same time feelings of sadness and anger would sometimes surface. The noises started up again at night, but she didn't want to put the gown away.

"Then I stared getting kind of paranoid, Steve. I began to wonder if Gordon was being faithful to me. I started to wonder if I should even go through with this marriage. What if he's not really sincere or committed?" At times she even thought that these feelings and doubts got stronger when she put on the gown. "I started to wonder if the problem was the dress or if the problem was me and Gordon."

She came to believe that the dress was cursed. Maybe her relationship was cursed. Maybe she was hexed. Confusion and self-doubt followed and, during a fit of anger, she tried to destroy the dress. Ripping at it only fueled her anger. It wouldn't rip! Cutting it didn't work either; the scissors broke in her hand. Trying to burn it, she just ended up burning herself. The dress wouldn't burn!

"I had finally decided to let go of the dress. I wanted it out of my life. I wanted to get back to figuring out what was real between Gordon and me. And that little old dress was suddenly indestructible!

"And then, Steve," she blurted out frantically, "yesterday, I boxed it up and put it in the dumpster. I was sure I was finally done with it. But I got up this morning and there, on my front door step, was the dress. It was sitting neatly folded in the same box just like I left it, like it was when I threw it out.

"I'd get rid of it again, but it might just come back. I'd like to be complete with it, finished. But I also know I need to learn more about it, and maybe resolve something with it. I can't just pass it off to someone else the way it is, and I can't seem to destroy it. I thought maybe you could help."

This seems weird, even to me. "I'd love to come by. I'm sure we can do something to get rid of the problem." We set up a time to meet.

Nishma, her friend Sally, and I gather in a circle, the boxed gown in the middle. The centering and invocation go smoothly, wonderfully. Their hearts are into it. But before I even have a chance to call on any entities that may be present, sadness washes over me. I feel alone, abandoned, rejected, so alone, so alone...

"SEPARATE, STEVE." That's Michael's voice. I'm glad Guidance is with me. "THIS ISN'T YOU. THESE AREN'T YOUR FEELINGS. SEPARATE!"

A deep breath wracks my body. I start talking aloud in order to include Sally and Nishma. It also helps me stay focused. "I see a young woman. She's on the East Coast of the United States. Her name is Virginia. She's wearing the dress. Standing, waiting, looking for someone who never comes. Waiting. So sad. Alone."

The sadness mixes with anger as Virginia starts talking…to me, to herself. I'm not sure. *"He left me. Went Out West and left me. He postponed the wedding, practically left me at the altar, and sent a message saying he'd send for me. He said he'd send for me! He said so…"* She repeats that phrase over and over again. A litany to the past.

"Virginia!" I almost yell it out. "Virginia, listen to me. We're here to help. That was a long time ago."

She's broken out of her stupor and, turning her face to me, I see the despair and the hard lines of bitterness. *"Then I get word that he's met someone else, betrothed to another. I hate him! I love him! For me there will never be another. So ashamed. So humiliated in front of my family and friends. I hate him. I love him. Maybe he'll still be back. Maybe he'll still send for me. That's it. He will. We'll still be together."* Virginia's obsession continues.

I see Virginia holding on to the wedding gown throughout her remaining years. She loves it. She hates it. Fondling it, trying it on, crying tears into it, she obsesses over it. She ignores her health, dwelling on the anger and sadness. No one can help. She will not be deterred from her conviction that her husband-to-be will return. Wasting away, she dies at a relatively young age…still holding on to the dress.

"Virginia. It's over now. You made it Out West. We're in Colorado now."

"Oh!" She brightens up, looking around, looking hopeful. "James?" Hoping to catch a glimpse of him, hoping she's finally caught up with him.

"He's gone, Virginia." I speak to her softly, kindly. "He did marry that other woman, but they're gone. He's been dead for so many years now." Sadness and dejection emanate from her, from me.

"HURRY, STEVE!" Michael prompts me. "YOU'RE LOSING HER. HURRY. BEFORE SHE DRIFTS OFF AGAIN."

Quickly then, I interject, "But you still might find him! You died many years ago, too. People who loved you, other people, also passed on. There's nothing for you here now, Virginia. They're in the Light. They're all in the

Light waiting for you, Virginia, waiting to greet you, hug you, and give you their support. James is in the Light as well."

She looks up, hopeful, anticipating. She starts to drift upward.

"Just let go of the dress, Virginia. You won't need it up there. There are other dresses, other opportunities. Let your love guide you. Let the Light guide you. There's still hope. But you need to go to the Light to find it, to find him."

In one quick breath, I realize I'm talking to thin air. She's disappeared, following the Light in search of him. I don't know if she'll find him there, but I know she'll be taken care of. Sweet relief washes over me as my awareness returns to Nishma's living room.

After the clearing, Nishma shared with me, while wiping tears from her eyes, that she'd been having more questions about her own engagement. Her fiancé had seemed distant, cold. They'd been arguing off and on, not resolving issues, muddling communications.

"I'd still like to get rid of the dress. I'll return it to the store where I got it," she said calmly. "That doesn't mean I'm letting go of Gordon, but the dress just doesn't work for me anymore. Too many sad memories. I can always get another one later."

Nishma assured me that she would talk more earnestly, lovingly, and honestly with Gordon. She would sincerely put some energy into bringing up and resolving their differences. She also needed to know if they did indeed have a good relationship, a lasting one. "Either way it turns out, I don't want to end up like Virginia. We'll see what happens. There's still enough caring that we can make a go of it. At the very least, we can learn to be more open and honest with each other. We'll see."

"Whatever happens, Nishma, I know you deserve to be happy, to be in the perfect relationship." Taking her hands in mine, looking into her eyes, I repeat a message I remember saying to Virginia. "Let your love guide you."

∽

Like attracts like. Nishma and Virginia had some similar lessons, and they helped each other gain insight, heal pain, and move forward on their journeys. Was it any accident that Nishma came upon the dress and felt compelled to buy it? Was it her own doubts, mistrust and uncertainty about her relationship with Gordon that resonated with the energy of the dress? Did Nishma's unacknowledged fears about her own wedding awaken Virginia, resulting in the dress calling to her? Who knows? Spirit, I think, sends us exactly what we need to awaken our soul. It is then up to us to hang on or let go, letting love be our guide.

Points to Remember…

- ✧ Objects may "house" a ghost.
- ✧ A person's energy may "resonate" with an object or spirit.
- ✧ We use whatever arguments are necessary to urge entities beyond their pain. The important thing is to get them to a better place. Spirit will take care of the rest.

Chapter 10

Moving Forward

Where is the line between our fear and our faith when dealing with angry spirits? A clearing may put to the test our trust in Guidance and our confidence in the healing process. We need to affirm that every individual, alive or dead, is a spiritual being deserving of love, forgiveness, and healing.

Soldiers Looking for a Fight

"I ain't done nothin' wrong. What's it to ya, anyhow?" That's Pete, the leader of the gang. I can feel a snarl cross my face as I channel his words to the group.

"Maybe you did, maybe you didn't, Pete," Beth, the counselor present, says in a quiet, yet firm voice. "That's not up to us to decide. We're here to help the people who live in this house."

I mentally review the circumstances that brought me to this property in New Mexico. Beth, an experienced, professional psychic had called me into the case. She preferred not to do this clearing alone because of the violence. It seems that a certain young couple was experiencing some traumatic events in their lives.

Beth knew that both the man and the woman were highly emotional, and she suspected the husband, Paul, of physically abusing his wife. "That's really none of our business," she told me, "but we've got to take care of the ghost problem."

About three months earlier, the husband, a six-foot-three-inch, muscle-bound ex-Marine, was physically thrown across the room. There was no one else present. Understandably, he was a little shaken. He related that no, he didn't trip! And, no, he didn't imagine it! It happened another two times over the ensuing three months, and he had the bruises to prove it! He wanted this entity out of his life!

Beth had agreed to come by, with several students, to take care of the problem. And she would be bringing someone, me, to channel the ghost. The couple was agreeable to this as long as we cleared up the problem and the husband stopped getting hurt.

"Pete. Are you listening?" Beth asserts herself. She's not about to let things drift in this situation. "Pete! Pay attention!"

Pete was one of three mercenary soldiers who died a long time ago, somewhere in the south. They knew they had committed many atrocities against others. Living a life of violence, they hired themselves out as ruthless killers. It didn't matter to them what cause they were fighting for, or who they hurt, as long as they got paid. All three died at about the same time, seemingly without remorse for their deeds. However, death got the better of them. As drifting entities, the three of them had hooked up again with plenty of time to review their lives. Sheepishly, they admitted to one another that perhaps they could have been a little kinder.

"But what can ya do?" says Pete, the acting spokesman for the group. "We did what we did. We didn't know nothin' else. So we's been movin' 'round looking for good fights ta fight. Fights that'll, you know, help somebody. So we find this here lady who's got this real angry guy, and he won't leave her alone. So we starts beatin' on him. It's a good thing we be doin'. We feel right at home here. You ain't got no business interferin'. You just let us be to do our job."

"Pete," Beth interjects. "It is our business. You're hurting him. He's done nothing to you."

"So? We got him dead to rights. He don't mind. He's lookin' for a fight, too. Ask him! And besides, he deserves it."

"But, Pete, you're hurting her, too. What you're doing is making things worse, not better. You've got to leave these people alone. They can work things out on their own. But you've got to go now. Focus on the Light…."

"What!" he shouts. "We ain't goin' ta no Light! We's got every right ta be here. We's stayin' put."

At this point I'm feeling uncomfortable channeling this ghost and letting Beth lead the conversation. The anger of the situation demands my involvement. Internally, I project my thoughts.

"Pete, settle down a bit. You're right. She is getting kind of pushy. But I'm here, too. Just listen to me for a second."

"Okay, but get that bitch off my back, will ya?"

"I can't promise to get her off your back, but I'll see what I can do."

"In the name of the Lord, in the name of the Christ…" That's Beth. "…with this Light I curse you for the evil people you are." *Oh no! She's overreacting.* In her efforts to help this couple and to keep the group safe, she's decided to immobilize these entities in the quickest, surest way she knows how. But I don't like it. I'm not in this line of work to condemn anyone to a living hell. I've got to intervene somehow, and fast!

"DO IT STEVE." Michael commands. "DO IT. I AM WITH YOU." I start talking with Pete silently, sending him messages while Beth continues. *"Hey, Pete! I know you feel a little bad about what you did, and about killing some of those people over the years. I know that, or why else would you finally be looking for the 'good fight'? You HAVE learned your lesson. I know you want to make amends for some of the stuff you did."*

"Yeah, I guess you're right. Just get that lady off us."

"I don't know if I can do that, Pete, without losing touch with you. If I start talking with her, then I can't talk to you. I can't handle talking to too many people at once. You can understand that, can't you? Just hang in here with me."

"Yeah. Okay, so what do we do now? I don't want to be listenin' to that lady." Is that a trace of fear in his voice? I can almost hear him wondering whether or not she can actually hurt him.

Beth's voice comes through to my awareness again. "In the name of Spirit, I command you to leave these people alone…" She continues with her monologue while I focus on Pete and his two cohorts.

"Pete, listen up! We've got to do this fast so we don't get in trouble here. You deserve to make things right for what you did while you were alive. I know you didn't know of any other way to make a living. But, you know you did some wrong things. At least that's a start."

"Yeah. But we can't do nothin' 'bout that now. We did what we did."

"That's right, Pete." I'm glad I've got him talking now, and listening. *"But you can't make up for it by continuing the violence, even if you think you're doing the right thing. Even if you feel they deserve it. You're only getting in deeper here, Pete. You're not in the best place to judge who's right and wrong, just like you don't want us judging you."* He's listening. He's getting it. I can start to see and feel his sadness. Loneliness and remorse are replacing the anger. The other two entities look to him for support, for guidance.

"In the name of Christ, our Lord…" That's Beth again. I almost forgot she was here, but she's been talking the whole time. Even though it seems like I've been communicating a long time with Pete, the whole interaction probably took only seconds. Beth continues, "…I collect HIS power, HIS energy, and screw you three into the Earth."

"Uh oh, Pete. Here it comes. Let's make this quick." I see a collection of Light, like a fist gathering, first above Beth's head, then above Pete and the other two soldiers. *"Who do you want judging you—a loving God, or this woman here? Make the choice Pete. Make it now! Are you willing to go toward the Light, toward forgiveness? God is all forgiving, even if we're not. Go toward the Light, and you can find better ways of making up for what you've done. Hurry!"*

I sense his confusion, his uncertainty. But above that, we both see a fist of power coming down, coming down to crush them, to drive them into the Earth, to condemn them for their sins. We both feel the terrible strength of that force. *"Hurry Pete! Grab your friends and go! Hurry! Go to the Light!"*

Pete gathers the other two, and starts to rise, starts being surrounded by the Light. At the last second, he turns to me. *"Thanks, man. You been good to us. Better 'n we deserve. But put that bitch on a leash, will ya?"*

Just then, the room is filled with an audible growl. It's from a dog they've had with them for quite some time, an angry mongrel that's been tagging along for the ride. The fist comes down with an enormous sense of power. The house itself moans and shifts its weight.

The three mercenaries get out of the way just in time. They're on their way to Spirit—not that they'll have an easy time reconciling their earthly deeds. But I am relieved I didn't have a hand in condemning anyone. I couldn't be at peace with that.

The group sighs almost in unison. Everyone feels the absence of the ghosts. I doubt the group knows the outcome from my perspective, since they could only hear Beth talking. *"Goodbye, Pete. Sorry we couldn't get your dog to go with you, too. But maybe that's for the better anyway. That was ONE angry dog! But it's nowhere to be found now."*

"Bless you, Steve." Was that Pete again? Or was that a message from my own guidance, from Spirit? Oh well. I guess I'll never know. But it doesn't matter. I did what I felt was right. Bless me. I'm glad I could follow through with what seemed most healing, and I'm glad this one is over.

Coming out of the trance, I squeezed the hands next to mine, letting them know it was over and that we could break the circle. Gently rubbing my face, I opened my eyes and turned to Beth. Her mouth was turned down in a grim frown, and every line on her face seemed to stand out. This pillar of strength was left visibly shaken by the whole experience.

I related to the group that it was my impression that at least one, or maybe all three, of the ghosts had gone UP to the Light rather than staying to be condemned. Giving no details about my inner dialogue with Pete, I expressed that I wished it could have gone more lovingly. "I feel that everyone deserves a chance to be forgiven."

Beth disagreed and stuck to her certainty. "Some people are just too far gone to accept the Light. They can't be allowed to hang out here and hurt others. They've made their choice, and I think it's right to confine them in a way that protects others."

Not wanting to start an argument in front of the group, I did tell Beth I disagreed, but I left it at that. While mingling afterward, however, I privately shared with her what I had done. She didn't like it. Perhaps she didn't even believe that the ghosts had succeeded in moving into the Light. I did concede that her actions might have clarified a choice for the entities, actually helping them to move beyond stubborn defenses. Looking around, we both agreed that the entities were gone from the premises, an important step in helping the residents heal.

Before leaving, I pulled the husband aside for a private conversation. "You know, Paul, it was your anger that attracted the ghosts. I know you and your wife have been having a hard time of it lately, but things have to change.

"Ghosts are attracted to a high emotional charge, especially the negative emotions. It would be real good if the two of you sought some counseling." I knew I was out on a limb suggesting this, and I definitely didn't want Paul's anger directed toward me. Still, I felt obliged to help him find an alternative to the fighting. "If you continue the way you have been, with lots of conflict, you might just as easily reattract the same kind of angry, fighting ghosts. Beth agrees with me on this, and we encourage both of you," I indicated his wife. "to find other ways of dealing with your anger and hurt."

Paul nodded his head, saying some words of contrition. He agreed to look at it and to do something about it. I suspected he was just saying what he thought I wanted to hear. But it wasn't my place to press the issue further.

"Just think about it. Okay, Paul?" Another nod.

Two things became immediately apparent to me after this session. The first was that I had better double check with a person BEFORE I work with them to be sure we agree on methods, options, and orientation. I do not feel it is up to me to condemn a soul to a possible hell. My experience has taught me that loving energy is more powerful than anything else. If we can stay focused on channeling infinite, divine love, even in the face of fear and anger, then we have created the best opportunity for healing. Because I am responsible and accountable for how I direct, with my own free will, the energy available to me, I must act according to my own conscience. Someone else may have a different experience or a different path. I trust them to heed their own guidance, learning their own lessons, doing what they feel is right. I, in turn, will heed mine.

The second thing that became apparent was that I was exhausted! Bouncing back and forth between the anger and the love was just too much to handle. Playing intermediary between Pete and Beth was tiring. Continuing the conversation between Pete and Beth while I was holding an entirely different conversation with Pete was, to say the least, disorienting. Trying to manage too many things at once took its toll.

For days afterward I felt drained. It felt like someone just came along and "pulled the plug" on my energy reserves. I was clumsy and accident prone, with headaches and sore muscles. To top it off, I came down with a whopping cold. It was the one time after a clearing that I actually sought out a fellow Spiritual healer for help. My friend and colleague, Linda Lee Landon, offered the insight and perspective I needed. *Thank you, Linda, for helping me to put things right. Thanks for helping me forgive myself for getting into that situation in the first place. Keep up the good work.*

With some regret, Beth and I never did resolve the difference in our approaches. The most I could do was ask her to consider what I had said. We didn't do any work together after that, even though we still respected and supported one another's intentions to facilitate healing. But about nine months after the clearing, she called me to report that Paul had contacted her. He said that some weird things were starting to happen again. She said she'd asked him if he'd gotten any counseling for his relationship, and if he'd found alternative means of dealing with his anger.

His response was, almost predictably, "That's none of your business."

Her reply, reassuringly, was, "Then call me when you have. Anything else we would do now may only put a temporary Band-Aid on things, and you'd probably end up attracting similar circumstances again."

Bravo, Beth!

Points to Remember…

✧ Throughout any clearing, we need to focus consistently on healing.

- ✧ Our goal is to serve in whatever form is for the Highest Good for ALL concerned.
- ✧ Every individual deserves healing, including us.

Just Following Orders

Brenda sighed loudly as she unplugged the vacuum cleaner and dragged it toward the closet, putting it away. "That makes three times this month," she thought to herself. Three times she and her husband Frank had awakened to a ring of fine dust on the living room floor. "How odd. A perfect circle of dust, or whatever it is. And always in the same place." Looking up at the ceiling, she could discern no obvious source.

Frank was in the bedroom overhead, checking once again for signs of dirt, bugs, or anything which could have created the dust which seemed to sift through the ceiling and fall to the living room. "There's nothing up here!" he called to Brenda. "Nothing at all!"

Brenda shoved the vacuum into the back of the closet and slammed the door. A chill ran up her spine, prickling the hairs on the back of her neck. She shivered, pulled her bathrobe around her more tightly, and headed to the kitchen for a cup of coffee.

Frank joined her at the kitchen table. "Don't worry, hon, we'll figure it out."

"Frank, I want to call someone." Brenda gulped from her coffee mug as she steadied herself for the conversation ahead. "It's not just the ring of dust in the living room. It's everything! When Aunt Marge was here last summer she cut her finger on that antique plaster frame in the guest room, but there's not a single place on that picture that's sharp enough to hurt a fly! Then last week, when your grandmother was visiting, she practically fell down the stairs because someone or something pushed her, really pushed her hard!"

"She probably just tripped, Brenda. She's old…."

"No! She definitely said she was pushed! And, Frank, I've felt it, too. I hate to go into the basement because it feels so creepy. No matter how many lights I turn on, I feel scared that I'm going to be trapped in the dark by something holding me there. It's like I'm being watched. And what about the time I was tripped on the stairs?"

"Okay, okay," Frank tried to sound reassuring. "You know I don't believe in any of this ghost stuff. But I care about you, Brenda. And if it makes you feel any better, go ahead and call someone. I doubt they'll find anything, but if it means we don't have to have this conversation again, it'll be worth it."

"I'm not crazy, Frank. I'm really not imagining all of this. You've seen the dust, you saw your grandmother almost break her leg."

"I know. It's just that this is all new to me. I never seriously considered that a brand new house, our house, could have a ghost. I don't even know if ghosts are real! But I do want to figure out what's going on, and I admit I can't explain it. Go ahead and give that guy Steve a call."

When Brenda calls and relates her story of events over the past several months, I feel sure of the presence of one or more earthbound spirits. It also occurs to me that there have been other stories of entities in that part of Colorado, an area with a history rich in Native American lore. This time I'll bring my drum, healing crystals, a smudge mixture for cleansing and blessing, and a friend, Sue, who is familiar with Native American energies. "I don't even need to come over and check it out, Brenda. I'll just set up a time with my wife and a friend of ours."

Marcia and I meet Sue at the property one Saturday morning. Upon entering the house, all three of us immediately feel surrounded by a stifling, heavy energy. A touch of paranoia has us furtively looking over our shoulders, as if we're being watched or followed while walking through the home. The living room feels crowded. The basement feels angry. The back yard is filled with sadness. There's a lot going on here.

We regroup in the living room, and I decide to vary the ritual for this particular clearing. I fill my ceremonial bowl with smudge, gently pinching the dry leaves as they sift through my fingers. I love the smell of that ancient mixture. As I light it, blowing gently across the top to get it smoking, I recall other times in sweat lodges and healing circles, where prayers were carried upward in the sacred smoke. Brenda, Frank, Marcia, Sue, and I stand in a circle. I look at each person's face—expectant, a bit scared yet excited. Frank has dropped his defenses of logic and surrendered to possibilities of helping in a new way. I'm glad he has chosen to be here.

"In the name of Spirit, I cleanse my body," I repeat as each person in turn washes the smoke over his face. "I cleanse my mind and my soul," as each person washes the smoke over his head and neck. Sitting now, half in trance, the people present watch as I cleanse and bless the ceremonial crystals. Sue drums, Marcia prays, "Mother—Father God, Infinite Power of the Universe, we ask that you join us here, that you watch over what we do, so that it may be for the Highest Good…."

The invocation continues as we bless the circle, ourselves, and the work we are about to do. "We pray to the four directions to aid us in this work and to help us create the sacred space. First to the East…" I reverently place a crystal on the floor facing an easterly direction, then continue to the South, West, and North. "We ask your protection and your cooperation to guide us in this work, to guide your brothers and sisters home. Mother Earth, we bless you and beg your protection, sustaining our energies. Grandfather Sky, help us to get above the pain and sadness of what has happened here. Keep us clear. Mitakuye Oyasin, All my Relations, we are all brothers and sisters in Spirit. Help us to bridge the gap between cultures, between peoples. Help us bring the Highest energies into this place.

"With the Spirits present, with the energies and intent of those present, we connect the crystals with the Light. Breathing Spirit into each crystal, we ward the space against intrusions and harm." To he group, "Fill the crystal to the East with Love and Light, send it to the South, connecting the two. Continue to the West, then the North, until we are surrounded with the Light…"

We are now ready to do the work. Sitting down, I take the hands of those next to me and encourage the lightworkers gathered to do the same. The smudge is still smoking slightly in the center of the circle where I placed the bowl. The drumming continues softly. Trance is but a breath away.

"*I can't stand it!*" an anguished voice rattles through my head. "*I can't stand it. What have we done? These poor people.*" It's the voice of a soldier from ages ago. "*We invited them here. We assured them of peace. I believed it. I was part of it. And then the horror!*"

I separate enough to relate my impressions to the group. I let them know I see a soldier. His commanding officer had invited some Native Americans here to talk, to come to a peaceful solution to some fighting that had been going on. Tired of the battle and trusting the intent, a small group of Ute warriors gathered. Feeling safe with an agreement of nonviolence, women and children were also present to witness and celebrate a laying down of arms.

"*The betrayal! The horror...*" the soldier cries out again. "*They sat down with us, and they even passed the pipe around once. We shared water, soldier and Indian alike, drinking from the same bowl. Then...then our troops came over the hill in a surprise attack. Under orders to massacre the Natives, my own people killed them all. I can't believe it! I didn't know! I can't stand it!*"

The emotions begin to overwhelm and confuse me. There's too much happening, too many different perceptions coming faster than I can keep up with. Staying focused on the soldier becomes impossible, so I come back to myself and speak to the group, relating pictures and impressions as they come flooding into my awareness. "It is a setup from the beginning," I explain. "The army has planned a massacre, but it purposely has not informed the soldiers who were sent ahead to meet in peace." I continue to share scenes with the group. Native women and children are running, but to no avail. They are cut down swiftly with bayonets and rifles. Ute Warriors struggle to defend themselves, but they are greatly outnumbered by the men in uniform. The earth is stained with the blood of innocents. A young child rushes to protect his mother, but the butt of a soldier's rifle knocks him to the ground. Lying unconscious, he regains his senses after the killing is over. He is the only Ute survivor.

The lone soldier who was talking through me sees what's happening. In shock, his fighting reflexes take over, but he is confused by the realization of betrayal. Through a veil of deception and panic his sense of decency prevails, and this single soldier rises to defend the Utes. Killing one of his own men, he is cut down immediately by another. Left to die slowly, he watches the bloodletting continue its course. "Too late...I am too late to stop it now anyway," he murmurs.

Past events begin to clarify the present situation in this house. The anger in the basement is from the Native Americans unwilling to let go of their land. The antique picture frame responsible for cutting someone's finger holds an old picture of a soldier. Ute warriors still trying to fight back trip people in the house on the stairs. The strange circle of "dust" that keeps appearing on the rug is the result of the sacred pipe spilling its ashes as the scene is played and replayed by confused souls struggling to create a different outcome. The sadness in the backyard is from the little child who survives the massacre. Injured and in shock, he lives for a couple of days and then fades away, his spirit wandering the area in bewildered sorrow.

With the information gathered so far, we can now begin the work of helping these tortured souls onward, beyond the pain and anger which have held them to the earth. Focusing first on the soldier, I must convince him that none of this was his fault. He didn't know what was going to happen. He was a decent man, and he did what he could do to stop it. "Forgive yourself, man!" I entreat. "You gave your own life in a supreme effort to protect those who had trusted you. You're not to blame. You've paid for your ignorance." I continue talking, reassuring him that his trust was given innocently. He never betrayed that trust. He did not know he was luring the Native Americans into a trap, and it is time to let go of that burden. Finally, he agrees to accept the forgiveness of Spirit. As he looks to the Light, his form shimmers and, joyously, I watch him rise.

Next, we turn our attention to the Native Americans. They are angry, defiant, and sad. We understand why they are suspicious and mistrusting of our little group claiming once again to come in peace. Sue drums softly as we call on their ancestors to help in the healing. Toward the center of our small circle, the five of us focus our love and our intent. I watch as individuals slowly come forward. First to step into our view are women in buckskins, naked children held protectively in their arms. Soon, more children follow them, peeking shyly around their mothers' skirts. I recognize the young boy who wandered off and, with our gentle encouragement, he comes close enough to locate and reunite with his mother. Men begin moving into the periphery.

The drum continues its song, awakening the Utes from their final drama of life on Earth. "Look to your ancestors," I speak to the growing circle. "Let go of the anger. It's over. There is peace now, at least of a sort, between the White Man and the Red Man. We are learning to be more honest with each other. It is time to stop the fighting. Your ancestors call to you. The elders of long ago invite you to their sacred fire. Reclaim the peace you deserve, the peace offered to you now. You are free to go on to a better home."

I see the Native Americans gathering closely. They are crying, wailing, mourning lost ones, mourning death. Arms from below begin reaching upward. More join in until all arms are stretching toward the sky in a unified gesture toward Spirit. A great circle of hands from above appears, all open and reaching downward through clouds of Light. The ancestors have come to bring these earthbound souls into their hearts. Fingers touch, hands clasp, and spirits rise homeward. My own heart feels like it has burst open with awe. A gentle beauty bathes the previously forlorn landscape in new light.

I am exhausted. My awareness returns to the house, the living room and the group. "We've done some good work here today, folks." I talk to the group as I open my eyes. "We've done what we could. Hopefully we've taken care of it all." In the back of my mind, however, there is some doubt. There was so much going on all at once, and so much to do that I can't be certain we paid attention to all of it. I realize that I'm speaking, in part, to reassure Frank and Brenda that they can relax in their own home. The other part is to convince myself.

Marcia, Sue, and I instruct Frank and Brenda on how to smudge the house for the next few days. They are to light the mixture and blow smoke into each corner of every room in the house. As they do this, they are to offer their apologies, their prayers, and their blessings. This will reinforce the intent to guide the spirits onward, helping to avert their return should any hesitate, among old memories and emotions, as they begin their new journey.

Packing up the crystals, drum, and other paraphernalia, we ready ourselves to leave. Through some tears of pain, sadness, and joy, we bid farewell. Everyone present has felt the intensity of emotions throughout this clearing. Sharing them has brought us together. Even Frank, our healthy skeptic, is deeply moved. "Thank you, Steve. I had no idea. I just had no idea. Thank you very much."

"Thank yourself for the willingness to stick around, Frank! Your participation was helpful. Having you and Brenda together on this made it easier."

I turn to include Brenda in the conversation. "Call me. Let me know if anything happens. Let me know if nothing happens. Again, I think we took care of everything, but I can't be sure. We can come back if there are any further problems. Just hold on to the Highest thoughts, affirming your intent. Cleanse, pray, and send your blessings. And get rid of that old picture of the soldier! We'll see how it goes."

I talked with Brenda several weeks later, and things seemed to have quieted down enormously. Aside from an occasional wave of sadness or anger hitting her, all was quiet. However, several months later she called again. Although there were no more "accidents" in the house, things were starting to feel slightly "weird." The circle of ashes had also reappeared. She agreed to talk with Frank and see about a time we could come over again to continue with the work. However, that was not to be.

As weeks rolled by, one date was set, then canceled. Another appointment was agreed upon tentatively, then rescheduled. Finally, I asked Brenda if she was serious about pursuing a resolution to matters.

"Well, truthfully, Steve, we have a friend who's into this type of work," she related. "And she's coming to town soon. So we'll see what she can do."

Belatedly, I supported her on doing what she felt was right. We went our separate ways, losing touch with one another for a while. I am still not sure how things ultimately turned out. A brief encounter with her a year later revealed that they "had resolved the situation." No further details were offered.

Not every clearing is successful the first time around. In this case, we knew we had taken care of some of the problems, just not all of them. Did our own emotions effect outcomes? Did Frank or Brenda hold on a little? Did we? Did our inexperience with Native American rituals hinder the process? Maybe some soldiers and Native Americans stayed behind to continue the fight. Or perhaps, after one last passing of the pipe, things took care of themselves over time. It would have been nice to know, but the situation was no longer in our hands. All earthbound spirits, after being shown the options, have the free will and choice to move on when they are ready; once again we can only trust that all has worked out for the Highest Good.

Points to Remember…

- ✧ Not all clearings are completely successful the first time around.
- ✧ We can only do our best at any given time.
- ✧ We need to trust the process of completion—our own, and that of Spirit.

Divination in the Dormitory

A fun and seemingly harmless occult game is the Ouija Board. It is one of several popularly marketed divination tools or devices used to contact spirits. The concept behind this one is rather simple. The board itself is printed with the alphabet, some numbers, and a few short words. Atop the board is a little plastic pointer called a planchette, allowed to seemingly float across the surface of the board. The players, putting their fingertips lightly on the pointer, ask a question. The pointer then moves, spelling out answers in response. With enough sensitivity and patience, whole sentences and complex messages can be communicated.

The nonmetaphysical explanation of this phenomenon calls for conscious and/or subconscious movements of the hands that direct the pointer. One could say the players themselves determine the outcome, even if they are unaware of their subconscious efforts. The metaphysical explanation, on the other hand, refers to actual spirits. A ghost could use the energies of the participants, the Board, and its own amassed energies to move the pointer.

I have never actually used a Ouija Board because I dislike them for a couple of basic reasons. First, I cringe at the idea of calling up strange ghosts for entertainment. I've seen too many ghosts with their own agenda decide to stick around and harass people, causing unwanted problems. I don't want to invite one into my space! The second reason, and to me the most important, is that, simply put, the Ouija Board is too easy to use. Anyone, regardless of awareness or intent, can conjure a ghost by opening a gateway for outside energy to come in. This means that even the most innocent players may unintentionally invoke havoc.

When we approach the spirit realms it is best to do so with centering, focusing, and the intent of healing. Likewise, approaching Spirit by summoning the Highest energies possible—calling on the White Light, our Spirit teachers, Guides, and Angels—will direct our energies toward an enlightened response. The Ouija Board does not demand any such intent. Labeled a "toy," it even presents itself as frivolous, encouraging recklessness and irresponsibility. When a person uses the board but does not focus on the Higher energies, he or she may well attract whatever entity happens to be around—whomever may be floating through the neighborhood at the time. I, personally, would like to have more control over who I am consulting for insight and answers!

Some people use the Ouija Board and do not get any results at all. Many others use it, have a definite response, and experience no problems afterward. Some, however, use it with regrettable results.

Several years ago, an instructor at a private boarding school for girls contacted me. It seemed that for weeks some of the high school students were having a hard time concentrating on their work. Grades were going down, girls were falling asleep in the middle of classes, more arguments were noted. The teacher knew something was going on, but he got no response from the girls when he questioned them.

Finally, one afternoon, a physical fight broke out between two of the students. That was it. He'd had enough! Calling the girls into his office, he sat them down and explained that they were grounded, on in-house suspension, and faced the possibility of expulsion if he didn't find out what was going on.

They gave up their secretiveness and blurted out the story: One night five girls decided it would be fun to use a Ouija Board and see what happened. They got it out, balanced it carefully on a bed in the dormitory, and started asking questions. The pointer moved! They continued, and it moved some more! Jokingly, they started asking personal questions. In response they got some pretty undesirable, lewd answers. This was too much to handle! The girls got insulted and began accusing one another of moving the pointer. Feeling a bit frightened and suspicious, they put the board away with a resolution to tell no one of the experience. Their secret would reestablish the trust between them.

"Thank goodness that's over with," they thought. "Good-bye and good riddance!"

Several uneventful nights passed, and the girls had almost forgotten their experiment with the Board, when some bizarre things started happening. One girl noticed her bed shaking in the middle of the night, but she thought it was another resident pulling a joke on her. Another girl had a similar experience the next night, but all of her dorm sisters fervently denied doing it. Things were starting to get strange.

A few nights later, one girl thought she was touched on her leg in the middle of the night. She bravely chalked it up to nerves and a bad dream. Then something happened that could not be explained away by "normal" means. One resident was drifting off to sleep when the covers on her bed were suddenly ripped off. She screamed and lashed out at the prankster, but no one was there.

For weeks, similar incidents occurred. The girls were losing a lot of sleep over this. They would lie awake at night feeling frightened and vulnerable, finally drifting off into fitful, often interrupted, dreams. Their mistrust of one another had increased, accusations against each other flourished, and many felt on edge both day and night. Yet, they had persisted in keeping things secret, still resisting the idea that anything supernatural might be taking place.

Upon hearing the whole story, the instructor called me and asked if I would be a guest lecturer at their spiritual psychology class. He felt that since I was a professional in the field of the occult, the girls would listen to me more than they would him. Perhaps I could help a group of giggling high school girls understand the seriousness of dabbling in the spirit realms. I was glad to try. I went to the class with the intent of being somewhat gentle, somewhat humorous and, of course, totally captivating.

I started my rousing, insightful lecture, and the students became fidgety. As I continued, they started snickering and sharing private jokes. Obviously, they still were not taking this thing seriously. So I went into professional ghostbuster mode, recalling some really scary ghost stories in order to get their attention. I exaggerated a couple just to make my point. "First the ghost shakes the bed. Then they touch you!" I warned them. "Touching leads to something more extreme, sometimes even violence." I wanted them to believe their safety and sanity could be at stake, and they had better take responsibility for their choices and actions.

The stories had their desired effect. The girls did take their situation seriously, perhaps acknowledging for the first time that they really could have called up a ghost. They were both chagrined and awed by their discovery. They unanimously agreed, with no reluctance on anyone's part, that they wanted the ghost gone. They would put the Ouija Board away and only approach metaphysics with sincerity and guidance. As I concluded the visit, the girls were asking thoughtful and sincere questions, thanking me for helping them put this behind them. They agreed to have me talk with their teacher to set up a time to do a ghost clearing.

A week later, I heard from the instructor who told me that since he'd had some experience with ghost clearings, he went ahead and took care of this one. The ghost turned out to be a previous resident who died on the campus several years earlier. She had been depressed and angry with other students right before her untimely death. Even though the present girls were not the exact ones she had been angry with, they would do. Awakened by the energies of the Ouija Board, she saw an opportunity for revenge. She struck out at whichever students were available, purposely scaring those who were more open to having contact with a ghost. According to the instructor, the ghost moved on quickly, eager to forgive, once she realized her own entrapment. Revenge never seems to hurt others as much as it hurts one's self!

Several months later, I ran across the teacher at a social function. He told me that the clearing must have worked since things had settled down and there were no reports of further incidents. He thanked me again for my help and my willingness to address the girls. Things were back to normal, and the administration, thankfully, was kept out of it.

This experience highlights the importance of education and information. In their innocence, the girls in the dorm played with what they thought was a harmless game. Yet, the game is attractive in and of itself because of the possibility that unknown energies exist. Thus, even to be inspired to sit down with a Ouija Board implies that one must be open to something mysterious; anyone totally closed would not waste his or her time. With neither intent nor awareness on a conscious level, the girls awakened an angry ghost. Their fear increased as their unexplained experiences increased. Surrounded by greater fear, anger, and mistrust, they inadvertently provided more energy for the ghost to interact on a physical level. The girls' initial secrecy and denial was, in many ways, a fear of their own power. Once they were able to acknowledge the validity of their experiences with the ghost and accept the possibility of ghosts being real, they were ready to take responsibility for their use of power. There were choices about how to respond to the situation.

Many young people have a curiosity about metaphysics and the occult. Students bring Tarot cards to school, play with pendulums, power beads, and crystals, read each other's palms at slumber parties, and ask profound questions about life and death. Perhaps it is time for us to respond to their curiosity more openly, to give them useful information about the responsibilities of personal power, to acknowledge Spirit more freely. In the course of such teachings, we can help them find much better ways to access personal guidance than relying on a Ouija Board!

Points to Remember…

- ❖ We are each responsible for the use of our personal power.
- ❖ Dappling in metaphysical realms without awareness or clear intent may bring about unexpected—and sometimes undesirable—results.

❖ Seeking the Highest, most loving Guidance available is an affirmation of our intent.

Loyal Pets

It's the middle of the night. Cold and clear outside, millions of stars create a great canopy of light above our isolated mountain home. Marcia and I had crawled into bed early, after an uneventful Saturday. I'm sleeping soundly when I sense Marcia stirring beside me, awakening. Was that a noise? I wonder. I listen for a bit, but nothing catches my attention. *No, it must have just been Marcia waking me up.*

I roll over and move to a more comfortable position, reaching out from under the covers to adjust the blankets. Now Marcia knows that I'm awake, too, and she mumbles, "I was just a little restless. Thought there was someone moving around, but everything seems quiet."

Sighing, I reply in a half whisper. "Yeah, me too." Enlightening conversation is not readily available at three in the morning! "But I do wish the dog would quiet down." Cheyenne, our Chocolate Lab, is lying right next to the bed. "She's snoring just like Sequoia did when she was with us." *I sure miss that big, beautiful Golden Retriever ever since she passed on a year ago.*

Marcia agrees that it's rather loud and disturbing. "Cheyenne!" she says sharply. If we wake her up, she'll stop making all that noise. "Cheyenne!" she calls again. "Good dog, you're a good dog, Cheyenne!"

We hear a noise coming from the living room. It's moving down the hall. Then, to our surprise, Cheyenne is standing in our bedroom doorway, tail wagging. She is looking confused but, I'm sure, no less than we are! Because, if it wasn't Cheyenne snoring by the bed, that means.... Marcia and I look at each other, nodding our understanding. *It's nice to have a short visit from Sequoia. Maybe it's our imagination, but we don't think so.*

We awaken to a bright, beautiful day with the morning sun shining through billowy curtains. We're just stirring, taking advantage of a lazy Sunday morning to awaken ourselves slowly, when our eight-year-old son tiptoes into the room. Climbing up on the bed, he snuggles into the warm space between us.

"Hey, Mom? What do you know about ghosts? Because I thought, last night…I thought…I'm not sure if it was a dream or not…but I thought Sequoia was sleeping on the floor next to my bed…."

Two years later, we were facing a health crisis with Cheyenne. Our beautiful Chocolate Labrador Retriever had suddenly taken ill. One day she was totally healthy and the next had contracted "canine hemophilia," a rare and usually fatal disease. After three days of blood transfusions, steroids and other medical emergency procedures, she was still under observation at the vet's.

Cheyenne's best chance of recovery was at the hospital, so we left her there one more day. Marcia dropped by to see her after work and told me she didn't look good at all. Feeling she would pass on soon, we made a vow to pick her up the next morning so she could make her transition peacefully amongst friends and family. I drifted off to sleep channeling Love and Light to her for healing.

I drive to the vet's office early in the morning. It's a gorgeous day. The sun is bright with little cloud puffs languidly drifting by. I park on the street. "That's odd," I think to myself. "Why didn't I park in the parking lot?" I get out of the car and start walking toward the building, hoping Cheyenne has recovered. For better or worse, I've come to bring her home.

Then I see movement. She has just run through the wall of the hospital, wagging her tail, running toward me. I'm flooded with relief. "Play!" she seems to say. "Play!"

I crouch down to pet her, glad that she's alive and well. Then it hits me. "Wait a second. She just ran through the side of that building. Dogs can't do that! This must be a dream. And this must be her spirit that's come to visit me. She must be dead. But she's alive—playing with me, forgiving me for leaving her alone." The loss I feel is tinged with joy. We are both okay. I love her. I'll miss her…

Awakening in the morning with that dream in my mind, I call the vet as soon as they open. It could have been just a dream after all, so my intent is to tell him we will be taking Cheyenne home shortly. His secretary transfers the phone to him. "Mr. Rogat, I'm sorry. But early this morning…"

"I know, Dr. Harris. I know. And thanks for doing all you could."

∼

What a wonderful gift our pets are to us. Full of unconditional love and everlasting loyalty, they offer a faithfulness and devotion which melts even the hardest of hearts. Dependent upon us for their well-being, they trust us completely and awaken in us our own capacity for giving and accepting love. They also have much to teach us about life and death. Because we outlive most of our pets, they help us experience the letting go that is necessary with the loss of a loved one.

We do our best with pets—we urge them toward the Light. Affirming our completion, we send them on to a better place. Yet we are occasionally blessed with a visit from them after they have passed on. This does not necessarily mean they are earthbound. They can just drop by to say hello, warming our hearts and theirs—a reminder of the continuation of life, the endurance of love, the connection with Spirit that intertwines us all.

Points to Remember…

- ✧ Yes! We can see our loving pets again in the Light!
- ✧ There is no loss. There is only change, movement, and the ever-growing awareness of Spirit.

Is My Husband Missing or Dead?

A woman called me and reported that her husband was missing. He had walked out suddenly and, for over seven years now, there had been no reports of his whereabouts. "Can you help me, Steve? I want to know if he is just missing or if he is dead."

I hate to get calls like this. I don't like the responsibility of answering with an unequivocal yes or no, alive or dead. Ethically, it would be wrong for me to say he is dead, even if that is what I perceive. My impressions might be incorrect, and my report could cause undue sadness, anger and upset. The reverse is true as well. If I were to say he is alive, and just missing, suppose I am wrong with that impression? I could then lead her to false hope, needlessly encouraging her to hold on to the possibility of his return.

The woman, Erin, did explain that there was no tangible reason leading her to believe her husband was still alive. She got in touch with me because she had been "feeling" his presence lately. She was just curious if this meant that he would be returning, or that he had passed on.

Taking a deep breath, I plunged in. I explained my reluctance at answering this type of question. But, I also empathized with her plight. Not knowing what has happened to a loved one is certainly a difficult emotional puzzle. I assured her that I would meditate on it and possibly dream on it. I needed to know that if I shared any impressions with her, it would be with the explicit permission of Guidance. I wanted to offer information only with the reassurance that it would facilitate healing. Promising Erin I would be in touch if anything became more definitive, I assured her we would talk soon.

Hanging up the phone, I walk into my living room. It's Sunday, my day off, my day to relax and put aside all my work concerns. I sit down on the couch. My son Joseph, ten years old at that time, comes in to talk with me about something. He asks me a question. I'm about to answer when both he and I look up in stunned silence.

There, behind the couch, is a movement. It's indistinct at first, just a sort of translucent gray color rising up. It takes shape. It's a large man! And then poof, he's gone! Joseph and I look at each other, then behind the couch, then at each other again. My son's eyes are round with fear.

"Joseph, it's all right. I just got off the phone with a woman who was wondering if her husband was dead. I told her I didn't know, but that I would be open to any impressions that may come up. I'd say that was a pretty strong impression!" I offer a reassuring laugh. Joseph knows of the work I do, and he is concerned about us actually attracting ghosts. I want him to know that this was not *our* ghost. "This ghost belongs to her. He was just visiting me so that I would call her back. He wants me to give her a little more information." Apparently satisfied, Joseph gives me a quick, easy hug and bounds outside to ride his bicycle.

I take a deep breath and, going to the phone, I dial her number. "Erin, hi. This is Steve."

"So soon? I didn't expect a call back from you so quickly, if at all. I know I kind of put you on the spot. Sorry, but I had to give it a try."

"Erin, it's okay. Just listen for a sec. You know I hate to answer questions such as yours, but something weird just happened. I use the term 'weird' because I don't attract ghosts. No matter how long I've been doing this work, very rarely have I ever had a ghost bother me or even appear in my home. They just aren't attracted to me except under certain circumstances, like when it's time for me to send them onward. Well, this is one of those rare, weird times."

Silence on the other end of the phone. Then, "What? What are you saying, Steve?"

I relate to her the experience that my son and I just shared. "I feel it was probably your husband, Erin. I can't be sure because I didn't get a good look at him. It all happened so fast. Then it was over. But since it did happen, I felt it was important to call and let you know, especially since this type of thing just doesn't happen to me."

Talking with her for a few more minutes, I hear Erin draw a deep breath of relief. I tell her I still don't know if her husband has definitely passed on or not. This, however, is a pretty good sign that she needs to let go of him. She needs to release him and go on with her life. To help her do this, I encourage her to meditate on what she wants to say to him in order to feel more complete.

"Just take some quiet time to open your heart and ask yourself what you would like to convey to him. Finishing that, you can then channel Love and Light to him and take care of any unfinished communications." I urge her to do this on her way to sleep that night, saying her good-byes and bringing the issue to a deeper level of completion.

She, too, feels that perhaps it is time to let her husband go, and she thanks me for my time and effort. I explain that it is really no effort at all. It was something I had to do because, if I didn't call her back, the ghost would probably just come back and bother me! And since I don't like ghosts hanging around the place, I've really taken the path of least resistance! Regardless, she thanks me anyway, and we go our separate ways.

Even though she and I didn't talk about it later, I trust that Erin took my suggestions to heart and carried out the deeper healing. In spite of my fears and reluctance to respond to this kind of situation, I felt good about how I handled it. I shared my experience with her, but I left the interpretation and the choices up to her. Guidance gave me the opportunity to help in a way that felt safe to both her and to me.

When we start having precognitions, when we open up psychically and Spiritually to perceiving ghosts, we have a certain responsibility. We need to act with integrity when sharing our experiences with others. We do not wish to give someone "false" hope and encourage them to hold onto loved ones who have passed on. Holding on may result in denying themselves further love and growth in this present, physical existence. Holding on may potentially inhibit the growth of the ghost, as well, in the nonphysical realms. On the other hand, neither do we wish to cause undue distress nor create fear. Deciding what impressions to share, how best to share them, and when to share what with whom, are constant questions a healer must ask. Thus, we do our best to keep our words and our work in tune with Divine Guidance, allowing Spirit to lead the way.

Erin was easy to work with because she respected my dilemma and did not push me to say one way or another something absolute and conclusive. With a willingness to look into herself and her readiness to let go, she realized that it was time to move on, no matter what was going on with her husband. This was a healing step for her, and she found a way to feel complete even without all the facts or information she had previously thought necessary. Once again, Spirit gave both of us exactly what was needed.

Points to Remember…

✧ In our anxiousness to offer comfort and hope, we must still heed the wisdom of Guidance.

✧ What a person *wants* to hear is not always what he or she *needs* to hear.

Part III

Communication with the Living and the Dying

Chapter 11

The Dream Body

Thoughts and feelings are alive with an energy of their own. By being aware of unresolved emotional conflicts and how they manifest, we can take the opportunity to heal ourselves and those around us.

The Angry Husband

It's Halloween. They got my name from a feature article in the local newspaper, my number from the phone book. The woman on the other end of the line sounds frantic. In the background I hear another woman shouting hysterically in Spanish.

Oh, God, I think to myself. *I've GOT to train other people to do this work. This is the seventh call in less than a week.* "Yes, I understand it's a bit upsetting," I reply in a quiet voice. *I hope this one is local. I don't have the time to go out of town right now.* "Yes, I'd be upset, too, if I came home and there was a strange man standing in my doorway." I try to calm her by speaking in a slow, steady voice. *I hope I'm not coming across as being bored. I'm really not bored, just tired.* "I do believe you when you say that he just disappeared."

"Yes, but Steve…" Maria goes on. "That wasn't the strangest part. A few nights later someone was banging on the front door in the middle of the night! My sister and I saw the same man outside. He looked real angry. There was no way we were going to answer the door, not with this man out there. So we called the police. But when we went back to see if he was still there, he was fading away into thin air. We felt pretty stupid when the police showed up and couldn't find signs of anyone having been there. No way were we going to tell them it was just a ghost."

"Maria," I'm trying to sound reassuring. "At least he's still outside. He hasn't gotten too bothersome yet."

"Yes, he has!"

Dang it! He's scaring her and she IS feeling desperate. I do hope it's in town because I've got to get to it soon. "Maria, whatever it is, we can take care of it. You and your sister and I can do this. I can get to it real soon. Where do you live?"

I hear a long sigh of relief on the phone. She answers more calmly. "Thank you. We live near downtown. When can you come?" *Thank God. And since there's been no violence, I could do this one alone, scheduling it soon.*

"Well, there's been no violence. Right?"

"Right…" She sounds mildly suspicious at my complacency.

"Well, since there's been no violence, I can make it within a few days because I can handle this one without additional people. But I'd like to get a little more information first. Okay?"

"Sure. Whatever you need." *Great! Now we're getting somewhere. She trusts me more.*

The story unfolds. Maria has just moved to town. She's come up from Mexico to join her sister, Carmen, who is going through an ugly separation from her husband. "That makes sense," I explain. "Some ghosts are attracted to an environment where there is intense emotional charge."

Maria describes the situation: Carmen and her husband had been living in their newly purchased house for a year. Everything seemed fine until about a month ago when Carmen discovered that Raul was seeing another woman. She wanted to go through some counseling, but he refused.

Carmen nagged him. She wanted to meet the other woman and tell her to leave Raul alone. She wanted to let the woman know this man was already taken!

"No way!" her husband responded. "And if you don't quit bothering me about it, I'll leave."

Carmen was determined not to let this argument drop. She'd put twenty years into this marriage. She was also a devout Catholic and, even under these circumstances, divorce was out of the question. She continued to pressure Raul until, one day, he stormed out.

While Maria talks, something starts nagging at me. An insistent voice prompts me to learn more about the husband. I keep the musings to myself but urge Maria to continue.

"And that is when I came up to be with her," she explains. "I just wanted to be here, to help if I could. I was here for a few days when Raul showed up. He wanted to talk with her. He wanted to get back together with her. I was listening from the kitchen. I was pretty quiet, but when he wouldn't promise to stop seeing the other woman, I guess I sighed kind of loudly. He must have heard me.

"That's when he got real angry and started threatening Carmen. I thought he was going to hit her. So I ran out and stood by my sister. I started yelling at him. My sister started yelling at him. Before he left, he turned back in a rage, screaming, 'You'll regret this. Both of you. You shouldn't have come, Maria. Carmen, get rid of her. Get her out of my house!' It was so ugly, Steve. I was afraid."

I hope Carmen's husband doesn't show up when I go over there. But then that little nagging voice from Guidance insists I get even more information. "What happened next? When did the ghost show up?"

"I'm getting there, Steve! Hold on a second," she answers sharply, critical of my impatience. "I convinced Carmen to get a restraining order against Raul. And that's when I think he sent this spirit after us."

Ah. The truth comes out. "Maria, does Raul have any training in what I call the black arts? Is there a way he could have done this himself?"

"No." Again, she takes affront, making it seem like I asked a silly question. "He doesn't have the training. But I know he was friends with some pretty scary people down in Mexico. I think he paid someone to do it."

"That's a pretty tough job, Maria, even for an accomplished sorcerer. Sending a little spirit or a bunch of negative energy is possible. I've even seen it. And if that is the case, we can take care of it easily. But to send a complete spirit, a man, that's practically unheard of. I've never seen it done."

"But, Steve!" she yells. "He HAS done it. We saw the spirit with our own eyes."

"I don't doubt at all that the spirit was there, Maria," I try placating her. "I didn't mean to question what you saw. I'm only trying to get more information." And then I grasp what has, until now, been eluding me. *What? Am I blind? Why didn't I see this before?* "Tell me. What did this entity look like?"

"Well, he was kind of tall, about six feet. He was wearing a plaid shirt and some old pants. We didn't really get a good look at him, but I think he had a mustache. And his hair was kind of a mess, too."

I'm going to ask this. But I think I already know the answer. "Maria, I just have one quick question. I could be wrong, but I need to ask. What does Raul look like?"

Silence. Waiting. More silence.

"Maria?"

"Yes. I'm here. Oh…I see. I didn't know that was possible. Is it?"

"Is what?" I haven't elaborated on anything.

"But you're right, Steve. Raul is about six feet tall. He always wears plaid. He's got a big mustache. And his hair is pretty long. But Raul's not dead. We got a phone call from him just a couple of days ago."

Silence. Waiting. More silence.

"Steve? Are you there?"

"Yes. I was just thinking. First Carmen and Raul separated. Then you got here, and then the restraining order was issued. And it was only after that that the ghost started appearing. What time did each of these ghost sightings happen?"

"Both of them were at night, about eleven o'clock or so."

I take a leap, relying on my intuition. After all, that's the only way to do this work. *Maybe I won't even have to go out there. This could be a rather simple matter!* "What we might have here is Raul's astral body, his dream body if you will."

"Huh?" She sounds confused.

"Lots of times, when we're asleep, we leave our bodies. We go floating around on the astral, in spirit. Most people aren't aware enough or conscious enough to control the dream body. But some are, and those people can even direct themselves to go places, to do certain things. Raul might not have that type of training but could be projecting himself there by accident. A lot of anger can serve as a strong focus. The target of his anger is his wife, but also you. He might feel he has a right to come back to his own house, so he unknowingly comes there while asleep. He's probably not even aware of it."

"But what can we do? This sounds even worse than a ghost." Now Maria starts whining, hoping I can make it all just go away.

"Actually, Maria, we CAN take care of it. I'm pretty sure. I'd like to take you and Carmen through a meditation together. I can even do it over the phone. Today! Is she there right now?"

"She's here. But she doesn't speak English real good."

"That's okay. I'll bring you through the meditation. And then later, you can bring her through it. It's a pretty simple exercise. It only takes about five minutes, and it's safe. Okay?"

She agrees wholeheartedly. "Maria, I call this the White Heart Meditation. . . .

"Relax and take some slow, deep breaths. Call in the Light, the Creator, and affirm your willingness to heal this specific situation. Affirm your willingness to communicate with love rather than with anger or sadness.

"Think of Raul. See him and hold this picture of him in your mind. . . .

"Take a few slow, deep breaths, and envision the White Light entering the top of your head, your crown. That Light represents God, Spirit, Unconditional Love and Acceptance, your Highest Potential. Breathe that Light in through your head, all the way down to the
, your stomach area. On the out breath, imagine that Light leaving your solar plexus. With every in breath, you are now breathing Love and Light into your crown and down to your solar plexus. On the exhale, you are breathing it out your solar plexus…

"Send a little white heart out your solar plexus, along a cord, and have that heart enter Raul's solar plexus. Keep channeling the Light into your head, through you, and to Raul. This way you are giving him more than just your own energy. You are giving him a Higher energy. Since you are channeling Raul the energy from an infinite source, you cannot be drained. You are empowering him AND yourself at the same time. You are communicating from your Lower Self, your subconscious, to his.

"Along that cord, communicate to him with a loving energy. It's important to do this with a loving energy, or he may not hear it. Anything that is incomplete or that you may have said earlier in anger can now be expressed with love. You can even let him know you are angry with him, but you can tell him you are angry in a loving way. Claim your anger as your own, without projecting blame toward him nor anyone else.

"See Raul as a frightened, innocent child. It was his fear that had caused him not to listen before. It was his fear that made him react with anger and made him wish to take control inappropriately of the situation. Think of how much power he must have given away or was robbed of in order to make him want to take power away from others now. Forgive that little child. It is always easier to love and forgive a frightened, little child than it is to forgive an angry, controlling adult.

"Send a lot of love to that child. Mentally and emotionally give that child a hug. Let that child hear and accept what you have to say:

'Raul, I'm sorry for overreacting the other day when you were here. I just felt protective of my sister. I thought you were going to hurt her. It's no more protective than you might be if you felt your brother or sister being threatened. I didn't mean to take control of Carmen's life and her decisions. I just want her to be happy.

'I know the two of you will work things out one way or the other. She asked me to come up here to be with her. She's having a real tough time right now, and I guess I get a little overprotective. We're not ganging up on you, honest. I AM encouraging her to complete things with you so the two of you can be at peace with each other and yourselves again.

'You're right, it's not my place to decide whether or not the two of you should be together. I just want everyone to be happy again. If you want to come back to your house, we can work it out. I'll talk with Carmen, and she could move out if that's best for the both of you. I'll even encourage her to get in touch with you so you can both meet at another place outside the house. That way, she won't get so angry, and maybe you won't feel so angry.

Part III   Communication with the Living and the Dying

'We know it's partly your house. We did not mean to kick you out of your place. It isn't going anywhere. The house is still here. It would be better for a while, though, if you would wait to be invited over. Then you would feel more at home, more welcomed.

'Again, I'm sorry if it seems that I'm interfering. I just want to help my family. Just like you love your family, I love mine. I am not going to try to stop you and Carmen from working things out. The opposite is true. I want to encourage you to work it out…whether or not you stay together. But, Raul, the best chance of working things out is without all the anger. It just makes her feel more threatened and angry. And it makes me feel overprotective.

'You and she can get together and get more stuff said AND done if both of you do it with a little more love, more gently. You have a better chance of getting what you want if you don't force yourself on her right now. She just needs a little space to cool down, to think things out, and to think about how to talk to you without getting you angry. She'll do it. I know she will. Just give her a little time.'

"Now review your relationship with him, Maria, and see if there is anything else which needs to be said. Send all communications with love. If you can send someone more love and Light than he can send you anger, then you have the situation licked. If you can send enough healing energy, the other person will either resist it and back off, or he will accept the healing and resolve things more amenably. At least you have done all you could to get back to a harmonious relationship.

"Mentally send him the following affirmation: 'I, Maria, communicate with love and understanding. I am rewarded by doing this.' Feel it, breathe it. Get in touch with a part of yourself that knows this is true. Send those feelings of peace and certainty to him. Communicate it in the 'I' form. Send the positive thought along with genuine feelings and clear images. Do it like you mean it!

"When complete, while still channeling the Light, see the heart within his solar plexus starting to grow. It continues to grow until it totally surrounds him. Still channeling the Light with your breath, make the heart get brighter and brighter, until there is nothing left but a big, bright heart.

"Know that he DID hear what you said. Whether he listens or not is his choice. Know that he DID feel the Love you shared. Whether he acknowledges that feeling or not is his choice, not yours! You have done what you could. The rest is up to him.

"You can slowly come out of the meditation now, feeling the love, the joy, and the new level of completion you have just given yourself…"

I hear Maria take a deep, freeing breath, letting go with a pleasant sigh.

"Maria, both you and Carmen might feel a bit guilty about the way things turned out the other day when Raul was there. Your guilt does nothing but open the doorway to his unwanted energies being able to effect you. You are entitled to feel the way you do toward Raul. But how you express those feelings, unleashing vast amounts of fear and anger, is what got you into trouble. If you blame Raul for the way things turned out with Carmen, he'll just get defensive and angry. Then he'll get on the offensive, trying to overpower your anger with his, just like he did the other day.

"Tell these things to Carmen. NO ONE'S at fault—not you, not Raul, and not her. Bring her through this meditation this evening, just before bedtime. When it is late at night, when we are about to go to sleep, the door between the worlds opens up. We are more receptive to psychic and Spiritual communications. We are also better able to send those communications.

"Have Carmen apologize for not getting her feelings across in a caring way that Raul could accept. Have her communicate that she will talk with a priest in the church to get advice, to see if there are any options open to her and Raul that will not hurt anyone. Have her communicate that she is willing to move out if he really wants the house. Have her ask for just a little more time.

"She can see him as a scared little child. Encourage her to find a place within him that IS lovable, and send it love. Have her forgive herself as well as him. Tell him to seek out from his past a time when he first let someone else take away his power. Who did he give his power to in the first place? That is to whom he needs to turn in order to get his power back, not to Carmen.

"Bring her through the whole meditation on her way to sleep. She can then merely drift off to sleep thinking, feeling, and channeling him those positive thoughts and feelings. He WILL get the communication on the spiritual level. And his spirit, his astral or dreaming self, will hopefully accept it."

"Will this be enough, Steve? Will he stop?" interrupts Maria.

"If you're sincere, I think he will, Maria. I want both of you to do this exercise every night for the next three nights on your way to sleep. If you fall asleep before you complete the whole thing, that's fine! It just means that it is REALLY getting down to the spiritual levels. Part of this is to get Raul to back off. But the other part is for each of you to feel more complete and more loving. Each of you can then have a wider range of responses available to you. Guilt and anger no longer control or limit your choices.

"This isn't really a substitute for talking with him in person. Communications ARE often necessary to clear things up. But at least this exercise is a start. It should take care of the unwanted visits at night."

"We'll do it, Steve. Thank you."

"Best of luck. And send my love and blessings to Carmen."

A follow-up phone call a few weeks later revealed no additional problems. Carmen had done the meditation and was seeing a counselor through the church. The couple had talked several times over the phone, and Raul had backed off, no longer demanding that Maria leave or that Carmen let him into the house. Even though things weren't resolved, all the parties involved were on the road toward completion. There were no more nocturnal visitations and, hopefully, everyone slept a little more soundly.

As for me, I made it through another busy Halloween ghost season. *By this time next year, I promise I'll have trained others to do this work. Maybe they can take over some of the extra caseload.*

Doppelgangers. The ghostly doubles of living persons. The astral body. The dream body. The individual's unique vibration of energy and light, without physical mass or matter. A true testimony to the realization that we are not simply flesh and blood created by our DNA's recipe for a specific combination of molecules. We are much, much more than we ever imagined.

Everyone has an astral body, but many people go through life without ever becoming aware of it. We think of our waking consciousness as comfortably housed in our physical body and, if by chance, we go cavorting off at night while this part of our awareness sleeps, we remain oblivious. Some of us, however, learn how to project our conscious awareness into the astral realms, giving us an opportunity to travel when and where we choose with intent and purpose. Moving in and out of time and space on a different plane, without physical mass, opens new doors for healing and communication. For many, this takes time, training, and plenty of practice. For a few, this talent seems to come naturally and easily once there is awareness of the possibility.

In this case, Carmen's husband, Raul, appeared to have no conscious realization that he was showing up as a doppelganger to intimidate the women. In all likelihood, his anger and his intense emotional charge provided the energy behind his visit. Strong feelings are like that. They leak out, spill over, and find ways to reveal themselves. As far as we know, Raul had not made any conscious effort to let go of his anger. Feeling justified in his discontent, he put his personal power behind his own fury until, even when he was sleeping, his anger sought release. Without conscious intent, his own astral body provided an outlet for his anger.

Carmen and Maria, also full of strong feelings, unknowingly created an opening for Raul to enter their space. Both women felt some regret about their interactions with Raul, and their guilt fueled the opportunity for his appearance by creating a hole in their surrounding energy. Guilt, as we have seen in previous stories, creates a weak spot, a self-doubting vacuum that often beckons to outside energies willing to support us in our self-flagellation. Raul was there to fill this void. Carmen and Maria were receptive to his evening visits because a part of them felt responsible for his anger.

One of my favorite tools for healing, in this type of emotionally charged situation, is the White Heart Meditation. It is particularly useful when there has been hurt, anger, miscommunication, and even a sense of physical threat between people. The White Heart Mediation helps a person move into a place of safety, where they can communicate without feeling threatened.

With less fear, they are free to let go of their own defenses and put more attention toward the honest expression of underlying thoughts and emotions. With the desire and intent to communicate their feelings lovingly, a person can create a healthier connection for sending and receiving information. This connection has effects well beyond the meditation itself; many people discover that the "difficult person" they had focused upon is now more open, cooperative, and trusting in subsequent interactions.

In the White Heart Meditation, I frequently ask people to visualize the person to whom they are communicating as a small child. There is an innocent child within each of us. Often frightened, confused, and uncertain of himself, that child wants the same unconditional love that we all want. If we can truly see the innocent child in another person, we are easily moved to forgive that child because we know that his struggle, pain, and need are similar to ours. Maria was able to reach out toward that part of Raul that felt scared and powerless. She was able to offer him genuine support for getting his needs met in a loving way. She was even able to understand how she had been a threat to him, and she sought his forgiveness as she forgave herself.

Carmen and Maria, by accepting responsibility for their own feelings rather than blaming Raul, had reclaimed their personal power. With safety and certainty, they could now encourage Raul to do the same. Wherever the future might carry their relationship, it was sure to be a place with more understanding, caring, and respect.

Points to Remember…

- ✧ Anger attracts anger. Forgiving others, we heal ourselves.

- ✧ Thoughts and emotions are alive with energy of their own; they can travel beyond the body's conscious awareness.

- ✧ If we can send enough healing energy, the other person will either resist it and leave us alone, or he will accept the healing and resolve things more amenably.

Chapter 11 The Dream Body

The Rejected Healer

Anger is a powerful teaching tool for personal growth. Our anger lets us know when we feel violated, hurt, or betrayed. It reminds us to pay attention to our thoughts and actions and to acknowledge our wants and needs. Left ignored, anger has a way of building up and leaking out at inopportune times or in unanticipated ways, helping to create a hostile environment. Many times this results in attracting other angry people toward us.

When we are willing to acknowledge our anger, embarrassment, or shame, we are then prompted to take a closer look at what is dominating our relationships with others and with ourselves. An opportunity for insight awaits! We can thank our anger and thank ourselves for our growing awareness. Such was the lesson for a young woman who received help in an unexpected form from a Spiritual healer. She first contacted me on a Friday afternoon.

"Hi, Steven? My name is Claire. I got your name from the bookstore. They said you do ghost clearings. Right?"

Her voice is high and thin, tinged with that shrill thread of fear I've learned to recognize quickly over the phone. "Yes, I do. What can I help you with?"

"Well, it's not exactly a ghost. I went to see a person who called herself a healer. And then we got into kind of a big argument." Claire seems to be hurrying now, as if she needs to blurt out the story or she won't have the courage to finish it. "I know I was partly to blame. I was upset, and I just wasn't ready for a confrontation on any of my personal stuff right then. But this woman was so determined to make me look at my own problems! I just got angry and lashed out. And now I think she's after me."

"Whoa, Claire! Slow down a second!" Silently, I am wondering if this lady's a little paranoid. I've encountered very few healers who are really out to get someone else. "Tell me who this person is and why you think she may be after you."

"Well, her name is Kathy. And what I did was sort of demand an emergency session. I was going through a tough time. My boyfriend got angry with me. He hit me and then left. I was frantic to talk with someone, so I called this Kathy lady. A friend had given me her card and told me she does good Spiritual work. I convinced Kathy it was an emergency, and she agreed to see me right away even though it was her time off."

"Go on," I prompt after I sense her hesitation.

"Well, Kathy said I should have known it was coming. She said all the signs were there, and she implied that I was blind not to see them. Anyway, to make a long story short, I disagreed. I got real angry and called her some names. I refused to pay her, and I walked out. I know it wasn't the right thing to do." Claire paused to take a breath. I could feel her waiting for my disapproval. I let the silence stretch on, choosing to neither reassure nor blame her.

"That night I cooled off a lot," she continues sheepishly. "I swore I'd call her the next day to apologize and to pay her. But then the weirdest thing happened.

"I was in bed, nodding off, when I felt what was, I guess, a 'presence.' I sat bolt upright with my eyes wide open and my heart pounding! There she was, standing at the foot of my bed. It was scary as all hell! She was standing there pointing at me, shaking her finger at me. I didn't know what to do, so I just yelled for her to go away. Then she disappeared right before my eyes!

"Is that crazy?"

"Claire, who was…"

"No, wait a second. I'm not finished. So anyway, the rest of the night was pretty quiet. By the time I got up in the morning, I figured it was just my imagination. I thought I probably dreamed up the whole scene. I wasn't ready at all when it happened again the next night, which was last night! There she was again, staring at me, pointing. Now I'm afraid to call her. I don't even want to talk to her. I think maybe she's evil or something, and I don't want to have anything to do with her." A big sigh signaled the end of her story.

"Claire, help me out a little here. What's Kathy's last name?" I try to plow on through this. She seems upset, but not necessarily delusional. Besides that, who am I to say she didn't see the spirit of this healer? My own experience with astral travel is that it can be sporadic, and it is not always within a person's explicit control. But, on occasion, our spirits do wander!

She told me the healer's full name, and the pieces started coming together to complete the picture. I knew Kathy and had great confidence in her abilities. I also knew she had a lot of personal power, most likely including the ability to send her spirit outward on the astral plane. But whether or not she did it purposely remained to be seen.

"Can you help me, Steve?" Claire is eager to find out if I am on her side. "Do you believe any of this? Is this woman out to hurt me?"

"Hold on, Claire! I believe you, and I'm sure it's been a pretty frightening experience. But there are a couple of things we can do immediately to clear this up. Are you ready?"

"Oh, yeah! Thank goodness! I was afraid you'd just think it was all my fault!"

"We can do this, Claire," I reassure her. "But I need your help. First, you sound like you're feeling guilty about storming off and not paying her. That's the door that let her into your space. So that's the most important thing to take care of right away. Call her as soon as possible. Apologize for calling her names. Leave a message if you have to. Promise to pay her immediately, and put a check in the mail.

"Do I really need to call her and talk to her?" Claire asks, letting the little girl in her voice sound helpless and pleading.

"Do you really want to clear up your part of this problem?" I ask, a little afraid that I might be sounding like Kathy.

"Yeah, I do," she concedes. "But would it be okay if I just write a note and send it along with a check? I really don't want to talk to her. She scares me!"

"Okay, write a note instead. Write it from the heart, and that should take care of your part of the situation." I want to keep her motivated to act on this. "But there's still more that needs to be done to clear up the nightly visits. I know this woman, and I really don't believe she would do this kind of thing consciously. She can be a little too direct, even brusque at times, but her heart really IS into healing. I don't think she would want to scare anyone. My guess is that she got more than a little angry with you following the session, but she didn't tap off that energy and let it go. Being the powerful lady that she is, I think she's astral traveling in her sleep. I'll bet she's not even aware of it!"

"Then how will she know to stop it?" Claire asks.

"Well, I have an idea. I'm willing to talk with her, sort of as a mediator on your behalf. If it's okay with you, I'll tell her about your experience. I'm positive that once she's aware of what she's doing, she'll stop. She really isn't evil or anything, Claire. She HAS helped a lot of people with her honesty and her directness, but she's only human. I think she's just angrier than she realizes."

"Okay, Steve. You can tell her whatever you want about my experience. But please tell her not to call me! I just want to be done with this. I've got enough going on. Plenty of people are already mad at me during the day. I don't want them yelling at me in my sleep, too."

I shared the White Heart Meditation with Claire, and I encouraged her to do it for several nights. Motivated to rid herself of Kathy's visitations, she promised she would follow through on the meditation, the note, and the payment.

When I called Kathy the next day, she was grateful for the opportunity to review what had ended in a frustrating counseling session with Claire. She told me that she did, in fact, have Claire in her dreams the past couple of nights. "I knew I was a little exasperated with her, but I figured the dreams were just a healthy release of my own anger. The last thing I would want to do is frighten or intimidate anyone."

"We're all human, Kathy," I reminded her. We all get hurt and angry at times, whether we are the client or the healer. Even when the anger feels subtle or unimportant, it rarely disappears until it is fully acknowledged. "Maybe you just underestimated your own power in this situation."

"Thanks, Steve." Realizing that personal responsibility was necessary while developing her abilities to astral travel, she agreed to do some processing on the matter. She would also do some forgiveness meditations for both herself and Claire.

"And, Steve? Would you please apologize to Claire for me?"

Checking in with Claire the following week, no further night visitations had occurred. Feeling in control again, Claire even voiced that she may give Kathy, "that powerful healing lady," a call for another appointment. "Y'know, Steve, she was right about a lot of things. I think I'm ready, now, to deal with some of my own anger."

We are all teachers, and we are all students. Claire attracted the perfect healer to help her deal with her guilt and anger. Claire could not ignore Kathy's judgmental apparition. Likewise, Kathy attracted the perfect client to remind her of the responsibilities that go along with personal power. Claire's impression of evil was so counter to Kathy's conscious intent that Kathy was also highly motivated to claim and redirect her own anger. She did not want to frighten or intimidate anyone. As for me, Claire and Kathy both provided a wonderful opportunity to welcome, acknowledge and thank my own feelings, positive and negative, for the lessons they invariably teach me.

Points to Remember...

- ✧ We are responsible for defining our own space.

- ✧ We have choices regarding how, when and where we release our hurt and anger. Awareness of the consequences of our feelings is paramount.

- ✧ Being in a state of completion, with clear communications, can resolve and prevent many problems—within everyday reality, and within the world of spirit.

Chapter 12

Fond Farewells

Earthbound spirits are individuals who are caught between physical and nonphysical existence. Time often ceases to move forward for them as they replay an emotional loop, relentlessly seeking resolution of past events. Thus far, we have focused on ghosts—*disincarnate* souls who have abandoned the physical body but not yet released past concerns on the earth plane. However, there is another type of earthbound spirit, one who has not yet let go of the physical body. This is the terminally ill, comatose or dying person.

While still connected to the body, these *incarnate* souls spend their energy trying to sort things out on a spirit level. They stand on the physical side of the precipice, reaching toward the etheric realms. They are, on deeper levels, still deciding whether or not to be here in the physical world. Those who are terminally ill or near death are learning things more tangibly. Reviewing past choices and current feelings, they still spend much of their time in the body. The comatose, however, focus most of their energy and awareness outside, beyond, the body. They have turned their back on the physical world as they struggle with decisions about what to hold on to and what to release before moving in a new direction. Like ghosts, the comatose, too, can get lost, turning in circles of confusion and uncertainty regarding the next step to take.

Earthbound spirits who are still physically connected to the body, just like those who are not, can be helped to move toward deeper levels of completion. Healing means helping the ill or comatose patient to decide, on a soul level, whether it is time to heal the physical body or time to abandon it.

As we have emphasized throughout, it is not up to us as helpers and healers to decide what is right or wrong for another. Our usefulness is not in making choices *for* others, but in awakening others to unrealized possibilities and available alternatives. When an ill or comatose person is ready and willing to move on to more life, he will do one of two things. He will either heal himself physically, experiencing more love and lessons on this material plane, or he will pass on, continuing his journey toward Spirit.

Through the resolution of past dilemmas, the soul is freed and able to leave its state of limbo. Moving in one direction or the other, the person invariably experiences more life.

Al and Edna

Al and Edna had been married for over forty years. He was a dedicated community leader in a small rural town, and she was a dutiful wife. Edna spent much of her time standing by his side smiling, being supportive, and coordinating what seemed like endless potlucks or bake sales. When their daughters were grown and Al retired, Edna thought they would finally focus on their relationship with one another, traveling and doing all of the things they had postponed for the sake of public service. She was wrong.

Change was slow in coming. Frustration escalated and tempers mounted, moving them to seek my counsel. After we met several times, understandings were reached and plans were made for mutual growth and meeting each others' needs. However, just as things started looking up, Edna was diagnosed with terminal cancer.

Given a prognosis of only six months to live, Edna sought my help in understanding and healing her cancer. Throughout several sessions with her, one major theme emerged: she wanted to leave Al. Both of them acknowledged that their relationship was no longer fulfilling and, now, with her cancer, Edna felt it was imperative that she live her remaining life to the fullest. She wanted to be true to her feelings and to quit sacrificing herself for others. To stay with Al, she reasoned, would be an emotional death long before her physical death. With Al's heartfelt blessing and the support of their two daughters, Edna moved thirty miles away, taking an apartment in the larger, adjacent city.

At sixty-three years of age, Edna began living. With newfound friends, she went river rafting, traveling, and camping. Her favorite story was of a two-week backpacking trip through strenuous mountain terrain with her close friend Jack. Her cancer had gone into unexpected remission and her life was full.

One year later her eldest daughter, Amy, called me to the hospital. The cancer had returned suddenly and fervently, leaving Edna's body ravaged and dying. This time, there would be no remission. The daughters knew this and, as I talked with them in an adjoining room, they expressed their greatest concern. "We don't know what to do about funeral arrangements! What kind of flowers would Mom like? Who should speak at the ceremony? What would she want us to do with her ashes?" As the girls fell over each other spilling out questions, I offered a simple solution.

"Ask Edna," I proposed. "She's in there. She can talk. Let her be a part of the plan."

Amy looked at her sister, Carol, in stunned silence. It had never occurred to them that they could actually discuss death with their mom. We ignore death, we cheat death, we deny death. To actually look death squarely in the eye, embracing and welcoming the transition, had not occurred to them. I left them pondering and went back to give Edna a light massage, my hands and heart offering love, reassurance and peace. I'd always had great respect for Edna's honesty with Al, and I rejoiced at her year of exploration and laughter with Jack. Before me lay a soul filled with courage, determination, and trust in life.

One week later, friends and relatives were invited to Edna's hospital room to celebrate her sixty-fourth birthday. Ninety minutes before the scheduled party, Edna died. Surrounded by family who had expectantly come bearing gifts and blessings, she slipped away quietly with a smile on her face, leaving the singing and the celebration to others this time.

Standing beside Amy at the funeral, I noticed that she was quiet and contained. While others openly grieved with sobs and sighs, she held herself slightly removed, almost observing rather than participating. Having gotten to know her through my work with Edna, I felt safe enough to tell her something I had been holding back since the funeral service began. "Amy," I said quietly, "I tried getting in touch with your mom after she passed on, but I couldn't. She must have crossed over and finished her journey pretty quickly."

A slight smile played on her lips as Amy leaned to whisper in my ear. "I talked to Mom like you suggested. Do you know what she told me? She said, 'Once I go, I'm out of here. I'm flyin' straight and true to the Light!'"

Two years following Edna's passing, Amy called again. Al was dying. Unlike Edna's quick departure, however, Al seemed to be hanging on, prolonging his pain in a wasting body. With each passing week the girls thought their dad would be gone, but still he clung to a life of morphine and semi-consciousness in his hospital bed. Could I do anything, they wondered, to help him be more at peace?

"Are you ready to say goodbye?" I asked. "Once I get involved, my intent is to help him see more clearly what his choices are. Sometimes people pass on fairly quickly, many times within just a few days…"

"Yes," Amy answered without hesitation. "Carol and I have talked about it. We're ready to help Dad move out of this painful state. Please come."

Upon arriving at the hospital, our greetings were tinged with both joy and sadness. We shared a few happy memories about Edna before gathering at Al's bedside. Forming a circle around him, Carol, Amy, and I held hands and prayed. His body was unresponsive to our communications, and I realized this work would need to be done in a trance state. With a few deep breaths, I expanded my awareness beyond my own body and mentally focused my energy on connecting with Al. Certain that my intent was only to do whatever might be for the Highest Good and in the name of Spirit, I found Al's spirit greeting me enthusiastically.

"*Hi, Steve. I remember how you helped us earlier,*" he confides. "*I was happy for Edna, you know, during her last year. It was good to see her so free and to know that I genuinely supported her on her choices. Too bad I was not so* kind to my daughter..." Al sighed before continuing. "*I never approved of Carol's marriage, and she knew it. That was unfair. She deserves to choose her own path, too.*"

"It's not too late," I assure him. "You can still let her know. She'll understand even if you don't verbally express it to her. What would you like to communicate? I promise I'll pass the message along."

With my eyes still closed, I watch in silence as Al pulls a gold ring from his pocket and reaches out to hand it to me. "*Steve, give this to Carol. Tell her she has my blessings. I want her to do whatever makes her happy.*" Smiling, I give Al a knowing nod of approval before returning to my normal wakefulness.

Hugs and tears follow as I relate Al's message to Carol. She is quiet, but her face is radiant with love. "I forgive you, Daddy," she whispers. "Thank you. I love you."

Amy called me early the next morning. Al had passed away late that night.

Points to Remember...

- ⬥ During life and during death, we can help souls become more aware of their choices.
- ⬥ Healing is for all those involved: the dead, the dying, and the living.

A Shared Journey

While working for Hospice in the early 1980's, I provided bereavement counseling to George. His wife, Carla, had succumbed to cancer several months earlier, and George's continued withdrawal and depression were worrying his two grown daughters. Realizing that they could not give him all the help he needed, they asked Hospice if there were a counselor available. I met with George many times throughout the next several months. Most of our sessions were held in his kitchen over a cup of coffee, just being there together with his grief and loss.

Gradually, George started coming out of his isolation and withdrawal. He began taking care of himself more, eating better, exercising, and displaying a brighter outlook on life. "I'm ready to move on," he cheerfully announced one day. He started cleaning out his wife's belongings, giving them away to charity. George even began oil painting again, something he had given up when his wife fell ill, a long time ago. Reclaiming his home and his life, he seemed well on the road to accepting more love and happiness. But then his own cancer, which had been in remission for several years before Carla's death, returned with a vengeance.

George's illness progressed rapidly and, within weeks, he was a patient in Hospice. Refusing food and water, with a "Do Not Resuscitate" order in place, he slipped into a nonresponsive, comatose-like state. This time my visit would not be over coffee as I greeted him in trance, my spirit seeking contact with his….

"Hello, George. I know where you're headed. You believe in the good life after death. You know where you're headed. We've talked about it several times. It's okay. You deserve a rest." Feeling his longing and uncertainty, I continue. *"Following your wife isn't anything to be ashamed of. I know your daughters will be confused, maybe even a bit lost, but they'll heal and grow.*

"You don't have to stay in order to take care of them. They'll get all the help they need. A dedicated group of people, including myself, are here to support them."

George is wavering. His spirit is ready to go, but he's not quite certain he's done enough for his daughters. *"It's not up to you make sure they understand or accept everything,"* I remind him. *"I'll help teach them about Spirit. We can hope they'll learn but, in the end, we both know it's up to them. I'll share my thoughts and feelings, my impressions of your spirit with them, and hope it'll be enough. They WILL get help in saying goodbye to their mother and father. Say hello to Carla for them…."*

Returning to this reality, I open my eyes and peer across George's frail body, watching his chest move in silence with nearly imperceptible breaths. I lean forward and, placing two fingers lightly upon his cheek, gently wipe away a tear.

I spend a few more minutes saying goodbye to George, and then I leave. He passes on peacefully that evening with his beloved daughters by his side, wishing him well on his journey.

Points to Remember…

✧ Sometimes death IS the healing.

Goodbye, Aunt Joyce

We often receive communications from others, alive or dead, within the dream state. Some dreams may be merely symbolic. Yet others, those I call "Dream-Visions," may contain messages from—or information about—other people. Noticing the difference between a dream and a dream-vision is not always easy. But, with willingness and experience, we can become aware that the visions are more tangible. With a sense of urgency, they demand more of our attention….

I had never been close to my Aunt Joyce, or at least I didn't think so. We'd spent time together at family gatherings while I was growing up, but I was usually too busy playing with my cousins to really notice or interact much with her.

As the years passed, we drifted slowly apart. I grew up, moved across the country, got married, and spent little energy connecting with distant relatives. Aunt Joyce was not in my thoughts, until one night I dreamed….

I am in Joyce's house that I remember well. The wraparound porch, five floors, the many windows, small bedrooms, all brought back a nostalgic feeling of joy.

I am attracted to noise, many conversations at once, filtering through the hallways. I approach the formal dining area and kitchen. It's a party! Joyce appears to be talking with five different people at the same time. Her mother, Roberta, has just moved out, she explains to a newcomer. This party is for Roberta….

I awakened with a start, having mixed emotions. The celebration was still with me, but there was also a feeling of loss. My Great Aunt Roberta, Joyce's mom, was gone. The dream left me with the impression that Roberta had died. Wondering if this was true, I called another family member in the morning. He reported that all seemed to be okay. *I guess I was wrong. It was just a dream.* Not having been particularly connected to that side of the family, I kept the dream to myself, not sharing it with anyone.

I put it out of my mind, until several months later when I had another dream....

"I've been here before. It's Aunt Joyce's house," I think to myself. *"This is a lot like another dream I remember." I'm walking toward the sound of voices, the noises of a party in full progress. I am shocked a little as I reach a group of people and realize we are no longer in Joyce's house. We are in an apartment. It's Joyce's. Her mother is gone, and there's another party going on. This one is for Joyce.*

She is playing the piano and, upon seeing me, she nods her head slightly. I return her greeting and, with a serene smile on her face, she turns back to the piano and continues to play. The scene fades away slowly as I awaken with the music going through my head.

I lay in bed for a while. This is no longer a coincidence, I thought. Two dreams within months of one another. Two dreams with similar stories to tell. I knew then that my Great Aunt would soon pass on, if she hadn't already. I realized that Aunt Joyce would celebrate that passing and move into a new, comfortable apartment, a new life. But for how long? The parallels in the two dreams left me pondering. I felt like I had been given a glimpse, a piece of information to pay attention to. However, with no more details, no time frame, and no information seemingly important to share, once again I kept my own counsel.

Within weeks of that second dream though, a cousin called to tell me that Roberta had passed on. She had been ill and in pain for some time already. The family was actually relieved that she had let go of her body and moved on. I sent a condolence card to Aunt Joyce, reinitiating contact with this long-lost relative. Pleasant memories arose of our time together long ago. Maybe we were more connected than I had thought.

The story continued to unfold several months later as Joyce sold the old house, moved into an apartment and created a new life for herself. I was happy for her. We still didn't find the time to spend with one another as we lived thousands of miles apart, but our brief telephone conversations had been warm and enjoyable. Gradually, the memory of the dreams faded. It was many months later that I found out through relatives that she had cancer. It didn't look good, but she was in treatment. We would need to wait and see what happened. Time passed, and then....

Marcia and I are sleeping soundly when the noise of a helicopter overhead awakens us. It passes, but we both lay wide awake. There is a glow in the room, a hazy violet color filling the space. We wonder at this as we try to go back to sleep. But it's useless. There is too much energy. It's just plain weird. The violet light intensifies, and I sit up with a start. I could have sworn I saw the silhouette of a woman standing in the doorway. "Who's here?" Marcia asks me. She, too, senses a powerfully loving, feminine essence.

I feel it's my Aunt Joyce. I acknowledge her presence, but we don't talk. I am finally able to drift off to sleep.

The rest of the night was fitful with vague dreams. They included Joyce as well as her ex-husband, Wade, whom she had divorced years earlier. *Now THAT was interesting! What does he have to do with anything? Do I need to do anything about this situation?* Obviously I was getting a bit involved. Maybe I would talk with Wade. Perhaps I would share my experiences. I closed my eyes to meditate on the situation, seeking a clearer direction in which to go with these impressions. Was there anything I could do that would be helpful or healing?

The next day, at the risk of total embarrassment, I decided to get in touch with Wade. We had not had any contact for years, and several of his closer relatives had judged him harshly when he'd divorced Joyce. He and I had never spoken about any of that. Yet, I felt compelled to write him a letter detailing my dreams of Joyce. I expressed my concern that though everything in the dreams about Joyce and Roberta was extremely vivid, references to him were vague. He figured in there somewhere. I just wasn't sure where.

I acknowledged to Wade that these could have been mere dreams, and that I could be imagining or reading too much into my experience. I let him know I could be entirely wrong and totally out of line in writing him about these things, but I felt Joyce was to pass on soon. Now, I encouraged him, would be a good time to complete on any unfinished business with her. They'd had a hard time during the separation and subsequent divorce, so I jumped at that bit of history and encouraged him to be at peace with those choices. Joyce had obviously gained a measure of peace with things, and she had gone on with her life. I also wrote of my experiences with people who had passed on, relating to him that it was a lot easier to complete with them when they were alive than it was after they died.

I apologized for bringing up anything that saddened or angered him. I explained that, as a result of all the dreams, I needed to share this sense of urgency with him. It was something I had to do to feel complete within myself. Closing with blessings to him, I sealed the letter and sent it off.

That same afternoon, I composed a letter to Aunt Joyce. I wrote her of my dreams, of my letter to Wade and of my love and appreciation for her. No fear of embarrassment here. I felt sure she would understand and respect my need to communicate honestly. She would recognize my intent. Several days later a family member called, telling me that Aunt Joyce had taken a turn for the worse. And amazingly, something else had happened: After being estranged for many years, Wade had gone to see her! They visited privately for quite some time. When "grilled" by family members, both Wade and Joyce said they were happy with the visit. Neither, however, would divulge further details, respectfully honoring the privacy of their short reunion.

Joyce passed on shortly thereafter. Even though I couldn't make the trip to say goodbye, three days after her passing I was deep in meditation....

I am drifting, feeling the quietude and peace, letting go of any stressful daily concerns. A thought occurs to me, "I wonder how Joyce is doing."

A chill runs down my spine. My eyes are still closed. Is this a dream? Is it a vision or just my imagination? I look up to see Joyce floating above the floor directly in front of me. "Hi, Aunt Joyce! Are you back here again?"

"No," she whispers, so softly that I am not even sure if her lips move. Did she actually say anything, or did I hear it in my head? "It's time to say goodbye. Thank you, Steve." She starts to fade away.

"Wait!" Tears of joy and sadness threaten to overwhelm me, but I mange to speak. "Thank me for what? I didn't do anything."

Again, in the merest whisper, "Thank you for the time."

She starts to rise up, floating higher and higher. There's a Light above her. She continues to ascend, almost completely surrounded by Light now. I mentally shout to her disappearing form, "Thank YOU, Joyce,"

She's gone now, but wait. There's one more thing. I hear a faint, almost silent message. I'm not sure if it's from her or from one of my Spirit teachers. "Tell the children."

"I will," I assure her, then myself. *"I will."*

Coming out of the meditation, I wrote down the whole experience, making it into a little story, and sent it to my cousin, Joyce's son. He didn't know what to make of it at first, but it admittedly brought him a sense of peace. "It can't hurt," he said. "I'll send it to my sisters as well."

My part was done. I felt complete.

I have no regrets for being drawn into this drama. It was seemingly "meant to be." I feel I was guided to get involved, or else why would I have had the dreams? True, they were precognitive dreams. They foretold the future. However, the future is NOT written in stone. The future could change. I could have misinterpreted the dreams. They could have just reflected my own hopes and fears. Bottom line, my impressions of unfolding physical events could have been wrong. However, because I had been drawn into it over and over again, I felt the need to get personally involved.

When telling people of precognitive dreams, we always take a chance on needlessly frightening someone. We always take a chance on being wrong. However, we can affirm this to the person with whom we share the "visions." In sharing, we are relating our experiences, our impressions, our interpretations. It is up to the other person to decide what to do with this information. I trust them to make their own choices according to their own needs. Sharing precognitive dreams is risky. But if we don't communicate, would we then always wish we would have? I do not want to give my fears of being judged crazy, or intrusive, more power than I give my potential to be loving and helpful. Therefore, I consciously choose to act from a loving space, acknowledging love for all the persons involved. I can then share with the certainty that, no matter their reaction, healing is taking place.

Points to Remember...

- ✧ Communication is the key to completion.
- ✧ Sometimes it is better to risk looking foolish and overinvolved, than to give in to fear and remain silent.

Chapter 13

Choosing a Direction

Helping a person pass on does not have to be done in their direct physical presence. Since there is neither time nor space in Spirit, we can connect with the souls of other people over any distance. For example, two of the previous stories dealt with people being "haunted" by others who were, at the time, merely sleeping. During the dream state, while the body is at rest, our consciousness is free to wander. Some people wander unconsciously, their spirit adrift, following emotions or events without their mind ever being aware of intent or outcome, just dreaming. Others can project their awareness consciously when there is a need, allowing for directed focus and intent.

Sleeping Beauty

"Steve. I've got a problem. And you're the only one I could think of to call."

That was Mary Anne, an acquaintance who had lived in Colorado for a time and then moved out of state. "I know you do trance work, and I'd like to get some information."

I remembered Mary Anne fondly and was willing to help with almost anything I could. "Sure. I'll do what I can. I do trance work over the phone or through the mail."

"Well, before you commit to anything, let me explain a little bit of what's going on."

Her voice began to falter. I could tell she was on the verge of tears, so I waited silently for a minute. When she didn't recover, I said, "Mary Anne, you sound upset. Tell me what's wrong. I haven't heard from you for a long time, but I can probably help. At least I can steer you in the right direction. Take your time. I'm here. We can work on this together."

"Okay. Here it goes. My mom had a stroke about a month ago. The doctors say she's recovered as much as she's going to. But she won't wake up. It's not exactly a coma. But they say she's damaged the part of her brain that's responsible for waking her up."

This must have been real tough on Mary Anne. She was such a caring person and had even moved to be closer to her family. She saw a lot of beauty in her mother and had always talked about her lovingly.

"I'm glad you're there to help take care of things, Mary Anne. What decisions do you have to make? Are they even yours to make?"

"Well, that's it in a nutshell. They're feeding her with a tube. But, other than that, she's on no life support or anything because she's just sleeping. They don't hold out much hope for a recovery. Actually, they don't see her waking up at all, ever."

"Mary Anne," I kept my voice even and unflinching. "Is it up to you to pull the plug, or is there someone else who needs to make that decision?"

"Oh crap, Steve." That's when she started crying. *God, I have a hard time listening to someone I care about cry.* "My Dad doesn't want to make the decision. My sister doesn't either. And my brother is freaking out. He can't even talk about it. So, yeah. I guess I'm it."

I waited until she was finished blowing her nose and catching her breath.

"So I guess what I want from you is some help in figuring out what to do. Is there anything that needs to be complete for her to pass on peacefully before I make this decision? Or maybe something I need to be complete with before I do anything else? Pulling the plug would feel so much like starving her to death. How do I know what she wants or needs?"

At that point I stopped and explained to Mary Anne that we could always hope and pray for a miracle, but she needed to be aware that the doctors may be accurate in their prognosis—Mom may never awaken. I also said that I'd be happy to get in touch with her mother's spirit and see what could be done.

Then with all seriousness, because I needed to know Mary Anne fully understood what I was about to undertake, I gave her a warning. "Mary Anne, I'll do this work, but ONLY if you're willing to let her go. Sometimes the person will wake up and come back. But often, when I do this work, if the person is ready to pass on, they will do so within three days. Are you ready for that?"

She started crying again. I suggested she take her time in deciding whether or not she wanted me to contact her mother. I encouraged her to call me the next day after thinking about it, just to be sure she really wanted to continue.

"Steve?" I recognized Mary Anne's voice as soon as I picked up the phone the next morning. "I guess I'm ready. That's why I called. Something's got to change. Is there any chance you can bring her back?" she pleaded.

It wouldn't be up to me, I explained. There's always a chance that a person will come back. I don't push people onward; I just help them to feel complete. The choice is theirs to make. "But Mary Anne, I've got to tell you. In three out of four cases, the person DOES pass on. And I just wanted you to be ready for it."

She was still with me and agreed to do the work. "I'm sure I'm ready, even though it isn't easy. It feels right, though, so much more right than just pulling the plug before knowing if she's ready. I want you to go for it, Steve."

I took her Mom's full name, Karen Lenore Johnston, and told Mary Anne I'd work on it overnight. "I'll get back to you sometime tomorrow," I promised.

I'm on my way to sleep. I breathe slowly and deeply, calling on the Light, calling on Guidance to help me in this endeavor. I breathe the White Light in the top of my head and breathe it out my forehead, my third eye. Projecting my consciousness outward, I call on Karen, trying to connect with her through her daughter, Mary Anne.

"Karen, Karen Lenore Johnston! I'm here to help. Your family is worried about you. They want to help. I want to help. Mary Anne asked me to help. Karen Lenore Johnston, talk with me, let me in." I keep calling on her. I keep breathing slowly and deeply, projecting Love and Light as I drift off to sleep. I start to dream....

I am in a house. I look down and discover that I am Karen. I am in my pajamas—white with red designs. There are people coming and going, but I don't find that strange at all. Neither do they. They don't give me a second thought.

A young man comes into the room. I know him to be my son, even though I've never seen him before. He looks lost and confused but makes his way straight to the refrigerator. He eats plateful after plateful of food. I can't understand how he could eat so much. What does he do with it all? Just when I think he's done, he gets more!

Finally, he belches, leaving the table and all its dirty plates. And who's going to clean up that mess? Not me. I've cleaned up enough. I try to tell him this, but he ignores me. He doesn't hear me. I may as well be talking to myself.

I follow him upstairs where he starts going through a closet full of clothes. He's looking frantically for something but can't find it. He almost starts to cry. I try to console him, but he's still ignoring me. He's crying. I reach out to hold him, but my hands and arms slow down as they get closer to him. I so much want to reach him, but I can't. Why won't he let me near? I have to help, but I can't. I can't. Sadness wells up inside of me. I feel like I'm going to burst at any second....

I awaken feeling sad and lonely. I know the dream was not mine. It was Karen's, but I feel as she did. I realize that I can communicate with her through the dream state. I need to meditate, to reprogram the dream and go back to sleep. I start repeating to myself, to Karen, "I give the perfect support at the perfect time. I allow others to accept it. I give the perfect support at the perfect time. I allow others to accept it." I channel the Light to 'my' son. I breathe in the Light and breathe it out to surround him. "I give the perfect support at the perfect time. I allow others to accept it."

"Karen," I mentally call to her. "You don't have to clean up after him. He's an adult. He is making his own choices. We know you love him. We know you've tried to help. It's up to him whether or not to accept the support. You give the perfect support at the perfect time. You give the perfect support at the perfect time."

I channel the Love and Light in my head and out my third eye. I project my awareness to her. "I give the perfect support at the perfect time. I allow others to accept it. I give the perfect support at the perfect time. I allow others to accept it." I drift off to sleep. I'm not aware of going to sleep until I start to dream....

I am an elderly woman. My back hurts. My legs are swollen, but I continue to work. I am in a butcher shop, chopping meats, taking people's orders, chopping meats, taking orders. A man walks in. It's Bob, my son. No it's not. It just looks like him. But the resemblance is close enough that I like to think of him as my own.

I don't realize I'm staring at him with my mouth just hanging open until he gets rather sharp with me. "Hey!" he calls to me. "Hey. Can I have some help?" This can't be MY son. MY son is nice. He's polite. Wait a second. I must be dreaming. Bob isn't so nice. Actually he's gotten kind of cranky these last few years.

The dream continues. I ask him what cut of meat he wants. He gets upset with me for even asking. Like I should know what he wants. I make some suggestions, but they are all seemingly bad ones.

"Oh, forget it," he yells. "Just give me one of everything." I am offended, so I glare at him silently. I carelessly stuff the meat into a bag and throw it to him. He catches it and walks off in a hurry. There's so much more I want to say to him, but it's too late. He's gone...

"Karen!" I mentally call out to her when I awaken. "Karen. He does accept what you have to offer. He just gets confused sometimes. He doesn't even know what he wants. Forgive yourself for not knowing. You've offered him everything. It's up to him to be grateful or not. It's up to him to decide how he's going to accept it, how he's going to use it.

"You give the perfect support at the perfect time. Thank yourself. You give the perfect support at the perfect time. Allow others to discover their needs and wants. Love him. Support him in growing up at his own pace, in his own way. You can't be everything to everyone. I receive joy from ALLOWING others to discover their needs and wants. I receive joy from allowing others to discover their needs and wants. I receive joy..."

I am at an outdoor picnic. I've brought my basket of food. I feel a little out of place, as everyone else has nice colorful coolers. They've got everything they need. What can I offer? I thought I brought some nice things, but they're nothing compared to the feast I am looking at. I start to turn away, but someone calls out to me.

"Mom. Mom. Did you bring it?" I am so embarrassed. How do I know if I brought "it" or not? I start wringing my hands on my dress. "Mom. Mom. Did you bring it?" He's insistent now.

"I don't know," I confess.

"Well, bring it here! Let me have it. It took you long enough. Everyone's been waiting." He reaches impatiently for the basket. I hold onto it. But then I look up and see my daughter. Mary Anne just stands there and nods, like everything is going to be all right. I hold on a moment longer, but finally I let him have it. This is still so frustrating.

He sets it down on the blanket, takes a deep breath and opens it. "Thanks, Mom. This is great. Thanks." Everyone's staring at me. I feel so embarrassed. I don't even know what's in there. "Sure." I stammer. "I just wish I knew…"

He turns away. He's busy talking with a woman, showing her what's in the basket. But I still don't know what's in there. I try to ask. I come a little closer. I try to speak up, but he's already moved on. "Sure. You're welcome."

I wake up. Still in a light trance, I am a little confused, a little disoriented, but feeling good. I realize I feel almost complete. "Karen, you've done good. Actually, you've done great. You've let go of the control. Other people do get what they need from you. You've given enough. Even if you're not sure what it is you've given, that's okay. You've given enough. Mary Anne will tell him you feel good about what you've given. She'll tell everybody who needs to know. You ARE appreciated. You ARE loved. You ARE loving.

"You don't need to understand everything. You don't always need to know what others need. Just accept that you've given enough, that they've gotten enough. You've given them what they've needed. Let them have it. Let them decide what to do with it. You ARE appreciated. You ARE loved. You ARE loving."

I drift off to sleep repeating that over and over. "You ARE appreciated. You ARE loved. You ARE loving…."

I am under the water. I am frantic to get to the surface. I've fallen off the boat, but I can't reach the surface. The water is tossing me left and right. I've got to make it to the top. It's rough. The currents are just playing with me—almost *letting me reach the surface, then dragging me under again. I feel like I'm about to burst. And then, finally, I reach the top. The water is calm. The sun is shining. The horror is over. I can float in peace like this forever....*

"Mary Anne?" I call her early the next morning, knowing that she hardly slept. "It worked. I don't know exactly what went on, but I know I did successfully communicate with your mom. She's at peace. You've done a good thing, Mary Anne. There's just one thing left to do. Then we'll see if she comes back. I think she'll wake up, maybe for just a minute. But remember, it will be up to her whether or not to hold on to the body when she does."

I tell her that I will send the dream experiences to her via express mail. She's to share them with her brother, who had to return home to his wife and family. She's to share them with her mom, affirming to both Karen and herself that the peace is spreading. She can do this aloud in her mom's presence, whether or not there's a visible response from Karen. "Call in the Light and speak from the heart, Mary Anne. She'll hear it. Let me know what happens. And God bless."

She called me a few days later to say her mom had passed on. She also told me that she was holding her mom's hand while reading her the letter. It could have been just her imagination, but she could swear her mom squeezed her hand ever so slightly, just for a second. The next day mom had coronary failure and made her transition peacefully "in her sleep."

Points to Remember...

- ✧ Communication can transcend the physical boundaries of time and space.

- ✧ Sharing from the heart is always healing. We give the perfect support at the perfect time.

- ✧ As the sick person reaches a new level of completion, he or she will most likely be ready to make a clearer choice: to come back to the physical body or to pass on.

What's Your Decision, Joseph?

While the dream state is often effective in contacting souls beyond the physical plane, we can also use Shamanic Journeying. This is a type of meditation that involves projecting our consciousness outward to communicate on a deeper, more spiritual level with others. Journeying to explore different levels of awareness requires training. It requires asking for and trusting in Guidance so that we may successfully focus our thoughts and safely return to this physical dimension.

No matter what method we use when doing healing work with ill or dying persons, one thing becomes evident: We ALWAYS need to ask the person with whom we are working for permission to carry out any healing. If that person is unable to speak for himself, we must ask the closest relative. Then, while in the healing trance state, we can ask the ailing person for his or her explicit permission to proceed. If permission is denied, we respect the choice, bless the person, and discontinue the work.

Following is an account of healing work using Shamanic Journeying.

Amy and Joseph were becoming new friends of ours. We had enjoyed sharing dinner several times, included our children in outings together and, most recently, joined in the celebration of Joseph's completion of graduate school. His return to college had been arduous and expensive, and Amy had worked many long hours to see the family through lean times. Now there was a wave of excitement and relief on everyone's part as Joseph accepted a high-level executive position in a prestigious marketing firm. We toasted Joseph with champagne and smiles, not seeing what was to come just a few weeks down the road....

It was a good day for some backcountry skiing. With cool breezes whipping around them, Joseph and his friend climbed the icy trail along a rocky outcrop high in the mountains. Two hours later, perched on the summit, they threw off their packs, sat down to face the sun, and downed gulps of bottled water. The view was spectacular and the blowing crystals of snow sparkled against the brilliant blue of the sky. Eager to slalom down the fresh,

Chapter 13 Choosing a Direction

powdery snow of the north side, Joseph had one ski strapped on when a sudden gust of wind lifted the other and sent it skidding across the icy ledge. He leaned to catch it before it could blow over the side. The ski slid; Joseph reached, faltered, and went careening over the edge, tumbling and bouncing several hundred feet before coming to rest in a crumpled heap on the rocks below. His horrified friend watched helplessly, seeing the moment in endless slow motion.

Miraculously still alive when helicopter rescue teams arrived, Joseph suffered several broken bones, head and internal injuries, and was in a coma. Although he temporarily emerged from the coma a few days later, he remained in critical condition. Drifting in and out of consciousness, he lay immobile and unresponsive.

Marcia and I visit with Amy at the hospital. Joseph's life is hanging in the balance. Will he live? Is the swelling of his brain going up or down today? Does he even know Amy is there by his side? Will he remember his two daughters? The doctors do not offer false hopes. Probable outcomes are dim, and they make it plain that Joseph could die.

As each day crawls by, Joseph's condition wavers, a roller coaster of encouragement and dismay. Amy is at a loss. Is she being selfish in her hopes for him to live and return to her and the kids? Or should she be wishing him a peaceful passage? What does he want to do? How can she help? Joseph himself seems undecided as his medical condition improves one hour and deteriorates the next.

Exhausted by the ups and downs, Amy accepts my offer to see if I can make contact with Joseph. She is ready to help him clarify his needs, and to support him on his choices.

...I focus my intent on healing. I invoke Spirit, calling in the Light, asking any Angels, Divas, Masters and Personal Guides to join us. I turn on a drumming tape to keep me in trance, to help me journey outward, to keep me focused, and to bring me back when the work is done...

The drums fill my head, my soul—steady, reassuring, like the beating of my heart. They drive me onward. I lay there in the dark with my eyes closed tightly. My heart goes out to Amy and to Joseph. I want so much to be able to help. What can I do?

"JOURNEY," a voice instructs me. "JOURNEY TO JOSEPH. ASK HIM WHAT HE NEEDS."

My vision shifts. It narrows. I go down a tunnel, a familiar cave that leads to the underworld. Visions, feelings, and thoughts pull me in different directions. I focus my intent once more. The drumming continues. I ask for Guidance. "Pull me through this one," I demand.

The tunnel opens onto a field of wheat, a tireless expanse of growth, of harmony and peace. The wind bends the grain in waves that go on forever. I hear the cry of an Eagle, my Eagle. He's circling above me. "COME! COME WITH ME, STEVEN. I'LL HELP DIRECT YOU. I'LL HELP YOU TO KEEP YOUR PERSPECTIVE, TO STAY ABOVE THE PAIN AND SADNESS. FOCUS!"

I am riding the air currents, calling in the Light, letting myself be guided to where I need to go. The presence of Eagle comforts me. "I can do this work," I remind myself. I spread my wings and fly. The view is great from up here. I can see forever. I can feel the strength...

"FOCUS!"

"Joseph," I call. "Joseph, I'm looking for you. Can we talk? I'd like to help. Let me know where you are." Almost immediately upon calling him, I come to a large stucco building. I am sucked through the roof and see Joseph lying atop a hospital bed. Amy is there. She's crying. She's talking to him, a monologue only she can hear.

"She wants so much from me," I hear Joseph's thoughts. "I can't give it to her." I feel his sadness and confusion. "Where do I go? What do I do?" he pleads.

"Joseph! It's time to get focused, Joseph. You've had a terrible accident, but you're still here. There are people who care about you here. They love you, Joseph."

"I know!" he moans. "I know. I just don't know what to do. I'm lost."

I feel his disorientation, as if he's in several places at once and yet nowhere at all.

He speaks again. "I don't know if I can continue. I've worked so hard at becoming independent. Now look at me. I can't go on like this."

"Joseph! Focus on my voice. Hear me. There is something we can do. This is YOUR life. These are YOUR decisions, but I can help. You CAN feel clearer."

He looks up, seemingly being aware of me for the first time. There's hope in his eyes—a flash of excitement, but also of fear.

"I'm not going to MAKE you do anything, Joseph. I just want to help you make some choices, to help you choose a direction, some place to go from here."

Anticipating my next question, he answers. "Yes, do it. Any place is better than here. I feel so lost. Confused, sad, angry at myself, a failure...."

I am aware of a cord stretching away from his body. A white cord from his abdomen disappears out the hospital walls. I am called away. I leave him mumbling, moaning. "Help me," *I call to Guidance.* "Help me focus. What's to be done?"

The drumming calls to me. Eagle grips me hard within his talons, passing me through the walls. Outside. Flying higher, faster, out of the city now, up to the mountains. And there, down there, is Joseph. He's sitting in the snow. Just sitting there, hugging his knees, shaking his head. He sees me and puts his head down further. Hugging his knees more tightly, he closes in on himself. "Go away!" *he screams.* "Go away. Let me be!"

I am about to leave when I remember the other part of him lying in the hospital. I remember being asked to help. "I can't." *I speak gently yet firmly.* "I can't. You asked me to help. Joseph is lying in a hospital, caught between life and death. He needs you to help him."

"This was supposed to be a celebration, Steve. I just joined a wonderful agency. Amy's been great these past few years. Supporting me, helping me, paying for my schooling. And now I'm supposed to go out and be successful. My life might as well be over. I'll be working so hard I won't be able to enjoy myself anymore. I'll have to support my family, but I won't be able to do that."

I take my cue. "Yes, Joseph, your family. They love you. Your daughters, your wife. They all love you. Do you think they'll only love you if you give up your life for them? They don't want that. They want you to feel good about yourself. They want you to be happy."

"But that's just it. They want me to prove that I'm strong enough to support them! Well, I can't! I've been real dependent on Amy for all these years. And now...now I'll have to be totally independent, strong. I'll need to carry all the weight. I can't do it, I tell you. I can't do it."

"TELL HIM, STEVEN," *I hear Guidance urging me on.* "TELL HIM."

"You're right, Joseph. You can't do it." *He looks up. Shock registers on his face as I agree with him.* "You're right, Joseph. You can't do it! And no one expects you to. They just want you to be stronger, not invincible. They just want you to be more independent, not totally independent. They want you to HELP carry the load, not to carry the whole thing yourself. They still want to be in it with you."

He sits up straighter. Releasing his knees, he stretches his legs, suddenly grimacing in pain.

"Hey, take it easy, Joe," I caution. "Let's do a bit of healing here. You don't have to do everything all at once. You don't have to jump into things right away. You can get stronger gradually, more independent one day at a time."

I call in the Light. We massage his head, a clear wind blowing out the fog. Sending that same energy to his spine, we help straighten things out a bit. He stretches as if to get up. We focus his energies on his legs, sewing a gash together so that each leg will hold his weight. I help him up, but he stumbles. His eyes are blurred. He can't see straight.

"Joseph!" I hold my finger up in front of his eyes. "Focus on my finger. Focus on getting stronger at your own pace. Focus on letting your wife and children help you a little bit more. You can do it."

He starts to sag, starts to drop to the snow again.

"Joseph! Listen! They love you. They WANT to help. You can let them help. They can get joy from watching you grow, from watching you get stronger and more self-reliant. They want to share your successes, not to force you to do things you don't want to do. They want to help willingly. These are their decisions. They're here for you, Joseph. There's no reason for guilt. Your healing helps everyone.

"They're waiting for you back in the hospital. Your family needs you back in the hospital, Joseph."

He looks me in the eye, and I see certainty there. He takes a deep breath. "But I'll need a lot of help with this one, a lot of faith." We startle at a noise from up the hill. It's a bear, a big, cinnamon-colored bear.

"It's okay, Joe. He's here to help." Bear comes closer and nudges Joe with his nose. Joe leans on Bear for support, for strength, for balance. Two words fill the air, coming from above, below, all around us. "BE STRONG." Amazingly, the words are spoken from Bear. "BE STRONG."

"It's time to come back, Joseph. It's time now." I stretch out my hand, palm up. Joseph nods. Reaching toward me, he grabs my hand. With my other one I grab a bit of Bear's fur. Taking a deep breath, I draw them to my heart, to my medicine bag resting on my chest. Immediately, I am pulled back to the hospital. The force with which this is done is unnerving. The drums roll on. Eagle circles above. "DO IT," Guidance commands. "DO IT BEFORE HE LOSES THE NERVE. DO IT WHILE HE SO STRONGLY WANTS IT, NEEDS IT."

I look upon Joseph in the bed. I bring my hands up, cupping them under my medicine bag, my Spirit Catcher. I take a deep breath, grabbing Joseph's returning part along with Bear. I breathe them from my heart. Holding them in my hand momentarily, I blow them into Joseph's navel, resting my hands there. My hands stay there of their own accord. We can hold those parts in there, so they won't leave again.

I reach into my bag again and blow the parts into his heart, then into the top of his head. Pressing my hands on his Crown Center and heart, I hold the parts in until I can feel them settling into his body. I feel the love and solidity of his body. A smile of contentment comes over his face as he drifts off into a peaceful sleep. "Rest well, Joseph. Rest, recover, become..."

Eagle screams at me. "FOCUS, STEVEN!" he reminds me to keep moving. This is not my time nor place to sit and rest. The drums roll on. They've picked up in rhythm and speed. They're calling me. Following the sound, I travel back through the fields of wheat. Personally, I'm glad I was able to do a Soul Retrieval for Joseph. I think he's decided to stay, decided not to pass on, but they are and will be, as always, HIS choices.

I come to my cave, up through the tunnel. The drums are calling. Life is beckoning. I rise from the tunnel into the sunlight, into my meditation space, back to where I started. With gratitude and wonder I open my eyes...

I talked with Amy that same day and dropped off a tape I had made of the journey. She agreed to listen to it and to talk with Joseph, even if he was unresponsive. She would share with him, with love and certainty, her feelings about what came up on the tape. She would reassure him and share in his successes. Together they would each grow stronger.

Within twenty-four hours, Joseph showed signs of recovery. It may have been the work that was done. It may have been Amy's unconditional love and support for him that pulled him through. It may have been a miracle. But the next day I was told he opened his eyes and kept them open for some time. He was able to focus more clearly, to speak a few intelligible words, and to consciously exercise control over a few of his muscles. He even gave a flicker of a smile to Amy before drifting off into a peaceful sleep, instead of a fitful semiconscious state.

It seemed he had decided to stay.

Good luck and blessings on your journey, Amy and Joseph.

Communication with this spirit took the form of Shamanic Journeying in which we spoke with each other both verbally and symbolically. Convincing Joseph's spirit to move beyond stasis was done through two avenues: speaking directly with him about his feelings, and using metaphor and symbols to redirect his thoughts to future possibilities.

Communication with Karen, the Sleeping Beauty, was accomplished through the dream state rather than through Shamanic Journeying. The concept, however, was the same: using symbols from the dream state to gain insight into her dilemma, and then speaking with her spirit to redirect her focus.

Regardless of the method used to attain the trance state—dreaming, journeying, or self-hypnosis, prayer and meditation—the goal is the same. We intentionally move our consciousness beyond physical existence in order to communicate with those whose awareness has already moved beyond their body.

Points to Remember…

- ✦ Communication with disembodied spirits can take many forms. We can be open to any method that presents itself, using whatever form seems most effective.

- ✦ Reaching a state of completion, a soul can then move forward, possibly choosing to continue life *within* the body.

Part IV

Personal Ghosts

Chapter 14

Getting Involved

The stories shared up to this point have focused on house ghosts, astral projections, and persons in transition between life and death. Earthbound spirits already introduced have been connected to a specific place, such as a house, neighborhood or geographic area. Their link is primarily with the location and/or the circumstances of a present household. Because these spirits and the property owners have few, if any, deep emotional ties to one another, these ghosts can often be sent on to the Light with relative ease. However, the relationship is more complex when dealing with a personal ghost.

A "personal ghost" is a spirit entity who has attached itself to the energy of a specific individual rather than to a place or a circumstance. Any living person who hosts an entity has, consciously or unconsciously, an emotional tie to the earthbound spirit. Likewise, the earthbound spirit has an emotional tie to the living person. Whereas a house ghost will stay put and tend to hold onto a geographic area, a personal ghost may follow its host from place to place regardless of location. The earthbound spirit's connection is with the feelings and energy of a particular living being and, due to a variety of circumstances, one or both parties involved have an investment in keeping the relationship intact. Emotions that perpetuate the situation often grow stronger and more complex as the intertwining bond deepens over time between the living and the dead.

Personal ghosts are not easily persuaded to depart from their host and move into the Light. Both the living person and the ghost may be convinced of a requisite interdependence, generating reluctance and fear at the thought of being separated. Attempts to rid one's self of a personal ghost by cleansing the house, moving to a new location, switching jobs or changing relationships are seldom successful. Holding onto the ghost, however, prolongs an unfortunate state of incompletion. Both beings stagnate as they strive to sustain a relationship that does not grow, does not move toward greater awareness, and is destined to become a dead end (excuse the pun).

Why do some people attract and hold onto ghosts, while others do not? The answer is simple: Guilt. Feelings of having betrayed oneself or another person, and feelings of having been betrayed, contribute to opening the doorway that allows a ghost to attach itself in the first place. Self-incrimination can result from many circumstances: incomplete communications, suppressed desires, judgments about our wants and needs, regrets about past deeds, feelings of inadequacy.

Most of us are well acquainted with guilt, and the resulting discomfort can be a powerful motivator for movement and growth. Our sense of guilt serves to inspire us to right action. However, sometimes we get stuck, consciously or unconsciously, in self-recrimination. We may be aware of the uneasiness, but feel unworthy of self-forgiveness. Believing that we deserve to feel badly for our transgressions, we stop our forward progress in order to take some time (days, months, years, lifetimes) to reprimand ourselves. We have lost sight of the self-healing, loving, and worthy part of ourselves. If these feelings of incompletion are strong enough or last long enough, we become vulnerable to attracting a ghost—one who shares similar feelings of inadequacy and incompletion.

This ghost may be someone we have known who passed on and may, in fact, be the very being with whom we need to clarify and complete our communications. Or this spirit may be unknown to us personally, but his or her lessons may be akin to ours. By conscious or unconscious agreement, then, our guilt invites the connection and enables the attachment to take place.

For a ghost to stick around a live, breathing, human being over a period of time, the ghost needs an energy source to support its presence in this denser, physical plane. The entity will subsequently draw life-force from the person to whom he or she is attracted. Plagued with guilt, the living person allows this "haunting" to take place. Rarely, though, does he anticipate its consequences. With part of his energy being tapped, the host may feel drained, listless, and less able to focus clearly. This leaves him more susceptible to disease, physical ailments, accidents, and emotional instability. Fatigue and depression become routine.

For the practitioner, sending a personal ghost on to the Light is more complex than sending on a house ghost. Not only do we need to counsel the ghost onward, but we also need to counsel the person being "haunted," helping him let go of the emotional ties that bind the spirit to him. When we coach the individual who carries the ghost, to help him send the spirit onward himself, there is then a greater probability that he will let go, complete the communication, and move on with his own growth. In effect, this will assure the ghost that his host sincerely wants him gone. This offers the spirit more certainty that he, too, is free of responsibilities within the relationship.

If a person who hosts a personal ghost is unwilling to help that spirit move onward, any healing work will likely be undermined. Under such circumstances, the practitioner may wish to rethink his involvement. No one has more control over another person's space than that person himself does. Therefore, if the client wants to hang onto a ghost, no amount of persuasive influence will override the client's true intent. In the ensuing power struggle, it is the client, not the practitioner, who ultimately decides who he lets in or casts out of his personal environment. Fortunately, by the time most people seek help in letting go of a personal ghost, they are ready and willing to complete the relationship and release the spirit. By the time someone comes for counseling to release limiting thoughts and feelings, they are usually ready for more positive thoughts, stronger self-esteem, and self-forgiveness.

A word of caution here: When dealing with an extremely angry or invasive ghost, call on a professional spiritual healer to facilitate the clearing. People who are trained extensively in working with ghosts can prevent the ghost from affecting their own energy field. They can use energy work on the living host to sustain and protect him or her from greater intrusion during the clearing. Also, because they are experienced and certain, trained metaphysicians can communicate more effectively with the ghost, maintaining a clear psychic connection.

However, in most cases, the ghost does not intend to be a threat or want to use anger or violence toward the host or healer. The entity may even be a loved one who has passed on, yet is still connected to the bereaved. Like people, ghosts get scared and are afraid of change and the unknown. Most personal ghosts need and want the same safety, understanding and insight craved by their warm-blooded host. Usually, a confident counselor can guide the living through a meditation or hypnotherapy session to help let go of the spirit. If, during the process, the client feels extremely uncomfortable, and/or the therapist starts to feel light-headed, dizzy, nauseous or sick, then it is appropriate either to stop or take additional steps to protect the space of both the client and therapist. (See Appendix for details.) If the therapist does stop, he needs to apologize to the ghost and assure the spirit that someone else will wish to talk with him or her at a future date. He then asks the spirit not to cause much trouble for the living, between now and then, because we would not "wish the spirit to feel bad about anything." The therapist ends the session with blessings for all present and then consults with a spiritual healer for specific guidance. Referring a client out for one or two sessions, or calling in a consultant, can be to everyone's benefit.

Throughout our work with people and with spirits, Marcia and I are constantly reminded that we are all in this together. Life is truly an unbroken circle. Each of us, within a body or without, is susceptible to sorrow, guilt, fear, pain, and disease as we learn our lessons. And each of us, when we are ready, can find the help, compassion and love to bring us healing. Joy and celebration await!

Points to Remember…

- ✧ Guilt, anger and sadness do not always attract a spirit! Those feelings merely open the doorway for that attraction.
- ✧ Healing sometimes takes the form of releasing ANY "negative energies" the client has attracted, while simultaneously closing the door that attracted those energies.

Where's the Party?

Neither Mark nor Kim could remember who first decided that they had a ghost, but both were now ready to get rid of it. The young couple frequently had fun dabbling in the occult and knew that their astrological charts showed them to be a perfect match. They liked to pull out Tarot cards on Saturday night and do a reading for each other. Never too serious, though, the session often ended in giggles and tickling, the cards lying disregarded on the kitchen table. Life was full of enough seriousness and pain. Better to look only at the surface sometimes and not let the heavy stuff get you down.

Over the past couple of weeks, however, some strange things were happening in their comfy little bungalow. Mark and Kim would drift off to sleep at night and awaken in the morning to find a picture in the living room hanging upside down. At first, Kim thought Mark did it. He must have gotten up in the night and turned it around, just to spook her. Mark thought Kim did it. While eyeing each other with suspicion, they laughed. But the laughter became more nervous when Kim and Mark got up one morning and found all of the pictures in their living room hanging upside down.

"C'mon, Mark. Tell me the truth. Did you do this?" Kim asked. Mark swore he didn't. Kim swore she didn't. They believed each other, shrugged their shoulders, and simply wondered how long it would go on. Out of the corner of his eye, though, Mark thought he had seen a small shadow scurrying across the living room floor. Okay, so they might have a ghost, but it seemed harmless. How cute, and a good story to tell their friends.

Last night Kim quit laughing. She was in the shower, humming as she lathered her hair, when she felt a poke through the shower curtain. "Hi, Mark!" Another poke. She giggled. "No, you can't come in. I'm not done yet." Poke, poke, poke. Kim could see where Mark's finger went along the geometric design in the blue plastic. She whipped back the curtain playfully, ready to pull him into the steamy shower, clothes and all. But Mark wasn't there! Nobody was there! Kim didn't know whether to be frightened or angry. Somebody, something was on the other side of that curtain, intruding on her private space. Time to get serious.

Mark called me the next morning. He was upset about Kim's shower experience the previous night and angry with himself for not being able to protect her. "This is getting just a little too far out of hand," he said. "When I saw that shadow in the living room, I should have called you then. I never realized a ghost could be so intrusive!"

"Has anything been broken?" I asked. "Or has anybody tripped and hurt themselves or felt pushed around?"

"No, no," Mark assured me. "In fact, the whole thing seems like a big joke. The upside down pictures were pretty funny, and Kim wasn't even as mad as I was about the shower thing. Once she calmed down, she started making a lot of jokes about a ghost seeing her naked and all. Now it feels like somebody is watching us all the time, no matter what room we go into. We never feel alone."

"Mark, has anyone close to you died recently?" My whole feeling about this ghost was that it was familiar, overly familiar. It seemed to pull pranks for attention rather than to frighten or intimidate. This spirit seemed to know Mark and Kim.

"You mean like a grandmother or something?"

"Anybody. A coworker, a cousin, a friend…."

"Well, it was almost a year ago, but my friend Jerry died."

The familiar tingling on the back of my neck told me we were on the right track. Mark was being paid a visit from an old friend.

"Omigosh!" said Mark. "Do you really think it's him? Wow! I guess it all makes sense now."

"What makes sense?" I asked.

"Of course! It's Jerry! Kim and I were at a party with some friends about six weeks ago. They dragged out their Ouija Board, and we started messing around with it. I wanted to contact Jerry. He was a good friend of mine who died. He killed himself in a motorcycle accident last winter." Mark's voice quivered. "God, I miss him. We used to hang out a lot together. I thought maybe we could talk to him or something, just to know he's okay.

"When we asked the Ouija Board to let us speak with Jerry, we didn't really believe anything would happen. But then all sorts of weird things did start to happen. It was like the room was filled with electricity and the whole table seemed to vibrate. We got scared, turned the lights back on, and put the board away immediately.

"We talked about it for days afterward," finished Mark. "But I never thought we actually got in touch with anybody. I didn't think that stuff could really happen. I mean, isn't a Ouija Board just a game?"

"Surprise, Mark! You invited Jerry to a party and he followed you home!" I said.

"What do we do now?" Mark asked. "Move to Alaska?"

"You invited Jerry into your space, and he responded because you and he may have some unfinished business. He is your very own personal ghost. If you move, he'll probably follow you. It's you he's attached to, not the house or the land. Are you ready to bring some closure to this?"

Mark responded with a tentative yes.

"Good," I stated. "That's good. But, listen. I'm going to have to see you here at my office. For house ghosts, I usually just go to the person's house and take care of things from there," I explained. "But for personal ghosts, I prefer to see the person in my office. It's more private. We won't be interrupted. And I'll need your help and cooperation in getting rid of Jerry. Since you called him, you'll need to get rid of him."

"Wait a second!" Mark interrupted. "I have no idea what to do. I can't just…"

Now it was my turn to interrupt. "No problem, Mark. I've done this with a lot of people. This is a pretty easy clearing to do. Jerry liked you. You liked him. There's no danger." And then I hooked him. "Besides that, it could be fun! Let's just set up a time to meet—sooner, rather than later. It'll probably only take an hour or so. We'll get it done, Jerry can be on his way, and you and Kim can have your privacy again."

We set an appointment for the following afternoon.

When Mark came over to remedy the situation and to send Jerry onward, he was very open to completing the relationship. He was ready and willing to let go of Jerry. This was an excellent place to start the work.

In counseling Mark to release Jerry, we first needed to explore why they were attached to one another. I wanted to know as much of the story as possible in order to help both Mark and Jerry let go of any present attachment. I listened carefully as Mark told me that Jerry was always a big partier, and that Mark encouraged this. Just before his death, Jerry was depressed and angry about the ending of a relationship with his girlfriend. Partying with his friends, he got high on drugs and alcohol. Then he got on his motorcycle, intending to go home.

Mark didn't stop him, even though he had the thought to do so. Later that evening, Jerry was found dead from a suspicious accident. It was suspicious because the police investigators were not sure if the crash was accidental or intentional. They could not tell if Jerry tried to avoid hitting the side of the overpass or if he actually aimed for the cement wall. Mark was stunned. He felt guilty about it but put his feelings aside, leaving his inner turmoil unresolved and incomplete.

Several months later, at another party, Mark was part of the group calling on Jerry with the Ouija Board. Among the gathered friends, Mark had the greatest emotional tie to Jerry, unwittingly calling his deceased friend to him. Naturally, Jerry seized the opportunity and latched on. I now had a framework from which to start, and an understanding of the guilt fostering the bond between these two souls. We were ready to do the clearing....

Together, Mark and I go into trance, saying the invocation, calling in the Light, stating our intent, breathing deeply, and relaxing.

I begin affirming that Spirit protects Mark's energy, especially his heart center-front and back. "Mark, your life force, because of the physical mass energizing it, is much more readily accessible to you than to the ghost. There is nothing to fear; the living always have more energy and strength than spirit entities. You are strong and safe, strong and safe. The Light is with you..."

Standing behind Mark, I lay my hands atop his shoulders, channeling him the Light, energizing him. I envision his aura and strengthen the boundaries of his energy field. I call on Jerry by name. I see him floating in front of Mark, and I direct Mark to see him as well. I physically put out my hand to stop Jerry from coming any closer. He looks confused at first, but then focuses his attention on me.

"Jerry, we've called you here to talk with you," I say aloud in a calm yet direct tone. "We know you've been playing tricks on Mark and Kim. Mark says hi, but he's a little scared by the stuff that's been happening. And Kim is starting to freak out, also."

Jerry looks down, despondent, guilty, and depressed. I can hear him thinking, *"Shit, I screwed up again. Maybe I should just leave..."* He starts to fade away.

"Stop!" I practically scream at him. "That's okay. We need to talk. Mark needs to say some things to you."

He stops fading and looks up, inquisitive, even interested. I continue. "I'll just talk for Mark at first. And if I miss anything, Mark will fill it in. Okay?" Jerry's continuing presence is all the permission I need. I go deeper into trance, feeling Mark's feelings, opening to the impressions. Thoughts, pictures and emotions crowd my awareness. *Please, God, put the right words into my mouth. Let me channel clearly.* My words, Mark's words, begin tumbling out.

"Jerry, I feel bad about not stopping you from driving that night. I thought at the time that everything would be all right, that you would get over losing Jen. I was wrong. I knew I should have been there for you, but I blew it off. I knew you blamed yourself for the breakup, but I blew that off, too.

"I could have helped more, but I didn't. I've felt real bad about that."

I feel Mark trembling and shaking with grief beneath my hands.

"I was just afraid to really talk about my feelings. I thought you would be embarrassed, so I didn't say anything. I'm sorry. We really were best buddies. I did and still do care. You had lots of friends. Sorry you didn't realize that until after you died. But, hey, Jen wasn't right for you, anyway. You deserved someone who would care for you as much as you cared for her.

"It's not Jen's fault she didn't appreciate you. Maybe she just didn't really know what she wanted. It's nothing you did or didn't do. I know you've let go of her mostly, and I support you on letting go all the way. I've blamed myself for not being there for you. Yes, I admit to being a little selfish that night, just wanting to get high and be with Kim. That was insensitive of me, but I figured you'd work it out, knowing that I really did care. I'm sorry I didn't say anything.

"I didn't know you'd end up killing yourself. But since then I've thought about it. I've gotten help in realizing that it was your life. You had more control over it than I would have. I now realize that it was your decision to die, whether or not you were aware of that decision. It was still your choice, not mine.

"I feel bad that you left us, Jerry. I've been blaming myself for that, but I can't do that anymore. It's getting to me. You're done here, Jerry. Jen felt bad about it for a while. But then she just couldn't keep on feeling sad. So she said her good-byes. Maybe she would have even gotten back together with you, but she knows that's over now.

"I'm glad you came back to visit for a bit. But I've got to say goodbye, too. Kim was freaked out about some things you did at our apartment, but I'll cool her down. I'll tell her you didn't mean to scare her."

I sense Jerry's acceptance. Maybe he just needed to know that people did care about him.

"Jerry, I never did say goodbye to you properly. I mean, I never cried or anything. I wouldn't let myself say goodbye because I blamed myself. And I just couldn't look at those feelings. I was miserable and scared. But now I know that I didn't do anything wrong. I was just too spaced out for my own good and maybe for yours, too. But, Jerry, I'll be more aware in the future.

"I can even thank you for that. Just by you coming back, I've learned to care more. You've helped me learn not to take things for granted. Thanks, Jerry. I'll tell the guys that you say hi. But it's time for you to go now."

I feel Jerry's sadness, a physical weight bearing down on me.

"Jerry, it's going to be okay. There are others in the Light to connect with. I know you didn't think much about all this stuff before. Neither did I. But it's real, or how could I even be talking to you now?"

"Oh, yeah?" I hear Jerry thinking. *"That's true! I never thought of that. But you are here talking to me!"* He looks up, but then back at Mark and me.

"It's all right Jerry. You won't be lonely. There's lots of people up there you can connect with."

Jerry starts to rise. *"Thanks, Mark. I got some things to think about. I'll catch you later maybe."*

I think to myself: *No! We don't want Jerry coming back, or even planning on coming back!* Aloud, I continue to speak for Mark. "Jerry, don't worry about it. We shouldn't really even be looking for you. That was selfish of us because you've got better stuff to do. There are Spirit Teachers in the Light who'll take care of you. They'll help you to understand all this. They'll even show you how to get more out of relationships and stuff. Just go to them. Follow the Light all the way up. They'll take care of you, Jerry."

Jerry looks up and continues to rise. I share this image with Mark, telling him to say anything else now that he might need to say to Jerry in order to feel complete. He can simply think the words if he doesn't want to say them out loud. I encourage Mark to "push" Jerry up to the Light, to say goodbye, and to open his eyes when Jerry's completely surrounded by the Light. A minute passes. Mark starts to breathe more deeply. He's more relaxed. There's a smile on his face, a light, airy feeling about the room, even the faint smell of flowers. His eyes flutter open.

It is done. So be it.

Mark and I thanked each other for sharing the experience and went our separate ways. A follow-up several weeks later revealed that all problems, all psychic phenomena had disappeared. Life was back to "normal."

This clearing is a good reminder to be careful what you ask for! Ouija Boards, séances, and any situation set up intentionally to contact the dead may broadcast an invitation to host a personal ghost. If our motivation for contacting someone is to relieve our own grief, then we would be well advised to look a little deeper at our possible need for completion. There are far more effective ways of working through sadness, loss, and guilt than becoming host to a personal ghost. Mark did not believe the Ouija Board was anything more than a game. He did not believe he could really contact Jerry. He did not believe he could be vulnerable to anything incorporeal. His intellectual beliefs, however, did not protect him from his more hidden emotional yearning. Mark got exactly what he asked for.

Points to Remember…

- ✧ When contacting the spirit world, we must do so for healing.
- ✧ With the clear intent of calling on the "Highest Energy possible," we will not open ourselves to attracting "unenlightened" or lost individuals.

The Overprotective Husband

At forty-eight years old, Jane had a lot to deal with. Her devoted husband, Dennis, was beginning to feel the ravages of a terminal illness. "Months now, maybe a year at most," the doctors said at his last appointment. Time together for the two of them was running out. Diminutive, reserved, and deeply committed to Dennis, Jane mustered her strength to help her get through the coming ordeal.

Meanwhile, Dennis had his own concerns. Jane had been a wonderful partner, and his heart filled with joy at the memories of good times shared together. He knew he was dying, and he hated to leave her. But even more, he hated the thought of leaving her alone. Who would share sunsets and laughter and tears with her? Who would cherish her, appreciate her, love her? Who would brush the hair from her eyes in order to look into them and see her heart? Surely Jane deserved this, even after he was gone.

Bravely facing his fate head on, Dennis decided there was something he could do for Jane even if he could not prolong his earthly presence. He could help her find a suitable partner to be with after his passing. "She will understand," he thought.

Dennis began encouraging her to date other men, to look around at the possibilities, and even to bring home her "prospective husbands." "I can help," he insisted, "by looking them over and letting you know which ones I approve of. I would rest so much easier just knowing that you're with the right person."

Jane was embarrassed. She didn't want to go out and date other men! But neither did she want to upset Dennis. So she humored him. She stalled. She promised him she would get to it soon. At one point she even brought Mark, a friend from work, home with her, pretending a deeper affection.

Dennis neither approved nor disapproved of Mark, but Jane's gesture of intent worked. Even if Mark wasn't the right one for Jane, Dennis was comforted in "knowing" that she would move on. He told her so. Relaxed and ready to go, just weeks after meeting Mark, Dennis passed on.

About eight months after Dennis' transition, Jane met with me. "I think I might have a ghost around me, Steve. But even if I don't, I could still use some healing and grief work to let go of my late husband. But…" she started fidgeting, averting her gaze, clasping and unclasping her hands, "I never did tell my husband that I didn't want his help, that I didn't want to bring men by for his inspection. I led him to believe that his request was fine."

"Hey, Jane," I interrupted her internal reverie. "You loved him. You thought you were being kind to him. So maybe you weren't completely honest. But you did care. Guilt is for those people who are mean intentionally, for those who are hurtful without regard for another's feelings. That's not the case here, is it?" It was more of a statement than a question, but she answered readily enough.

"No! I loved him!" Defiance mixed with her sadness. "I DID love him. I was just afraid of hurting him, of disappointing him."

"Okay, Jane. That's okay." I leaned forward, putting my hand gently on her forearm. "It sounds like you've had a hard time of it. You're pretty clear on this, though. So, what's the problem? What makes you think there's a spirit hanging around you now? And if this spirit happens to be Dennis, that's actually pretty normal. When people are very close, they often visit for a short while after one of them has passed on. When you're ready to let go, you will. When…."

"I AM ready!" Straightening her back, leaning forward toward me, Jane returned my gaze without a blink. "I'm ready now!"

"Oookaaay," I drawled, trying to diffuse the rush of emotional energy that was building. I needed a little more background, a little more history to grasp the whole picture. "First, tell me what's taken you to this point. What's been happening that brings you here for my help?"

"Well…I think, I'm almost convinced, that he's still here, still trying to help. Actually, he's starting to be kind of a pain. He's getting in the way!" The story unfolded. She really did open up to other relationships after Dennis passed away. After all, she felt like she had done much of her mourning *before* his death.

Several months after his transition, Jane dared to make a date with a gentleman. But a problem arose. On the evening of their planned engagement, his car wouldn't start. Calling to say he would be late, he fixed the car and headed down the road. Twenty minutes later, he called to say he was delayed with a flat tire. He was apologetic, she was embarrassed, and their relationship ended in awkwardness before it ever got started.

Time went on. She met someone else who seemed interesting. Amidst scheduling difficulties due to unforeseen meetings and last-minute appointments, they finally agreed on a date. He didn't have any car problems and made it to her house on time. But, ascending the three steps to her front door, he tripped, badly spraining his ankle. All plans were abruptly canceled as he hobbled back to his car and drove home to put his ankle on ice.

"I did feel Dennis' presence at various times during these past several months, but I shrugged it off," Jane explained. "After all, like you said, it's pretty normal to have a loved one stick around for a little while after passing on. I trusted that things would work themselves out." She glanced at me with one eyebrow raised, searching for agreement. "I wasn't sure or not if Dennis was influencing things, if it was coincidence or just my imagination. So I dismissed it. I wasn't really attracted to either of those guys, anyway."

Her story continued. Weeks passed. She finally met a man that she WAS attracted to. They had been introduced at work, eaten lunch together several times, and become fast friends. Then they took the plunge, agreeing to "do dinner" together—a big step. A date was set. He picked her up; no car problems, no accidents. Everything was going fine. He had chosen an elegant restaurant for dinner, quiet and charming. After some initial self-consciousness, they settled into a comfortable meal. Sensing their mutual attraction, they talked, laughed, and relaxed over a glass of wine… until a chandelier came loose from the ceiling, crashing to the floor beside his chair.

"That's when I decided to call you!" She took a deep breath, relieved to have made it through the whole story. Her exasperation was obvious. "I'll never be able to get on with my life at this rate! If a man should ever try to kiss me, he may end up with a broken neck!" Even though we both laughed, hers was tinged with nervous fear.

I said that it really did sound like Dennis was still hanging around, possibly screening potential candidates. True, he could be a little more subtle and gentle when expressing his disapproval, but he was definitely getting his point across.

Jane gave a wan smile. "So now what do I do?"

"Well, let's look at it from Dennis' perspective. He never got the message that you didn't want to submit other men to his inspection. He never did get the message to quit interfering. He passed on in that state of mind—caring about you and wanting you to end up with the right person. But, his emotional investment may definitely be past the point of appropriateness. Even the best intentions can lead things awry if he is trying to help too much."

"Can you help me fix this?" she pleaded, adding with a sense of finality, "I'm ready…."

Jane sits on the stool in front of me. "Just relax. Sit straight. And breathe. That's it, relax. Breathe slowly and deeply. Relax with each out breath. It's as easy as letting go of the breath."

I place my hands on her shoulders from behind her, gently rocking her forward and back. Rocking, breathing, swaying with the breath, letting Spirit be our guide. "Mother-Father God…" I continue with the invocation. I feel Jane's body relax under my hands. My breath matches hers, letting go, swaying, breathing, trusting.

"We're here to talk with Dennis Handleman. We'd like to talk with Dennis Handleman. This is for healing. We mean no harm. Jane needs to talk with you. Please, Dennis. Please come and be with us for a moment or two." Nothing happens. Is he just being stubborn?

"Dennis. We know you've been around for quite some time already." There's a stirring in the air in front of Jane. I hold my palm up, facing outward, channeling the Light to him, and keeping him at the edge of her aura. I see a face, old, worn, tired, a bit angry. "Dennis, we're just here to talk.

I hear him now. *"I don't want to talk!"* His resentment at my interference is tangible. Heat pulsates towards the two of us.

"We're here to help Jane. Let's help her together," I say aloud. He lightens up, backs off. He looks almost quizzical, but definitely interested. Good. I've got his attention.

"Jane," I speak softly, almost reverently. "Dennis has agreed to listen to us. I'll speak: at times I'll even speak for you. Just stay with me. Send your thoughts and feelings to him as I do. Back me up. Stay with me. Can you sense his presence?"

"Yes," she whispers. And then in awe, "I didn't know it would be this easy."

"It's not always this easy. It's because of our intent. And because the two of us are in this together."

My dialogue with Dennis begins. "Dennis, thank you for coming." He nods, but I can feel his impatience. "We called you here to be honest." I can start to feel Jane's sadness, to see her thoughts. I speak them to Dennis, Jane's words coming out of my mouth. "I've missed you, Dennis. I'm sorry you passed on, but I'm glad you're rid of the pain."

"It wasn't that bad, Jane." He's gentle and loving with her. *"Mostly, it hurt to be leaving you, and to have you take care of me for so long."*

Aloud, I relate his words to Jane. I go deeper into trance, swaying, relaxing, breathing, drifting. "It wasn't that bad, Dennis. I wanted to do it. I loved you so much. I still do. But I need to let you go."

Dennis gets angry at this. He puffs up his energy. He grows, starting to tower over the two of us, wanting to reach me, to get me to stop. I channel the Light fiercely now. He doesn't like my interference one bit. *"Wait, Dennis! Wait!"* I mentally call to him. *"We're just here to talk. All the decisions are still yours and Jane's. Just listen."* I smell sulfur, the heavy smell of charcoal. That's his anger. God, I hate this part.

"Dennis, remember when you wanted me to bring men by for you to look over?" He nods, distracted from his angry response. "Yes, I know you remember. Well, I need to apologize because Mark, the first guy I brought over, was really just a friend. I wanted you to think we were getting closer so you'd feel good about seeing the type of person I would be with. But he was just a friend.

"I didn't know what else to do. I couldn't just tell you then that I didn't want to bring anyone by. I loved you too much to hurt your feelings, but I lied. I felt bad about bringing anyone by. I knew that when you died you'd need to let go of me, but I didn't say that to you then."

Jane starts to sob. Dennis is focused on her, tenderness and love reflected in his eyes. "But I've got to say it now. You've got to let go, Dennis. You trusted me enough to choose you as a husband. You know, I didn't do too bad there, did I?"

Dennis starts to respond, *"But, I can't just leave you like..."*

"Yes you can, Dennis. I loved you enough to understand that it was time for you to leave. I need you to love me enough to understand that now it's time for ME to leave. I've got to move on, Dennis."

Acceptance starts to dawn on him. He looks down at the floor, embarrassed at being so pushy.

"That's okay, Dennis. I know you love me. And that anything you did was because of that. But it's time to trust me now. It's time to go."

He looks up now, staring at me, pleading with his eyes. *"Is this true, Steve? Have I done too much?"*

"No, Dennis. You didn't really do too much. No one was really hurt. You just got a little carried away." He reaches out, trying to caress Jane. Once again, I hold up my palm to keep his distance.

"Jane, breathe in the White Light. Breathe it in the top of your head, down to your heart. That's it. Now breathe it out your heart. Surround Dennis with it. Caress him with that Light. Take his hands in yours." I watch Jane's body expand with her breath.

"It's time, Dennis," I speak for Jane once again. "I know you still care for me, that you still want to help. But if you really want to help, you can go to the Light first. You can go to Spirit. You can learn better ways of helping. But you need to go first." He squeezes her hands. I hear her gasp at the same time. *Did she actually feel that?* I continue the dialogue, "I've kept you long enough. That was selfish of me. I've kept you from other loved ones, friends, and family waiting for you in the Light. Forgive me for holding you back."

The love on his face shines through. A refreshing breath of cool air fills the room. "Jane," I relate to her. "He wants your forgiveness as well."

"Of course I forgive you," she says between sobs of sadness and blessing. "Of course I do!"

I squeeze her shoulders. "Jane. If there's anything else you want to say to Dennis before he goes, just say it now. If there was anything you said before in anger, say it now with love. If there's anything that wasn't said, say it now. Channel it to him with the breath, with the Love and Light."

She nods her assent and starts whispering. I mentally step back now, still breathing, still channeling the Light, making sure he stays at the edge of her aura, that he only holds her hands.

Moments pass as Jane finishes. "Jane, if there's anything you feel he wanted to say to you before he passed, see him saying it now. Saying it with Love and Light." Dennis' mouth barely moves, but he's sending her his love. I let Jane collect his words on her own. Dennis looks down at their hands intertwined; one set flesh and the other light, and squeezes one last time.

I step back in to bring the dialogue to a close. "I love you. I bless you. I release you, Dennis. Go to the Light. There are loved ones, friends, family, and teachers waiting for you there. Go to Spirit." I speak the words aloud, focusing all of our attention on the Light.

To Jane: "Now, with each breath, Jane, surround him with the Light. With each breath, urge him, nudge him into the Light." I see Dennis rising, becoming indistinct. The Light surrounds him.

To both of them now: "That's it...the Light. Look up. The Light. Spirit welcomes you. If it's right, you'll be with each other again. That's it. Blessings to you, Dennis." And he's gone, leaving behind the fresh scent of flowers, a gift of Spirit, a blessing for us both, for all three of us.

Speaking with Jane several months later, I was happy to hear that there were no more incidents or accidents with any prospective suitors. She had gone home to a phone call from a gentleman but decided to decline his offer for dinner. The following week she called a male friend, just to spend time together, with the limits clearly defined as friendship.

Jane had become pickier, more discerning about whom she would go out with. The urge to date was not as profound, and she related that the changes were all for the better. She would spend more time alone, but not lonely. Spirit was on her side. When it was right for her to find the perfect man to be with, she would.

Two years later she got in touch and wanted to introduce me to her fiancé.

There are several details of this clearing with Jane and Dennis which highlight important reminders whenever we work with personal ghosts.

As a spiritual healer and trance medium, it is my job to contact the spirit world. It is also my job to serve and protect the client. When inviting contact with a personal ghost, the connection with his or her host is initially strengthened. Yet, we do not want this energy to become overpowering or invasive. Thus, we start the clearing by strengthening both our own and the client's energy fields. We channel and surround ourselves with Love and Light through imagery, deep breathing and hands-on energy transfer.

At the appearance of the entity, we strengthen our boundaries, allowing for contact but not intrusion. If the entity becomes angry or feels threatened, we channel the Light with greater focus and intent, knowing that when we channel more Love and Light than someone else can channel anger or fear, love will prevail. Anyone engaged in this type of work must be aware of options to keep himself and others safe.

Additionally, during a clearing I discourage clients from going too deeply into emotional catharsis while connected to the Spirit world during a clearing. A deep emotional charge may unintentionally increase the bonding with the earthbound spirit, making the subsequent release much more difficult. In Jane's case, by keeping things moving, staying focused on the need to change the relationship, and helping her engage in the dialogue, she easily moved from sadness and regret to helpfulness and certainty about her own needs. There's always time later for catharsis—AFTER releasing the spirit.

Finally, I want to reiterate that a personal ghost clearing is significantly more effective when the client participates in helping the spirit to move onward. By coaching Jane on her interaction with Dennis and giving them both the chance to say some final words, we increased the probability that they completed with one another. Jane was certain in her request for Dennis to go to the Light, and he heard it best coming from her heart. Both people involved were loving and supportive of one another, making it easier to facilitate completion.

Points to Remember…

- ✧ We start the clearing by strengthening our own and the client's energy, channeling and surrounding ourselves with Love and Light.

- ✧ It is often normal to have visitations from a loved one who has passed on. However, inviting them to stay, letting them stay, and relying on them is inappropriate.

- ✧ Holding onto the past only fosters a deeper state of incompletion, keeping both the living and the dead in an unhealthy relationship. Stagnation then settles in.

Chapter 15

Empower Yourself

Performing personal ghost clearings is rewarding to all involved, resulting in increased love and healing for everyone. Some clearings, however, can be more challenging and emotional than others. Anger and negative judgments, our own fears and limitations, may prevent us from effectively severing the attachments that were created. Sometimes we lose sight of Spirit, forgetting to empower others and ourselves. As healers, it is imperative that we stay focused on Love and Light. Yet, as you will see in the next case, I lost my objectivity and became too emotionally involved. I lost sight of the unconditional love coming from Spirit. My connection with and receptivity to Guidance was severely strained.

The Family Curse

"This is a long time coming," says the woman sitting before me. "I didn't really believe in curses but, as the years go by, I'm starting to." She pauses, waiting for my reaction.

"Go on," I encourage her. "I don't know if I really believe in them either. But whatever it is, we can deal with it."

Carla, a gentle, unassuming forty-year-old, first called me because of a "hex" or curse that was put on her family decades ago. I had told her over the phone then, and again in my office now, "Yes, we can take care of it. We can raise your energy level enough to throw off any curse. We can also explore why and how you may have accepted the curse in the first place. Clearing up the thoughts and feelings would prevent you from taking it on again sometime in the future."

I had really been looking forward to meeting with this woman. I don't get to handle many cases dealing with curses. They're usually not that big of a deal, having more to do with a person's fear of the curse than any actual power behind the curse itself. But now, as Carla sat in the chair and recounted her family history, the hair on my neck and arms started to rise. *This IS a spooky story! Maybe she really has taken on a curse.* She continued to relate the story to me, almost in a whisper, looking around as if someone were watching, looking, listening.

It seems that years ago her grandmother fell in love with Eduardo, a very nice man living in the same village in Mexico. The Catholic Church blessed the engagement, and family and friends celebrated their happy union. Everyone, that is, except Bendita, Blessed. She accused Carla's grandmother of stealing away Eduardo's affections. As his former girlfriend, Bendita felt she should have become his wife! The young couple tried to placate Bendita with apologies, invitations to family gatherings, and kindnesses, but to no avail. Bendita was determined to hold a grudge against them, refusing to let go of her anger.

Following the marriage, there was little contact between Bendita and the newlyweds. Things would normally have ended there, with the two women going their separate ways. However, Bendita was a bruja, a highly trained sorceress. For the most part, brujas are just like anyone and everyone else—normal people with extraordinary gifts. But just like normal people, there are nice brujas, and there are hostile ones.

In her anger, grief and jealousy, Bendita put a curse on the grandmother. Summoning vengeful energies, she pronounced, "From now on, every woman born to your family will have a curse on her! She will be sickly and never able to please a man! Yes, you can be happy with Eduardo, your husband," she said with contempt. "But none of your daughters, nor theirs, nor theirs will ever find that happiness."

Years went by, and the couple shook off the threat, never having heard from Bendita again. When a beautiful, healthy girl was born, they dismissed the curse altogether. More children were born to the couple. The family grew and prospered. But then their eldest daughter came of age. Puberty struck with unexpected force. What was supposed to be a time of celebration became a time of tragic misfortune.

First, the girl's youngest brother was killed. Following this, Dad lost his job. Tension, fear, and uncertainty dominated the household. Then, this newly budding adolescent became seriously ill. As Carla was told, the girl, later to become Carla's mother, never fully recovered her strength after a terrible bout with pneumonia. Her growth was stunted. She was always getting sick with one thing or another and was reportedly "weak-willed." It was as if her inner Light had just turned itself off.

The story didn't end there. Following community traditions, the frail daughter eventually married and started a family of her own. Carla was born. "I remember having a fairly happy childhood," Carla related. "I mean, Mom was always complaining about something. And she was in bed as much as she was out of bed. But I got to play and have friends and go to school. The house we lived in was small, but I only had to share my room with one other person, my little sister.

"We got along. I don't really remember all that much. But I think I was happy. And then I started my first woman's cycle." Tears started forming in her eyes as she continued.

"I had bad cramping and bleeding. I was scared. I was nauseous and just wanted to be taken care of. I just wanted some reassurance, to know that everything would be all right. But that was not to be. Grandmom had been living with us for quite some time. Things were okay, but she was getting pretty old.

"So right then, when I felt like I was already in Hell, Grandmom's health took a turn for the worse. She was starting to die, right there, right then. It was painful in every way. I was in pain, my mom was always in pain, and Grandmom was sick, hurting, angry, and dying. I remember thinking, 'Don't die. Don't leave me!' It was then that I heard Grandmom ask mother if she had told me about the curse. Grandmom was wondering if I got the curse, too, since I was so sick.

"Grandmom passed on within minutes of mentioning the curse. I'll always remember that night with horror. It was shrouded in pain and fear.

"Talking with my mom later, I learned about Grandmom's history and Bendita's curse. Mother didn't give it much credence, but it scared me a lot at the time."

The years progressed and Carla matured, putting all that "nonsense" behind her. She grew up and moved to the United States. Although she never focused on a particular career, after years of poor jobs and conflicts with employers, she finally settled into what she called a decent job. After many unsuccessful relationships, "bad luck" according to her, she finally married and settled down. She reported being fairly happy. Her husband was a good man, one she could rely on. All her experiences seemed to fit neatly into the category of "I guess it's been a tough life, but I've survived."

Carla reported that the last few years had been "mostly okay." She got a lot of satisfaction from her home, her job, her family, and especially her children. But now, as her eldest child, a daughter, was approaching adolescence, the past was surfacing. Carla's memories and fears of the curse kept invading her conscious thoughts.

"What if the curse is real?" she asked, not really wanting an answer. "I don't want to pass this on to my daughter!" The pleading in her eyes, the shakiness of her voice got to me.

I kept my thoughts to myself, but they were running rampant in my head. *What a vindictive, cruel person that bruja must have been! How heartless to do this to a family throughout the generations. Such misuse of power.* I also felt sorry for Carla and her family—how sad that they had accepted that energy into their lives.

"Don't worry, Carla." And then, a bit too forcefully for my own liking, I said, "We'll take care of it!"

Seating her on a stool, standing behind her with my hands upon her shoulders, we start the invocation. "Mother-Father God, Infinite power of the universe, White Light of the Lord..." I feel the Energy, the Love, the Power starting to build, starting to flow through me. "We ask that You join us here, that You watch over what we do..." Everything feels great.

But then a wave of dizziness comes over me. I start to waver. *Oh, crap! What's that?* My certainty falters. I feel angry, hurt, jealous, and possessive. *Wait! That's not mine. That's coming from Carla. No, not Carla, from outside Carla. A black cloud, projecting its energies toward me. I don't want to give this power like Carla has.*

"I'M HERE. EVERYTHING IS FINE." Ah, that's Michael, one of my Guides. My Gatekeeper. I trust in Spirit. I call on the protective Light of Spirit. Michael continues with reassurances. "YOU'LL DO WHAT YOU NEED TO DO. STAY FOCUSED. DON'T TAKE IT ON." I take a deep, centering breath.

"Thanks for coming, Bendita." I say aloud. "We just need to talk for a bit."

"*I don't want to talk. You're up to no good. She's mine! Stay away!*" Her thoughts materialize in a bleak fog of anger.

The cloud starts to descend. Getting bigger, darker, closer. I call on the protection of Spirit. I remember my power animals. I am here to help Carla. We will do whatever it takes to get through this. My black panther shows up. He growls, pacing the perimeter, warding the space, guarding both Carla and myself. The cloud backs off slightly.

"Bendita, what was done, was done a long time ago. Carla's grandmother didn't mean to hurt you."

"*Yes, she did. She didn't care. That whore! She knew Eduardo was mine. He loved me. She stole him with her lies and her fancy clothes and her oh-so-important family. I'll show her. I'll show them all. They can't get away with this. They...*"

"Bendita! Listen!"

A blast of foul-smelling energy surrounds me. I feel Carla shudder under my hands. *Jesus! Help me! Michael! Keep her away.* I call on my protective Spirits. *Give me the strength!* I feel us gaining ground again. Bendita backs off. But, God, she's powerful.

"Carla's grandmother was in love, just like you were, are. You let your love take hold of you. Grandmom was just doing the same thing. Have some heart. It's not right to keep haunting her family. Forgive..."

"*No!*"

That last blast gets me dizzy again. Even a little nauseated. The smell of rotten, putrid toxins fills the air. I can taste Bendita's bitterness. Unwittingly, my anger takes hold. "You're a nasty, self-serving, evil woman. You abuse your power. You abuse your privilege. You can't do this anymore. You have no power here anymore. You're dead! You've been dead a long time. Carla's Grandmother has been dead a long time. It's not too late to seek forgiveness, and to seek Eduardo in the Light."

"*No!*"

I can't keep this up. I feel shaky on my feet. Thoughts bound rapidly through my mind: *I need to resolve this before I lose ground again. Before I get sick. Before Carla gets worse. Before Bendita invades Carla's daughter. Oh no, Bendita's picked up on that thought. She's looking around, looking for a way to leave, looking for the daughter. I need to hurry.*

"*No!*" I shout with my internal voice. "*You can't go!*" Panther surrounds her, keeps her there.

I hear Michael speak to me, a mere echo in the back of my awareness. "STEVE. KEEP YOUR LOVE. DON'T DO THIS. EVERYONE DESERVES BETTER. EVEN BENDITA." But I'm too scared and too enraged to listen.

"In the name of Spirit," I speak aloud once more, "I command you to leave this woman and her family. I call on all my protective Spirits to contain you, to keep you away from this family. You can keep your anger. You can keep your blame. But you can take it with you to Hell. You've had your chance." I'm rambling now, only later realizing that my fear and anger were driving me.

I push her down, deeper, deeper. I see the fires of her Hell. Pushing her further down, through the flames, I stuff her into a coffin of her own making and chain it closed amidst the searing heat. There's no escape for her. Around me the fires continue to blaze.

But I feel safe. Finally. Carla, too, takes a deep breath and relaxes. She can sense that the fight is finished. I've regained my balance. My thoughts are already becoming reflective. *It's over. I did what I needed to do. I had to do it. Bendita's curse was going to hurt Carla's family. If we hadn't helped Carla end this here and now, she'd hold onto it and pass it down to future generations. I couldn't let that happen.* The cloud is gone. The anger is drained.

Carla and I look at one another. We chuckle tentatively. "It's over, isn't it?" she asks.

"Yes. It is. It was a tough one. She was real powerful, real angry. She wouldn't let go. But with your help, we got rid of her."

We wrapped up the session rather quickly. I was exhausted. I told Carla to call me if there were any other problems. I didn't expect any. I reassured her that she could just do her best as a parent, and that she could keep affirming her daughter's strengths. She could love her daughter and do her best to teach the girl to be loving toward herself and others. "You'll be fine!" I shouted to her with a big smile as she got into her car and drove away.

I stepped back inside and collapsed on the couch. I felt sick. I had a terrible headache. The nausea still persisted. I was glad Carla was my last session of the day because I was beat. Ah, well, sometimes this work is taxing, but I felt good about helping Carla.

That night, my sleep was restless. My dreams, even though I couldn't remember any of them, seemed tiresome. Arising the next morning, I found myself in a fog, so I did some simple centering and channeling exercises along with some aerobics to get me back on track. Feeling more energized, I put the spirit expulsion behind me. Life goes on.

A couple of days later, while working on an outbuilding near our house, I stood up too fast. Hitting the top of my head squarely on the underside of the eave, I was knocked flat on my back. Dazed and shaken, I reprimanded myself for being so clumsy. Then I put it behind me. Life goes on.

However, within weeks, I realized my neck wasn't healing properly from the outbuilding incident. My back was also thrown out of balance. I did some stretches, got a massage, and discovered specific exercises to help straighten my neck and back. For the most part, the pain cleared up, so once again, I put it behind me.

After a few months, I finally admitted to myself that my neck problems had become chronic. They would come and go, and I was barely staying on top of them. To aid in my healing, I finally looked back. *What was going on in my life just before the accident? Is there something emotionally incomplete from that time? Did I try to put something behind me that I'm not yet finished with?*

Of course! How could I have overlooked it? I then realized I had been feeling bad ever since the expulsion. I knew that particular ghost clearing was different than anything I had ever done before, but it was also upsetting, so I had stuffed it away. I didn't want to look at it. But it was surfacing, demanding attention. I realized I felt bad about how I had treated Bendita. The guilt was getting to me. Something had to be done....

I call in the Light, doing the invocation slowly and deliberately. I make a specific request for Michael's presence, as well as my panther and any other Spirit Allies. Filling myself with Love and Light, I start the drumming tape to keep me on track. This is definitely one journey during which I will not drift. I can't afford it.

"IT'S ALL RIGHT. WE'RE HERE." That's Michael.

"Thanks, Michael."

Barely acknowledging my thanks, he talks rather loudly this time. "IT'S ABOUT TIME YOU GOT TO THIS! CONGRATULATIONS ON FINALLY WAKING UP."

"Thanks again, Michael."

I let the drumming take me to my safe place, my power spot in the Middle World. Panther greets me and leads the way. I enter a hole in the ground. I drop almost straight down, spiraling to I don't know where. It's getting dark. A light appears in my hand. Panther is still with me. Eagle has joined in the dive.

We enter a big cavern. It's hot and stuffy, but the Light surrounds me. Coolness envelops me. *Ah. There it is!* A coffin surrounded by flames. I'm actually a bit surprised. I wasn't sure if it was even there or if I'd find it. I guess I shouldn't be all that surprised. Whether or not this place exists in spirit is a moot point. It is also a part of me, and I need to heal it!

The drumming brings me back to the task at hand. Panther continues to patrol the perimeter. Eagle nudges the chain around the box. *Well, here goes nothing.* I unlock the chains and cautiously lift the lid.

She's there, just coming out of a deep sleep. Opening her eyes, she takes a moment to focus. Recognizing me, she starts to get angry, then changes her mind. Curiosity fills her aura.

"I'm here, Bendita, because I did wrong," I tell her plaintively. *"It was wrong of me to put a curse on you, to damn you. I did to you the same thing you did to Carla's family. I know you were hurt and angry. You had every right to* be." Feeling her sadness now, "I'm sorry, Bendita. But everyone has suffered enough already."

Her remorse comes through clearly. *"I'm so lonely. I had it all. Then I lost everything."* There is nothing threatening, nothing hurtful emanating from her. A shroud of sorrow and emptiness envelops her.

"Bendita, listen. You've lost a lot, but you can get it back. You CAN have the love and the support and even the power. I know there's nothing you can do to change the past." She nods. "But we can change the future. There's more forgiveness, more love and power in the Light. Maybe even Eduardo is there along with others who love and support you."

She starts to rise, shakily at first, then with more certainty. I put my hand over her heart, filling the hole that's been there seemingly for an eternity. Looking into each other's eyes, we have an understanding. Two souls, out of place, out of time, trying to fit the pieces of life together. Panther growls. Bendita and I look at our surroundings. *Such a dreary place. Let's go,* we think to one another.

We rise together, Panther behind us, Eagle ahead of us. Up, out of the cave, through the tunnel, above a landscape filled with wheat. Up through layers of mountains, clouds, light. We could keep going, but suddenly we stop. *"Bendita, we're not there yet. We've got further to go."*

"No, Steve." That's the first time she's addressed me by name. I'm momentarily startled by her acknowledgment of me as a person, and I realize she actually does have a heart. "This is as far as I go," she says with finality. I notice a presence off to the side. A caring, benevolent entity welcoming her to this level, this higher plane of Spirit.

"Goodbye, Bendita. I'll send Carla your regards. I'll let her know you're aware that you wronged her, just as you felt wronged. She's stronger because of it, and her daughter, too." She starts to fade, surrounded by a milky, white glow. *"Bye, Bendita. And thanks for letting me help this time."*

Coming out of trance, I feel light-headed. But it's a good feeling this time—lighthearted as well. I realize I just let go of an enormous weight that I didn't even know I was carrying.

"GOOD JOB, STEVEN." There's Michael again.

"Thanks. But where were you during all this?"

"YOU MUST KNOW BY NOW THAT YOU NEED TO LEARN TO DO THIS ON YOUR OWN. I WAS THERE, WAITING, WATCHING, READY. BUT YOU DID FINE."

I feel the love coming from him, the caring, the patience. And then he yells, "NEXT TIME, IF THERE IS A NEXT TIME, GET TO IT SOONER! BE MORE AWARE!"

"Thanks again, Michael."

Can someone truly put a curse on a yet unborn child? Can one spirit's anger and vengeance affect generations to come? If Carla's case is any evidence, then the simplest answer would appear to be yes. And yet, I feel compelled to look a little deeper.

We don't know what really happened between Grandmom and Bendita. Did the Grandmother, in fact, feel guilty about marrying Eduardo? My experience tells me she must have been open to accepting the curse at some level, consciously or unconsciously, thereby allowing the energy into her space. And the subsequent generations? Maybe there were agreements at a soul level, before the daughters even came into a physical body, to share in the lessons. Perhaps Carla's physical and emotional trauma during the onset of puberty opened her up to accepting the curse.

The result, however, of Carla's experience and subsequent healing, would be her newfound strength and awareness of her own personal power. None of us are blind victims, and our awareness has the capacity to grow well beyond what we consciously perceive in our present state. I choose to trust that it is all perfect, according to what we need and want, in order to heal ourselves and awaken to the beauty of our own soul.

Another question to be raised is the concept of Hell. Does it exist? Can entities truly be sentenced to an eternity of pain and suffering among fire and brimstone? Once again, my own experience tells me that we are the creators of whatever hell we imagine. It is we who sentence ourselves based on our own projections of guilt, anger, jealousy, greed and fear. Were Bendita in a more loving space, emanating forgiveness and caring, I have no doubt that her ability to choose for herself to go to the Light would have been far more powerful than anyone's ability to lock her in a fiery coffin. Love is ALWAYS stronger than anything unloving. But whatever judgments we pass on others, so we bring upon ourselves. Bendita's hell was a self-confinement created by her own blinding rage, the flames fueled by years of hostility and resentment.

Likewise, my choice to act out of fear and anger in taming Bendita led me to bring several things down upon my own head, literally. During the clearing, I lost focus of that which was for the Highest Good of *everyone* concerned. I clung to my own judgments about Bendita's misuse of power, letting compassion for her go by the wayside as my outrage and alarm grew. I forgot about being loving; I forgot that Guidance would help me if I asked; I forgot that behind Bendita's anger there was great pain. I forgot that everyone deserves healing.

Immediately following the clearing, I chose to acknowledge feeling good about helping Carla, but I did not want to look at my sentiments toward Bendita. I stubbornly held to the beliefs that she deserved what she got, that I had no other alternative if I were to protect Carla and her daughter, and that Bendita chose to become a victim of the pain that her anger had created. I brushed aside my headache and nausea after the clearing, my restless sleep, and even my knock on the head. Thankfully, my body continued trying to tell me something and, thankfully, I listened.

My experience with Bendita only confirms my many understandings about doing this type of work: Keep it loving! Be aware! Stay in touch with your personal reactions, and be willing to acknowledge your own feelings! None of us is expected to do everything right all the time; we have our lessons, too. But Spirit always gives us another chance to pay attention and, in doing so, we can save ourselves from additional suffering.

Taking the opportunity to help Bendita in a more loving way, she and I both benefited from the healing. My shoulder and neck returned to health and, hopefully, I learned my lesson. Time will tell.

Points to Remember…

- Not all spirits ascend directly to the Light. Some, with Divine Guidance, may choose to stop at a different place along the way to further their healing. We can still bid them farewell, trusting they are in good hands.

- That which we overlook on an emotional level often manifests on a physical level, in order to focus our attention on healing.

- We may not be able to change the past, but we can change the future.

- Healers also are vulnerable to personal judgments and emotional involvement.

The Medicine Man's Hex

"I was dropped off in the small town of Otowanga. I wanted to do a good job setting up this clinic, so I worked hard to gain the trust of the locals." Tom spoke quietly, determined to recount the story that had led to others telling him he was crazy, making things up, or overreacting. He had recently returned from Africa, participating in a volunteer program to establish a medical clinic in an outlying village.

Soft-spoken and gentle-mannered, this twenty-five-year-old, six-foot-two, African-American male was the perfect picture of health—strongly built, handsome, assertive, open, and honest. On the surface, everything seemed to be going well for him. But there was this minor problem of a possible hex put on him by the town's local medicine man. Tom came to me for some advice, some healing, and whatever else I could give him.

"I was given a hut to sleep in, an assistant from the town, and plenty of medical supplies. At first it was slow but, as people got past their shyness, they started coming regularly. Scrapes were bandaged, deep cuts stitched, minor medications dispensed. The more serious cases were referred to the hospital several miles away." Tom felt that things were getting off to a good start.

Then there arose an unforeseen problem. Traditionally, the inhabitants in the area had gone to the local medicine man for much of their health care. Now they were coming to Tom. There was a division growing within the community: those who wanted newer, more modern health care, and those who wished to follow the traditional ways and support the medicine man.

The medicine man himself got involved. He visited the clinic, asking Tom to pack up and leave, saying, "Things had been going fine until now. The people here were perfectly happy seeing me and letting me take care of them, until you showed up."

Tom tried to explain that things could still be as good, if not better. "We could work together on some things," he had explained. "I don't want to interfere with your ministrations, your Spiritual practices or herbal, natural remedies. I just want to do my job and offer alternatives."

Tom sighs and leans back in the chair across from me, shrugging his shoulders.

"No go!" Tom relates to me. "The medicine man wouldn't buy it. The more I tried to gain his cooperation, the more resistant he became. He got angry and told me to leave. But I told him I had a job to do, and I was going to stick it out. I put my foot down, and I thought that would be the end of it. However, a few days later the medicine man came to me again. He must have realized I was serious about staying, so he made a threat."

"'You should go now,' he said to me. 'We have ways to make you leave, ways to make you regret staying, and a curse upon you if you do stay.' That spooked me a little."

Tom went on to say that even though he was getting a bit frightened by the threats, he held to his convictions about supplying medical care. He decided to stay. Yet, within three nights he would change his mind.

"Steve, I'm a fairly rational man. I'm healthy. I'm certain. I practice martial arts. I had a right to be there in that town. And there were many people supporting me there. That night, I went to bed and, although I was a little nervous, everything was fine. But, in the middle of the night, I heard strange noises from outside the hut, noises that seemed part animal, part human. I went out to see what was there, but things had quieted by the time I went to investigate.

"The next night was a repeat of the first. The strange noises were there. And this time I heard a deep rumbling sound coming from all around the hut. Again I got up and went outside to investigate, but there was nothing to see.

"It was the third night that clinched it, though. I was just starting to drift off to sleep when the noise started—the animal sounds, the rumbling. As I swung my feet over the side of the bed to get up, the wind picked up outside. I guessed it was the wind, but I'm not so sure anymore. I heard bushes rustling, and the frame of the hut was creaking. Then the whole structure started to shake! It felt like an earthquake, but right under my feet. The floor was shaking. The walls, the roof, everything seemed alive and threatening. So I ran outside. But the second I did, everything was quiet. It was a perfectly calm, peaceful night.

"That was the final straw," Tom said. "I'm not really a superstitious man, but I felt like running away right then and there." He seemed embarrassed telling me this, not even looking at me. "The next morning, I just packed my bags and got out of there. I asked my assistant to watch over things until my supervisor came to take care of the clinic. And I was gone! I walked and hitched rides to cover the twenty miles to my supervisor's office. I looked him square in the eye and demanded a ticket back home."

I said little, nodding and encouraging Tom to continue. I knew we were approaching the tougher part.

"Glad to be back in the States, I put that experience behind me. And that was nearly a year ago." He finally looked up, almost pleading with me to understand what he was saying. "But there have been too many weird things happening in the past year. And talking with someone recently, they sort of jokingly said that maybe I had a curse or something around me. I felt this chill come down my back. I got dizzy and nauseous and remembered the medicine man. That's when I looked around and got your number."

When asked about the "weird" things happening in his life, Tom related several events to me. He had dated three separate women during the past year, and they had all been healthy when he started dating them. However, within a couple of months each one had come down with stomach problems. He didn't think he was the cause, but when the third one became sick, he did think it might be more than just coincidence.

"That could be a sign of a curse or hex, Tom." I told him rather nonchalantly, not willing to commit myself yet. "For an entity to hang around a person, that entity needs energy from somewhere, and it will usually get it from the person to whom it is attached. That person usually feels it in the stomach area, the power center in body-mind terms. But since you consciously work to stay healthy, those entities may have needed to get their energy from elsewhere, from someone close to you."

He started to look a bit guilty, perhaps taking responsibility for the three women. Quickly I reassured him, "I know you're thinking that you caused their illnesses, but you didn't! If there is a curse in effect around you, then it is the medicine man who helped put it there, and you unconsciously took it on."

Giving me an unbelieving, rather challenging look, I realized that he was having trouble accepting the possibility of his own story. "I mean it!" I said, leaning forward and speaking a little more forcefully than intended. "Really! So what else happened that makes you suspicious of a curse?"

"Well, now you're going to think I've totally flipped. But I've had two dogs die in the past year. And when I got another one, he got sick." The sadness was obvious. What he couldn't get in touch with regarding the three women, he did when talking about his pets. "One got hit by a car. The other one hung himself with his chain when he jumped a fence. And the third one is still on special food and strong medications."

His voice started to crack at that point. I wanted to reach out and touch him, to reassure him, but I held myself back. If, in fact, his space had been invaded, I did not want to touch him without some permission from him. "That IS a situation that points toward an entity or something hanging around you," I shared with a little lump of sadness in my own throat. I had also lost pets in the past. "Pets, dogs in particular, will frequently intercept any negative energy directed at their owner. They will often take it on, making themselves sick or becoming carelessly unaware of their surroundings in the process. So illness and/or accidents can happen as a result of this. That, too, isn't your fault."

I didn't know what else to say except that it wasn't his fault. He seemed like such a nice guy. I just didn't want him to feel any worse than he was already. But now I had the story, and I was ready to move toward a resolution. Opening up my intuitive centers, I started channeling him Love and Light, surrounding him with a protective envelope. And that's when I perceived the entities.

"Tom, I do feel like you picked up something a little bit nasty from your time in Africa. I've tried to get a sense of the energy but can't pick up much. And that's pretty good." I leave a pregnant pause for things to settle in there.

"If I picked up on it strongly, that would mean a lot of power, and maybe even the ghost of a person around you. But at this point, all I pick up are what I call heebie-jeebies, little nondescript entities. I like to call them that, because the name itself prevents us from crediting them with too much power. They're almost like little animals that just like to feed on energy. Sometimes I call them lower astral entities. They are attracted to people who are angry, or to people who may feel guilty about something…"

He interjects quickly when I pause for breath. "Yes! That's what they are!" He's getting excited now. "I had a dream a couple of times about some little animals. They were around me, just nipping at my heels, trying to bite me. The second dream ended when one of the little buggers actually bit me. But I thought they were just dreams, not real!"

"Well, they might be real or they might signify unresolved issues trying to catch your attention. Either way, we can take care of them. Even if you don't have a curse hanging over you, we can, at the very least, help you to feel more complete about your assignment in Africa. We can help to put it behind you. And if there are other reasons for the spell of 'bad luck,' we can discover those and take care of them."

After Tom mentioned that he had seen a body worker in the past and that he was currently seeing a chiropractor once a month for minor back problems, it felt safe to proceed with some hands-on healing. Explaining to him the process of contacting and communicating with the spirit world, I had him sit on my trusty office stool while I walked around behind him. Putting my hands on his shoulders and having him close his eyes and take some relaxation breaths, I continued with the invocation. Taking him deeper into a trance state, I started talking…

"With each breath you relax more and more, feeling the safety and the power within this room. Relax. Breathe in the Light. Breathe it in the top of your head straight down to your solar plexus, your power center. Now breathe it out your power center. Be in touch with the Love and Light of Spirit…

"Breathe it out the solar plexus, and send a little white heart along that cord to the medicine man. Hold a picture of him in your mind. Travel along the cord to the village you were in last year, and seek out the Shaman…"

I feel him starting to shake beneath my hands. "Relax. Feel the power that the two of us are channeling from Spirit. We are totally protected here. 'When two or more are gathered in My name, so shall I be there'… Relax. That's it." Tom's shoulders drop, and I'm ready to proceed.

"We would like to speak to the medicine man of this town, to the helper and protector of these people. We would like to…" I feel lethargic, like a fog has just dropped over my mind. I breathe deeply and channel more energy to myself, to Tom, and to the Shaman. "We just want to talk."

"No you don't!" I hear this thundering voice from the ethers. *"No you don't! You're just trying to trick me into listening again. The time for listening is done. It's time for action."* I see a black cloud thundering towards us.

"Breathe deep, Tom. Channel that Light. He's not too happy about our presence. But then, we're not too happy about his either."

The storm subsides, leaving me shaken, but none the worse for wear. To the medicine man, and also aloud for Tom's benefit, I say, "Tom is gone from your space. He has no intention of returning. He's just tired of carrying around your energy."

"Well, tough! He knew what he was getting into when he stayed." The sharpness of the Shaman's words is meant to sting.

"Yes, but he now realizes his mistake. He's paid dearly for his intrusion."

"Good!" That's all the reply I get from him. He is eager to dismiss us, but I'm not yet willing to retreat. More of Tom's energy, support, and participation will make this easier.

"Tom, he's still angry. Maybe things didn't exactly settle down after you left. Let's try it again. Breathe deeply. Continue to channel the Light. If we can channel more Love and Light than he can channel anger, then we've won. Send your thoughts and feelings along with my words."

To the Shaman, "We come this time in peace."

"I don't care. People are still coming here, trying to bring their ways, but we were fine before you ever came."

Again, to the Shaman. "But now we are doing our best to make things right. What's done is done. Tom felt bad about disrupting your life there. He felt bad about how things turned out. He even told his superiors that you weren't pleased with us being there. He recommended that they leave things alone there. It's not his fault if they kept on coming back. He's paid enough for his ignorance.

"All we ask is that you remove the curse that you put upon him. We ask that you call off your angry energies."

I hear a grunt from the Shaman. The dark energies around Tom start to grow. They start to smell like rotten garbage. They're getting excited, active, trying to get closer.

"Breathe, Tom! Channel that Light!" I almost shout. I hear Tom's breath coming faster, steadier.

"In the name of the Lord, in the name of the Christ, I command any energies, any entities that don't belong here to be gone!" I see the Shaman breathing and sending more anger. *This will never do*, I think to myself. *The negative energies surrounding Tom are not even cognizant. I can't convince them to go to the Light if they don't even know what I'm saying.*

I breathe the little beings the Light, but it's absorbed as soon as I send it. I try to push them into the Light, but my hands go through them as if they have no ethereal substance.

"Go away! Leave us alone," the medicine man shouts. *"This is his problem now. You deal with it. Now go!"*

Great! Now what? I wonder. *I can't just send these little demons down to the underworld. I remember the last time I did something like that. What a mess! I need a different resolution.*

To the Shaman, "Okay. We'll go now. But I do hope you'll find forgiveness in your heart. You're wasting your energies here. They'd be better put to use in helping your people." I hope he's heard that, but I'm not sure because at that moment I sense a door being slammed shut…tight!

"Tom, breathe in the Light. Breathe it out your heart and surround yourself with it. Surround yourself with a great white cocoon made of Light. Its walls are like a fine mesh, a screen through which only the Highest energies may pass. Any limiting energies just bounce off, like reflections in a mirror, going back to the source."

I speak to the negative energies surrounding Tom. *"Go now. Your job here is done. There is nothing left for you here, nothing to feed on. There is only death and loneliness waiting for you here. GO! Go back from whence you came. You will just rot and die here if you stay. GO!"* Visually I push them back to their source, back to the Shaman. They resist at first, but then give in. Homing in on his energy, they shoot out of here, going, going, gone.

There's a substantial lightening of the room, the smell of flowers. Spring rain. Cleansing, fresh, full of life. *I do hope that the Shaman is aware of his little heebie-jeebies returning to him.* Tom takes a deep breath under my hands, and I turn my focus on him.

"The cord has been cut between the medicine man and you, Tom. Let's surround him with the Light and hope that he gets it. His little animals have just returned to him. If he's not aware of them, they might just curse him right back. But then, that's his problem now, a problem of his own making. Bless him. Surround him with the Light, and pull away. Leave him with his creations, and let's hope he knows what to do with them. They'll never bother you again…"

Tom left with a big smile and lightness in his step. I never did hear from him again. Reviewing the healing, I felt good about how I dealt with the situation. I didn't get angry or resentful. I didn't wish the medicine man or his animals any harm. We sent Love and Light and gave him the chance to accept it. Our compassion for his circumstances was real. Sincerely, I do hope he was aware of the return of his curse. I do hope he got back in touch with his loving energies so he could continue to help himself and those who relied upon him. But then, that is his choice. It always has been and always will be.

～

Tom's situation reminds me that there is always a bigger picture inviting us to broaden our perspective. His intentions at the medical clinic were in earnest, and he diligently dove into his mission of helping and healing. That the clinic would divide the village and appear threatening to the local shaman was beyond Tom's initial awareness.

Upon realizing the impact of the clinic, Tom was open to working together, but that option was unacceptable to the medicine man. Tom dug in his heels, proclaiming his right to stay. But he felt badly about it. Once he had a glimpse of the bigger picture, he was questioning the advisability of the project. By the time he felt threatened enough to leave, he was actively encouraging his supervisors to reconsider their mission.

Tom felt guilty about his ignorance, guilty about his inability to work with the medicine man, and guilty about being part of a mission that seemed to be creating a hurtful situation. Although none of these things were expressly his "fault," he tended to take responsibility for the outcome. This is what opened him up to the menacing energies sent by the shaman. As Tom accessed a bigger picture, he did something even more damaging: he beat himself up for not having seen things sooner! I wasn't surprised when he mentioned back problems. Many times, we will "stab ourselves in the back" with our guilt, possibly creating health problems in the mid-back region between the shoulder blades.

Tom also put himself in an ironic paradox: he blamed himself for not having enough personal power while at the same time fearing that he might have too much! He felt inadequate and ineffective in his ability to remedy the situation in Africa before he left, blaming himself for lack of power. He also felt he was the cause of illnesses and loss of girlfriends and pets, taking responsibility for an abundance of power. He had created a kind of straightjacket for himself with his guilt, feeling at fault because he couldn't do enough, and because he did too much!

The way out of this predicament, of course, was forgiveness. One of Tom's lessons throughout this experience seemed to focus on accepting that all things happening around him were not his fault nor within his power to control. The villagers, the medicine man, and the people who hired Tom all had their parts to play. His girlfriends, even his dogs, on some level, had agreed to be with him for reasons and lessons of their own. All he could do was act with integrity according to his best awareness at the time.

After our session, I had no doubt that he would assess what is and is not within his control, and he would make more choices guiltlessly—for the Highest Good of everyone concerned. He would be a better emissary in the future because of his willingness to learn from past experiences.

Points to Remember...

- To protect ourselves from attracting an entity or having an entity latch itself onto us, we can surround ourselves with a White screen, only letting in those energies that are for the Highest Good.

- On a body-mind level, the drain on our energies may show up in our solar plexus region—the Power Center. The guilt-ridden "stab in the back" may be reflected in the region between the shoulder blades.

- No one can curse or hex us unless we are open to taking it on through guilt, fear, incompletion and lack of boundaries.

- Not all negative energies manifest as disincarnate souls. Although less tangible, their influence must still be addressed.

- Even though we might have dreams of one or more ghosts around us, they do not, in and of themselves, prove that we have attracted unwanted attention from the spirit world. The dreams might signify unresolved issues trying to "catch" our attention.

- We are responsible for releasing guilt and setting our own boundaries.

Chapter 16

Family Patterns

Occasionally, I will be working with a client, doing some healing to address physical or emotional symptoms, and I will unexpectedly pick up on the presence of a spirit. The client may not be aware of any ghostly energies hanging around. There may be few, if any, overt signs of an entity. No objects are being displaced, no doors are opening and closing, no beds are shaking in the night. Yet, I will sense the influence of a spirit who has passed on.

Such was the case with Gloria, who came to me seeking counseling, healing, and help in addressing her current relationship difficulties.

Parent and Child

"Steve, I've been having a real hard time in my marriage," Gloria begins our session. "I know Bill and I agreed when we first got together that I would support him on his self-employment. We agreed that he should do his best to follow his dream, but things haven't been working out so great."

Gloria has been married for five years. In her early thirties, she has a two year old girl and is pregnant with her second child. Her worries are mostly financial, but they are affecting her relationship with her husband.

She lets out a long sigh of exasperation and continues. "We're a little strapped for money right now. I feel real guilty about pushing Bill to make more money, but what can I do?" She's almost pleading with me, as if I can snap my fingers and get her husband to generate more earnings. "I know he loves me. And he's got a good heart, but I can't keep working extra hours to take care of him. I've got the kids to think about…."

She trails off at this point, waiting for me to say something. Knowing that I can't magically resolve their relationship issues right here and now, I decide to focus on her tendency to take care of others. If she can release the tension and guilt about speaking up for herself, then there is a much better chance she and Bill can communicate honestly. They would both then be able to resolve things more quickly, easily, and lovingly. I go right to the heart of the matter.

"Gloria," I lean forward and look her directly in the eyes. "Do you have a pattern of taking care of others, of being a caretaker?" Silence on her part. "Has there been anyone else you feel you've taken care of at your own expense?"

Her soft brown eyes glaze over for a moment and then clear up as if she has made an internal decision to explore the pattern. She talks to me of a past relationship in which her boyfriend was cheating on her. Knowing he was sleeping with someone else, she couldn't bring herself to confront him. She had felt unworthy of demanding monogamy from him, and so she let her needs, wants and feelings go unspoken.

While we are talking, I sense a presence enter her space—just a little blurring in the air around her. I interrupt her. "What happened to him, Gloria? Is he still alive? How did you split up?"

She looks down at the floor, accessing memories. "I don't know where he is now. Last I heard, he was still alive. We had been seeing each other for almost a year, and I thought things were pretty serious between us. I suspected he was messing around, but I thought if I could just be nice enough, if I could meet all of his needs, he would give her up. But then one night I bumped into him at a restaurant. He was there with this other woman!" Her anger starts surfacing. "I just couldn't keep my mouth shut after that. I got real angry at him. We talked the next day. I confronted him, gave him an ultimatum, and stormed out of there. Well, the next day he called me to say that it would be better if we didn't see each other anymore."

The blurring in the air around her is getting darker, thicker, almost tangible. Gloria may even be feeling it because she starts physically shrinking into herself, hunching her shoulders and pulling her arms in across her stomach. She turns and glances over her shoulder as if she senses someone watching her. I keep pushing forward, hoping to discover and heal any past experiences that are contributing to the present pattern of limiting energy.

"Gloria, that must have been real tough. You finally spoke up, and then you were shot down. But I'm sensing a whole history of being taken advantage of and being taken for granted. It feels bigger than one or two incidents here and there. Did you have anything earlier in life where you felt the same?"

"YES!" She almost jumps up out of the chair as her hand comes down from overhead and hits the table in front of us. "My dad! I felt the same way around my dad!" She goes on to explain that she grew up with an alcoholic father who was emotionally and verbally abusive. "I guess you could say I grew up with a Cinderella complex. Everyone else got to have a good time. My father, my mother, my sister; they all got what they wanted, but I had to stay home and clean. It seemed like I was always the one to get in trouble. My little sister was perfect. Growing up, she was always busy doing things, having friends over, getting out of the house to do stuff. But I was stuck there, having to put up with a lot of crap from my dad."

The air around her seems to be taking on the form of a dark, angry cloud. Her voice falters, her breath loses strength.

"Did you ever resolve things with your dad?"

She leans forward at this point, a slight sneer curling her lip in uncharacteristic bitterness. "Yeah! We resolved things! He died when I was seventeen."

That isn't exactly the answer I am looking for, so I ask her point blank, "Did you ever talk with him about the way he treated you? Did you ever confront him on his behavior? What I really want to know is…did you end that pattern of abuse with him before he passed on?"

"No. I never stood up to him, never told him how I felt." The bitterness is gone. Now she is almost whimpering.

"You were only seventeen, Gloria. But now you're a grown woman. Now you know that you don't have to fear that anger. We can move past this. Are you ready?"

"Yes!"

"Then let's do it…"

I ask her to sit up straight on a bench I use for healing as I brief her on the procedure. "I'll be doing some energy work around your navel area. On a body/mind level, the navel relates to your psychic connection with your parents, the metaphysical equivalent of the umbilical cord." As I talk, she relaxes. I make the work we'll be doing sound as routine as possible even though I really never know exactly what to expect. But I trust Guidance, and I'm being urged to continue. "I'll also be working on the back of your neck, the place where we connect on a thought level with others and where we are sometimes prone to taking on others' negative judgements. We'll go a step farther in completing the relationship between you and your dad. Is that okay?"

She nods and settles into the bench more comfortably.

"Now, breathe deeply and relax.…"

I place my hands gently on her shoulders, rocking her slightly to and fro. She continues to breathe, relaxing with each outbreath. "Mother-Father God…" I almost whisper the invocation, setting the sacred space.

Matching my breath with hers, I slip into trance, connecting with her energy at all times. "Gloria, what was you father's full name?"

"Cameron Elliot Croft."

"Good. Now let's call on him, although he may already be here.

"We'd like to call on Cameron Elliot Croft. We'd like Cameron Croft's presence here, please. Cameron, please come and talk with us. Mr. Elliot, we only want to talk." I know I'm avoiding the whole truth here. We really want to do more than just talk, but I need to make it safe for him to listen to us. What he does after we talk will still be his choice, but I need to call him here first.

I had almost forgotten about the cloud that surrounded Gloria earlier. But now it suddenly detaches itself from around her head and shoulders. It moves about two feet in front of us and turns around!

We got him! Wow, he is one big guy! Instantly I greet him, eager to keep things moving. "Welcome, Mr. Elliot. I'm glad we could all meet at this time." The cloud just hangs there expectantly.

"Gloria, your dad is standing in front of us now. See yourself connected to him by a gold cord extending from your navel to his… That's it. And a silver cord from the back of your neck looping around to connect with the back of his neck... Good."

Cameron recognizes the connection we've just made. He realizes that he is still, and always has been connected with his daughter. I sense uncertainty from him. Fright, shame, embarrassment, then anger. *Ugh. That's sulfur I smell! It smells toxic, like smoldering waste, pent up emotions festering in the soul.* He starts to withdraw, to shrink in upon himself.

"Wait!" I say forcefully. "Wait! We need to talk with you. Your daughter needs your help. She's been having some problems in her life and needs your help."

I feel Gloria almost flinch under my hands. She doesn't want to be here, doesn't want to be near this angry, hurtful man. I whisper to her. "Stay with me, Gloria. Let me talk with him. Just project the words I use, along with the feelings, straight to him. Let me help you take care of this. Trust me. Trust yourself. He can't hurt you anymore, not here, not now." She relaxes once more.

I turn back to Cameron. "Gloria's been having some problems lately. She's attracted abusive relationships in the past, people who would take advantage of her."

"What's that to me?" I hear him reply. *"It's her life. She can do what she wants."* The anger and defiance oozing from him is palpable, forming a moat around him to keep us away.

"We're asking for your help here, man! By God, Cameron, she's been your daughter for over thirty years! Please bear with us."

"So what?" he replies. *"You can go on, but make it quick. Don't waste my time."*

"Gloria's been having a problem communicating with her husband, Bill. She needs to take care of her kids better. And she's been trying to get Bill to take more responsibility. But he keeps coming up with excuses, reasons for not contributing more, and promises that are never fulfilled. She wants to confront him but needs your help...."

I feel the love and Light of Spirit flow through me in the midst of this man's pain. Healing. We must go for the healing. I deepen my trance state.

Whispering to Gloria, "Gloria, I'll speak for you a little bit here. Just send the thoughts and feelings to him with Love and Light."

"Dad, I've never learned how to say 'no' to anyone. I love Bill, but I'm afraid if I say 'No, I won't take care of you anymore,' that he'll leave. I'm scared, Daddy. I loved you. You were my dad. But I was so angry with you that I couldn't even talk. I wanted to kill you sometimes. You purposely made me feel so inadequate."

Cameron's energy starts to fade, but I continue relentlessly. He needs to hear this. And Gloria needs to say it, even if it IS through my mouth. "I hated you, Daddy, but I also loved you. You were my father. It was getting near the time when I was going to be leaving home. Oh, God, I so much wanted to tell you off, to get you to stop embarrassing me and making me feel bad. But I was afraid of your anger. I was afraid you'd kick me out before I was ready. I was afraid I'd lose you, even though we weren't close. I was so afraid I would lose you. And then I did, Daddy. You died on me."

Gloria starts to cry quietly. I continue, not wanting to drag this on anymore than is necessary.

"Daddy, I never got to say 'stop it!' I wanted to so many times. But what could I do? I was just a kid, a scared teenager. My space wasn't my own. I couldn't leave because I didn't have the money, and I wasn't old enough. I couldn't stand up to you because you'd just start yelling, doing your best to put me down. You were always more powerful than me, Daddy."

Cameron's making a face—disgust, boredom, disappointment. "Tough luck, Cameron. You're stuck listening to this. She's older now, and she needs to say this to feel more complete, to get on with her life and to let you go. This can help you, too, even if you don't realize it yet."

"I couldn't even talk about my feelings, Daddy. You'd just give me that face to shut me up. I didn't have my own thoughts, my own feelings. I didn't have my space, my privacy. You were always there, judging me. I need to let that go, Daddy. I need to let that go now! Please try to understand, Daddy!" I find myself almost pleading with him, praying that he will respond with some kind of compassion. And then his heart visibly softens. The bilious green pool around him dissolves as he takes in Gloria's words. *"Thanks for caring enough to listen this time, Cameron. You can help a lot now,"* I project to him.

To Gloria I whisper, "He hears us, Gloria. He finally hears us."

I continue her words to Cameron. "Daddy, I've got to let you go. I've been carrying you around with me for years. It's all I can do sometimes to stop being afraid that others will judge me wrong if I talk about my feelings. But they're MY feelings, Dad. They're mine! And they're important to me!

"I forgive myself for not standing up to you earlier. I forgive you for being so scared that you felt you needed to control me. I realize now that I was trying to save you. I was avoiding making you feel bad. You'd get down on me, but you'd also feel bad. I thought that if I could just save you, if I could keep you from ever being angry with me, you'd turn around and love me more. But I couldn't, Daddy. I couldn't."

I'm almost sobbing with Gloria's words and feelings that are channeling through me. Gloria IS sobbing. "I couldn't," she cries aloud. "I couldn't!"

To Gloria I say, "Know that his pain is HIS, Gloria. Sometimes people set it up to feel the anger, pain, and sadness. Sometimes they have to wait until it gets bad enough in order to have the motivation to change. That means that the pain, anger, and sadness are part of the healing process. Let your dad have it back, Gloria. You've been holding on to it for him far too long.

"He has a right to it. Only he can heal it. It's not up to you anymore. Everyone is healing themselves at the perfect time, in the perfect form. This is just his way. He WILL heal. Give him a chance."

I see Cameron reach out tenderly to caress her cheek. But he pulls back, embarrassed. "It's okay, Cameron. It's never too late to love someone…."

Turning back to Gloria, I continue. "Think of how badly he must have felt about himself in order to make other people feel so bad. See him as a scared little kid, Gloria. That frightened child is still inside of him. It's a lot easier to forgive a scared little kid than it is to forgive an angry adult. You can do it. You deserve to forgive him for yourself, for your life and happiness."

I resume speaking to Cameron for Gloria. "Daddy, I know someone robbed you of your power long ago. I know that because that's why you kept trying to get power from me, from mom, and from sis. But you've got to get your power back from whoever stole it from you in the first place. Look to Spirit, Daddy. Look to the Light for that. They can help you. You're dead, Daddy. You're dead. And I need to move on with my life. I need to finally say 'goodbye.' And you can go on to Spirit for help, for healing…"

It's time to move toward completion. I take a focusing breath and give Gloria specific instructions. "Gloria, if there's anything else you want to say to him, if there's anything else you need to communicate, say it now…with love and forgiveness…and POWER! See him hearing you. Speak with the certainty of your own heart. Just think the words to him. He'll get them. Then, if there's anything you think he truly wanted to say to you from a loving space, but never had a chance, see him, hear him saying it now…"

I give them a few moments, and then I gently squeeze her shoulders where my hands have rested the entire time.

"Gloria. We need to say goodbye to him now."

I continue with words for her. "Daddy, I love you, I bless you, and I release you. I need to push you to the Light, Daddy. This doesn't have to be a final goodbye. But you need to go to Spirit first. You need to say goodbye now. Then, if it's right, sometime later, you can always come back to say hello. But you've got to leave now. We are no longer father and daughter. We are just two people in Spirit, two souls just trying to do our best to learn and to live and to grow. Goodbye, Daddy…"

"Gloria, I'm going to put my hand on your abdomen now. Take a real deep breath and hold it… good. Now tighten those muscles up. Tighten them up hard. Push them against my hand. And when you let go of the breath, take any energy of his that you've been carrying around, reach in, pull it out, and give it back to him. At the same time, cut the cord at the navel that's been connecting you for so long. Sever it! Use scissors, a sword, or some dynamite. Just cut it and let your breath blow it away…"

Gloria releases her breath in a sudden gush, and I feel the foreign energy moving away, out of her body and into the Light. Her abdominal muscles relax. "Feel the healing breath, the healing energies filling that area. Feel the freedom…

"Now take another deep breath and hold it. Hold it tight and squeeze your eyes closed." I put one hand on her forehead, another behind her neck. "Squeeze them kind of hard. And when you let go of the breath, relax, and we'll cut the cord at the back of your neck." I grab on to some of her hair, pulling it slightly. "Now let it go, Gloria. Let it go!"

She slumps forward on the bench as she releases the energy. She did it. She let her dad go. The dark, strangling energy is no longer binding her.

Gloria cries a little longer, but I can't tell if it's sadness or relief. Neither can she.

Gloria's story is a good example of how undesirable patterns in our life may reflect a limiting thought or belief we have adopted and continue to carry with us. In this case, Gloria embraced the role of caretaker at a young age, doing her best to please others at the expense of her own feelings. She did not want to risk being rejected nor abandoned, so she pushed aside her own wants and needs. She wanted to save her father from his own guilt and anger, so she resolved to be impossibly good. Feeling abused and powerless, she watched her father pass on with a mixture of guilt, anger, and relief. But she never stood up to him. She never claimed her right to fulfill her own needs. She never really let go of the energy that her father brought to their relationship. So familiar, in fact, was this energy to her, she did not realize the hold it had on her, even after her father's passing.

In the healing process, it was important for Gloria to go back to that paternal relationship with new awareness and a commitment to healing herself. As in the previous stories involving personal ghosts, Gloria needed to be involved in sending her father's spirit on to the Light. Because her dad was abusive, and because he himself did not yet seem to have the insight needed to move beyond his controlling stance, we went through a process of cutting the cords connecting these two souls as father and daughter.

Parent-child bonds are typically seen on an energy level as one cord running between the navel of the two beings and another running between the backs of their neck. In most cases, these cords form at the time two souls embrace a parent-child relationship. They remain intact throughout the death of one or the other, continuing until, on a spirit level, one or both beings decide to sever them. Typically, such a bond feels supportive, helpful, and loving. When a parent passes on and the child is filled with fond memories of warmth and encouragement, the connection is healthy. When the parent and child feel complete in their communications, when they have realized acceptance and forgiveness, the connection is healthy. With healthy connections, the disembodied soul is free to go to the Light while still connected to, but complete with, the child. In Gloria's case, however, this connection with her father was unhealthy and destructive.

Cutting the cords with her father, first of all, freed Gloria to move out from under the influence of this man's dominance. She acknowledged her love for him but also identified her hatred of his anger and mistreatment. There was certainty in her willingness to let him go. In effect, Gloria was saying, "I am no longer living my life as your daughter. I am a free spirit, my own person. I am independent of you." Secondly, severing the cords freed her father. It was time for him to go to the Light where lessons awaited; he would learn more quickly about love, forgiveness, and understanding in the close company of spirit guides. Hanging around Gloria, fueling his own inadequacies by continuing to convince her of her shortcomings, was only hurting both of them. Gloria realized this before he did, though, so she made the first move to let go, to quit taking on her father's pain and sadness, to surrender her father to the Light.

When a loving parent passes on, letting go of him or her is rarely easy. We often still long for the encouragement and support that were so tangible during the person's lifetime. But it is that shared love and respect that prompt us to bid them a safe journey into the Light. We would not want to hold them back from a resting place of peace and reconciliation with other loved ones who have passed on. Ironically, letting go of an abusive, angry parent may, in many cases, be far more challenging. Still craving their approval and support, we may continue to play out a self-defeating pattern in our struggle to earn their love. We agonize over the lack of support until, like

Gloria, we are ready to move toward healthier ways of giving and receiving love. Fortunately, Spirit endures. It is never too late to heal.

Unborn Child and Parent

Similar to the process of releasing a parent who has passed on, I work with clients to cut the cords with an unborn child. Before doing this, however, it is important to process some of the emotions around the potential birth and the resultant passing of the child. Whether the termination of a pregnancy is planned or unexpected, the result is the same: two souls come together, forge a link for purposes of growth, and then choose different paths. After the physical separation, they continue to help one another become more aware of personal lessons bringing the relationship to a new level of completion. We neither condone nor condemn abortions; those issues are best left to one's personal, religious, and spiritual beliefs. We are here not to judge whether an abortion is right or wrong, but to help heal the individuals involved after the baby has passed on.

My work with Bonnie provides a good example of the ongoing process of release and renewal. Coming to see me about her relationship with her husband, she thought she had put a teenage abortion behind her long ago. It quickly became apparent, though, that the energy of the baby was still with her. Bonnie was going through life feeling guilty, openly allowing her space to be invaded by others, unsure about deserving to get her own needs met. Now in her early thirties, she was ready to make some different choices for herself. Together, we began the process of cutting the cords with the unborn child.

"Do you know if that baby was male or female?" I ask Bonnie.

"A girl, I think. I've always felt she was a girl."

"Okay. Great! Imagine that baby in front of you right now, a healthy, happy little girl. See yourself connected to her with a gold cord running from your navel to hers. See a silver cord coming out the back of your neck, looping around to connect at the back of her neck. Can you see it?"

"Yes. Oh, she's so beautiful, Steve…"

"Of course she is. Just as you are to her, Bonnie. And both of you deserve to be free. Thank her for coming, Bonnie. And know that it was HER choice to connect with you in the first place. Her soul made the agreement with total awareness. She wanted to help you, just as you would also be helping her. You were, and are, in this together, even at this time of letting go."

I feel Bonnie relaxing, trusting, acknowledging the wisdom of Spirit. "I'll be talking with the baby, Bonnie, and I want you to relay the messages silently to her as I say them aloud. Just stay with me and put your feelings behind the words. She'll get them. She'll hear you."

I feel Bonnie nod as I take a breath and focus on the baby. "Thanks for coming, both now and so many years ago." As I speak the words for Bonnie, I feel a subtle shift as her energy joins in the channeling. "I'm sorry that we couldn't have this life together at this time, but I'm glad you could join me, no matter how briefly. You came to me during a very hard time in my life. I was having trouble in my relationship with your father, Kerry. We weren't even sure we wanted to stay together.

"I know I really wanted a child, but it just wasn't the time. It was hard for me to let go of you, but I felt I just needed to. I was young. I didn't know what I wanted. I didn't even know where the next meal was coming from, or the rent. I was scared.

"Thank you for helping me to commit more to my own life rather than committing to someone else's. I know it didn't work completely. I did realize, after the abortion, that I needed to take care of myself. I left Kerry and I got a better job. Making those changes worked, at least back then. I'm sorry if it was sad and painful for you, but I guess I really needed to wake up to life. I needed to take care of myself.

"To have you with me then would have been horrible. I couldn't take care of Kerry. I couldn't take care of myself. And I wouldn't have been able to take care of you either, at least in the right way. Letting you go was actually what seemed the best for all of us." Bonnie's shoulders shake under my hands as I feel her long-ago sadness. This was not a decision she had made lightly.

"I know I didn't learn that lesson completely. I STILL take care of others. You know I'm married right now, to Wade. We love each other, but he can be so domineering at times. It feels like he wants to control me sometimes. We're working on it. I know I've had my part in it. I've just supported him on whatever he wants. I have never said what I want. I was happy to do that for a long time. But now I realize I've been living in his shadow, still taking care of other people instead of myself.

"I need to learn that lesson again. I think he still loves me enough to support me on my strengths. I guess I'll see. But I've got to take care of myself, and I'm ready to ask him to help me do that. I DO love you, and I realize now how you've helped me be aware of all this. But you can't just keep hanging out, trying to help.

"Letting go of you earlier helped me at that time in committing to my own life, my own space. And I need to let you go again, only this time even more. You can't help anymore. I know it's taken me a while to really forgive myself for not being able to take care of you. But now I understand. Now I see how much your coming AND your going have led me to be more aware of my own needs. I promise to take care of myself again, without the guilt this time. I'm sorry it took a lot of pain and sadness for me to learn this lesson the first time around. But it doesn't have to be that way anymore. You and I both deserve to get more of what we need and want."

Bonnie has stopped shaking, her shoulders under my hands feeling stronger, more resolved. With Guidance at my side, I continue.

"If it's right for you to come in as another child of mine, then so be it. If it's right for you to be with others, then I'm sure they'll be very happy. I know it's up to you, just as it was up to you to be with me then, and now. But I need to let you go. I need to push you into the Light. I know it's a little selfish, but I guess I'm learning how to be selfish in a healthy way. I need to be able to take care of myself first. Only then can I be here for others and support *them* on taking care of themselves."

I lean down to speak softly in Bonnie's ear. "Bonnie, if there's anything else you need to say to her in order to let her go, say it now. Send it to her with Love and Light. If there's anything you need to tell her in order to assure her that you'll take care of yourself, do so now. Just send the thoughts and feelings to her. She'll get it…Let me know when you're done…"

After several minutes, she lets out a long sigh and nods her head. "Done," she states with finality.

I speak to the child once again, gently, apologetically, lovingly. "I need to let you go now. I need to say goodbye. I love you. I bless you. I release you to the Light. You need to go to the Light now. Seek guidance in the Light. You'll know how and when to help others, and yourself. Just look to the Light."

I take Bonnie through the steps of cutting the cords. First she breathes into the abdomen, holding the breath until she's ready to let go. As she lets go of the breath, she cuts the cord at her navel and heals the opening. With another breath she cuts the cord at the back of her neck. Together, we push the baby to the Light, surrounding her with Light, until there's nothing left but Light.

Still basking in the glow, Bonnie acknowledges the necessity of taking care of herself, and she vows to do that in loving ways. She'll be more aware of the pattern she's had of giving up her space to someone else. And she'll take it back more gently, more lovingly, without the pain, anger, sadness, and guilt.

Finally, I encourage Bonnie to enfold herself in the Light, feeling her eternal connection with Spirit. She can know that we are ALL children of God. In the grand scheme of things, we are all here but for a short time upon the Earth to live, to grow, to learn, and to love.

Ancestors and Descendants

The psychic cords, although always present between biological parent and child, may also be present between a surrogate parent and child. The cords may be present between the child and whichever family member may have been instrumental in raising him or her. These surrogates may include a grandparent, uncle, aunt, stepparent, foster or adoptive parent, or even a much older brother or sister. The need for cutting the psychic cords with a surrogate parent is an important consideration in the healing.

In rare cases, we can cut the cords with someone who is still alive, but this is done in only two circumstances. The first situation pertains to the parent or child being terminally ill and close to death. The second situation pertains to the parent or child being abusive to themselves and/or others. When all means of trying to resolve the situation have failed, when the relationship is so unhealthy that separation becomes necessary, we can cut the parent-child cords. This does not necessarily sever the relationship between the two but, rather, redefines it. The relationship is no longer between parent and child, but between two "people."

Points to Remember…

- ✧ By cutting the gold cord at the navel and the silver cord at the back of the neck, we redefine the parent-child relationship.
- ✧ In Spirit, there is no parent-child relationship. We are merely teaching, learning from, and sharing with one another.
- ✧ By focusing on our *own* healing, we naturally create healing opportunities for others.

Chapter 17

Boundaries

The tendency to attract earthbound Spirits is not limited to people whose parent, child, or loved one has passed on. It can extend to anyone, particularly to those who have let go of their boundaries, those who may have a deeply ingrained thought that "my space is not my own." There are many situations and life experiences that often contribute to this limiting belief.

An isolated or neglected child growing up with minimal attention may spend a great deal of time in his own little world. As he naturally searches for companionship and connection, he may encounter the world of spirit. If people have been unavailable or unsafe to be with, then maybe spirits are safer! The child then gives up his space and unwittingly opens a doorway for disembodied friends.

Additionally, a child growing up in an enmeshed family may be prone to the same limiting thought, "my space is not my own." In such a family there are few, if any, psychic boundaries. When one person is experiencing a strong feeling, the domino effect takes hold and the emotion travels along to every member of the family. If Dad comes home from work feeling angry and disgruntled, by the end of the evening Mom and children are also irritable and annoyed. If Mom is feeling depressed and hopeless, then Dad and the kids find themselves discouraged and pessimistic about life, too. Whatever the dominant emotion, the whole family takes it on without distinction of ownership.

Children in this situation may grow up without permission to feel their own feelings because they are expected, instead, to feel whatever someone else is projecting. They are not allowed to be happy or excited for themselves. For instance, if Dad is angry about his circumstances, no one else should be too happy. If Dad is elated, no one else in the household may be allowed to feel sad. Without the emotional and psychic boundaries, the child loses the ability to distinguish himself from others. It is drummed into his head that he is NOT the authority in his own life. Instead, he sways with the emotional tide of those more powerful around him. His space, emotionally and psychically, is not his own.

Traumas can have a similar effect, as can drug or alcohol abuse. An emotional and/or physical shock, or continued substance abuse, opens up a person's space. Either circumstance causes a person to leave his body to one degree or another, "jumping out of his skin," so to speak. This may be recognized by a sense of detachment, as if the everyday events around him are unreal or in slow motion. The energy that once occupied his body is no longer there, leaving a void that the universe is anxious to fill. In spiritual or shamanic terms this can be referred to as "soul loss." A person who is not completely in his body is ripe for attracting someone or something to fill in the empty space, opening the doorway to spirit attachments.

A physically and/or sexually abused child will often have the tendency to attract unwanted attention from the world of spirit, both at the time of abuse and later in life. Not only is his emotional and psychic space not his own, but now his body, his physical space has been violated. Overpowered, the child has perhaps even learned to survive by allowing intrusions to come and go without a fight.

As this exploited child grows into adulthood with the thought that he does not have, nor deserve, his own space, he will often attract relationships that are intrusive and disrespectful. Then, with people crowding in on him, he decides to reclaim his space aggressively, followed by guilt if someone has been hurt during the power struggle. Conflict ensues. This is evident with people who manifest one abusive relationship after another. They are trying to heal themselves through current relationships, creating the patterns over and over again as they struggle to regain their power.

The high emotional charge, the sense of vulnerability to outside forces, and the belief that it is unsafe to be in one's own body may all attract the attention of spirits. In addition, entities from the spirit world may feel free to float about with little loyalty toward the person to whom they have attached. Ghosts are attracted to high-energy emotional situations, especially anger. Aggressive, controlling people are therefore ghost magnets. By extending their personal space to overpower others, they give up their boundaries, inadvertently attracting ghosts. When we think of someone walking around with a "dark cloud hanging over his head," we may be perceiving one or more entities hovering around him. A spirit may even transfer its attachment to someone else if another susceptible person comes along. In other words, if we are open to attracting ghosts, we can actually "pick one up" from an angry person who hosts them. Like a cold or virus, if we continue close contact with the dis-eased person, and if our own immune system is fragile, we can catch the illness.

All of these scenarios have the same resolution within the healing process. A person needs to get rid of any spirits who have attached themselves, and he needs to close the open door that has invited the violation in the first place. By paying attention to unwanted patterns in his life, by continually assessing his feelings, and by moving toward forgiveness and completion, he can end the habit of giving up his own space. Committed to claiming his own life, asserting authority over it and setting healthy boundaries, he becomes free.

My Space Is My Own

Robbie was not a complainer. Resilient and caring, she provided a foster home for teenage boys along with raising her own son in the single-parent household she had worked hard to establish. Life was sometimes tough, but Robbie prided herself on being tougher.

"But I think I need your help now, Steve." Not an easy thing, I gathered, for this high-spirited woman to admit. "I've got a flood of paranormal activity going on...." Robbie went on to report noises coming from the kitchen in the middle of the night. Cabinets, even the refrigerator, would apparently open and close. Yet, upon getting up to investigate several times, the house was quiet with everyone sleeping soundly in his own bed.

Additionally, the delicate tinkling of a small wind chime hanging in the hallway, well away from doorways and drafts, was heard at different times during the night. Robbie finally contacted me when she felt someone staring at her while she was lounging on the sofa watching television.

"It feels like a benevolent spirit, Robbie," I told her when I first entered the house. "I sense a woman, somewhat lost and confused, but otherwise harmless."

A sigh of relief escaped as Robbie began to feel safe. "Then we don't need to do anything about it, right? I mean, if she's not a problem, then I can live with it."

"Sorry," I apologized gently. "But for a spirit to hang around, she's got to get her energy from somewhere, and that may be from you or your kids. And we don't want that. Besides, we can make the spirit more comfortable by sending her on to a better place."

She almost looked disappointed, as if the ghost had become a fast friend. We went over the benefits of claiming her space as well as the importance and responsibility of helping the spirit onward. With less regret and more understanding, Robbie was ready to start the work.

The spirit, Annie, was a middle-aged woman whose own children had been taken away from her. She had not been allowed to care for them and had died, seemingly of grief, shortly afterward. Having never completed in helping her own children grow up, she had naturally been drawn to Robbie's group-living situation. She was there to help.

Robbie and I led Annie through the process of forgiving herself for letting go of her own children. We reminded her that her kids did, indeed, grow up to be fine people and that they had lived full lives before passing on many years ago. Now, we explained, Robbie needed to learn how to take care of the kids under her roof herself, and she was getting plenty of help from friends and family. She had chosen this lifestyle and needed to prove to herself that she could do it herself.

"Annie, your kids are waiting for you in Spirit," we conveyed to her. "There is nothing standing in your way now. Others forgive you, and they know that you really did love your children. They trust you with them now. You need to go to loved ones in the Light."

Annie completed her journey quickly, easily, and gratefully. It was so easy! The work felt right. It felt complete...until I got a call from Robbie several weeks later.

"Steve! I need you real bad! Things were quiet for a couple of weeks, but then I started feeling weird. The noises all stopped. Well, all of them except the wind chime. But I've been having some scary dreams." I interrupted, not wanting her to work herself into a frenzy of fear and helplessness.

"Robbie! Listen to me. The worst thing you can do is to give up your power to this situation. You don't want a spirit to think it's really got you running scared. They might feed on that and act out more. Since you haven't been hurt...."

"That's just it, Steve!" It was her turn to interrupt my rebuke. "The dreams were all about a man coming into the house. He would break through the front door and just stand there looking around. A few nights ago, I dreamed he was standing over my bed, and I woke up sweating and scared. Then last night I was asleep and felt my bed shaking. I thought it was one of my kids teasing me. But then the covers were ripped off of me. I screamed and turned on the light, but no one was there. God, Steve, I'm even afraid of going to bed now!"

That sounded kind of extreme. Plus, I don't like it when there's more than one ghost present. Maybe I didn't notice this guy when I was there the first time, or maybe Robbie got herself a new one. Either way, it can point to a person's pattern of attracting ghosts, of attracting unwanted people into her space. I canceled my appointments for the morning and went right over.

This time the clearing was a little more involved. The second ghost was an angry man who had lived in the area. His wife killed him when he had abused her and the children one too many times. He was angry at all women, still trying to take his power back. As a child he had grown up being mistreated, and he had continued the fight. Robbie, who took in neglected or abused children and protected them, was a natural target for his anger.

"This woman is NOT your wife!" I almost screamed at him during trance. "You're dead, and your wife is dead as well. Robbie is not the object of your anger!" As the clearing continued, we assured him that his own abusive parent was in Spirit waiting to apologize, waiting to make amends. He didn't believe us at first, but we convinced him that the only way to find out was to go to Spirit.

"Go to the Light. Find your power in the Light. Find the peace you've been looking for. There's nothing for you here. This isn't your wife. These aren't your kids. They all have lives of their own. Go to the Light. Get help in finding your family and in healing yourself. You need to leave these people alone now. It's best that you do this by choice now, since you already know you can't stay." That got through to him—helping him to realize that there was more power in choosing to leave than there was in waiting until he HAD to leave.

After completing the second clearing it was time to talk with Robbie about some of my suspicions. There were too many patterns to ignore. As it turns out, yes, Robbie did have a history of abuse. Her ex-husband had just dropped by a week earlier. She had divorced him because she was tired of constantly having to protect herself and her son from his abuse. He had ignored the court's most recent restraining order and would be going to jail this time.

Robbie and I talked about how she could claim her space and take her own power back from her ex-husband. She readily agreed to carry out some exercises and to do some healing on those issues. When she came for some personal follow-up counseling over the next few weeks, she shared that after experiencing the White Heart Meditation relating to her ex-husband, she began to feel much more in control of her physical and emotional space. She was able to see that it was HIS choice to violate her space and HIS choice to provoke the consequences. Finally forgiving herself for him ending up in jail, she was on the road to setting better personal boundaries without feeling guilty.

Things had quieted down in her household—everything was quiet except for an occasional tinkling of the wind chime. "It's not bothersome, Steve. It even feels kind of friendly." She was happy when I told her not to worry about it. If it felt good, it could be a spirit teacher, a helper, even a friend saying hello. She could take it as a reminder of her own growth.

Robbie and her household seemed to be back on track. Having reached her goal of stopping the hauntings, we discontinued the private therapy. One of the foster children moved out. Her son, Spencer, moved to a downstairs bedroom—a big step for him even though he was already twelve years old. Life was moving on at a steady pace. But then another foster child moved in, disrupting the status quo. Spencer felt ignored, "dethroned" if you will, and became angry. He still had his own room, but the new kid was getting "far too much attention."

Robbie called me for some advice on parenting, and we discussed it at length. She would need to stay on top of setting personal boundaries for herself—not only with her son, but with the recent arrival as well. She needed to reassure Spencer that there was enough love to go around.

Wanting to do her best, she took the advice to heart and acted on it immediately. She gave Spencer more responsibility at home, but with more privileges to go along with the jobs. She started spending more quality time with him, and the situation became more loving. Spencer was still angry at losing his father and sharing his mother with these "strangers," but he was more appropriate in expressing that anger. His grades in school picked up, and he was following through with responsibilities at home on a regular basis. Peace was achieved.

Five weeks later Robbie was notified by one of Spencer's teachers that he was falling asleep in school. He was starting to get behind on his schoolwork again and seemed apathetic. Concerned, Robbie helped him more with his work, let up on some of his responsibilities at home, and scheduled more study time. She also addressed his diet to make sure he was eating healthier foods and enforced an earlier curfew so he would get the rest he needed. He was seeing a counselor at the time, and things seemed to get back to normal once again.

Things were not as normal as Robbie had hoped. One morning she realized that Spencer's habit of occasionally falling asleep on the living room couch was getting out of hand. There were mornings, she knew, when he would creep back to bed and fall asleep in his room. But here he was again this morning, sleeping right on the couch when he should be getting ready for school!

Until that time, Robbie had not shared her previous ghost experiences with Spencer for fear of frightening him. But now she needed to approach the subject. As she told him of the two ghosts we had taken care of, he became increasingly

Chapter 17 Boundaries

agitated, then relieved! He'd had several bad dreams and, once, the covers on his bed were ripped off of him in the middle of the night. He'd even heard someone laughing but, when he turned on the light, no one was there! Lying wide awake in the middle of the night, he'd felt not only scared, but stupid as well. Restful sleep over the last few weeks had become impossible. This was the first time he had talked with anyone about these strange occurrences.

That's when Robbie called. Could I please come over again and take care of the problem?

"No, Robbie. I need to talk with you first, privately, so we can decide the best way to approach this. Tell Spencer that I'll be over in a few days to take care of things, and that he shouldn't be too concerned right now. He's safe. We WILL take care of it, but I need to talk with you first."

That was agreeable, and Robbie came the very next day, which was commendable since it reflected her willingness to resolve the situation.

As we talked, a bit more of her history came out. Over the years, she had gotten into the habit of letting Spencer sleep in the same bed with her. This was allowed when her husband was out late and she suspected he would come home drunk and abusive. She had feared for her own safety and that of Spencer. Yet, when the mother and son were together, the husband did not cause trouble for either one.

Spencer's move downstairs had been well accepted at first, even enjoyed. But, increasingly, he felt insecure about having his own space. With the ousting of Dad, he had also lost his role of protecting Mom, leaving him questioning his importance in the family. Additionally, with Mom setting firmer limits, he felt ignored and shut out.

Talking with Robbie, we uncovered a fear of hers that she would be abusive like her dad and her ex-husband. Yes, she was taking care of herself more easily, setting better boundaries, and following through on consequences more consistently with the children. Spencer would then accuse her of being "unfair and mean," and the old guilt would take hold, leaving Robbie blaming herself for being abusive. She would sheepishly let go of her boundaries and stop encouraging her son to be responsible for his feelings and his space.

The two of them were seesawing between being angry with one another and being overly protective of one another.

When the anger escalated, Spencer took on his mother's tradition of attracting spirits. This current entity harassing Spencer could have been one of the same spirits returning or a new entity who had entered the house. Maybe the spirit had been there all along but kept a low profile when we did the clearings. We'd find out.

First, Spencer and his mom met with me a couple of times to talk about their living situation. We discussed how his mom needed to take care of herself. And, out of respect for him and his strengths, she needed to encourage him to take care of himself. We explored different ways for Spencer to resolve his sadness and anger. He acknowledged that Robbie had grown stronger and was better able to take care of herself. He no longer needed to give up his space or deny his own needs in order to take care of her or to let her take care of him. He could also redefine his relationship with his dad, choosing not to see him if it didn't feel safe. He didn't have to "give up his space" in order to take care of Dad, either.

The first step was for Spencer to tell the ghost to go away and leave him alone. He tried it for a couple of nights and things changed, but only slightly. The covers were no longer being ripped off his bed. At times, though, the bed would still shake, and Spencer would hear quiet laughter from the corner of his room.

Spencer was motivated and willing to claim his space, but needed help in doing so. We could now take care of the problem—hopefully for the last time. We met at their house for another clearing, and this time Spencer was invited. Even though I usually prefer to exclude children from the ritual, he needed to be there to put his energy into getting rid of the ghost.

As it turns out, the entity was a teenager who had been in the house all along. He had been an orphan while alive, shuffled from one foster home to another. Dying in a car accident, with nowhere to go and no one to call family, he went to the nearest foster home. He went to a place where he could feel comfortable with the people living there.

He really wasn't a mean spirit, just a young man being a trickster. He liked to rile things up a bit and watch the results. He actually thought he was being a friend to Spencer. We affirmed Spencer's ability to take care of himself. We affirmed Robbie's choice to limit the number of children she would take under her roof. And we assured him that Spencer had the willingness and ability to make more friends, ones that were living, not dead.

Encouraging the spirit to find friends and family in the Light, we sent him on.

This time we spent a few more minutes checking the entire house for any earthbound spirits who might still be there. We asked, challenged, then dared any others to let themselves be known, but none were found.

Following the clearing, Spencer started seeing a counselor on a regular basis to help him sort things out. The situation never became as bad as it had been, and he made good use of the support offered. Robbie got back to her part-time arts and crafts business. Foster children, some short-term, some long-term, came and went with only minor problems. The ex-husband kept his distance and didn't violate their space again. A healthy environment had been attained.

Several years later Robbie called, thanking me for all the help she'd received. She had moved out of town and was living in another part of the state. She was in a wonderful relationship with a gentle man. Spencer was doing great. And she really didn't mind the occasional middle-of-the-night jingle of the indoor wind chime.

Points to Remember…

- ✧ Limiting patterns control us only if we decide to hold onto them.
- ✧ We can't change past experiences, but we can change how we presently respond to those experiences.
- ✧ We close the door to intrusions by claiming our space.
- ✧ We can accept into our space only those people who support us on maintaining healthy boundaries.

Part V

Journey's End

Chapter 18

Completion

Throughout our work, whether it is with disembodied spirits, people who attract ghosts or those who are making the transition between life and death, we have encountered lessons of completion. We use the term "completion" when referring to a state of being in which a soul, residing within a body or without, is at peace with itself, others, and the world. Completion means there is no obligation left ignored, nothing tugging at the edges of our attention, nothing awaiting resolution. Being complete allows us to relax with contentment in the present moment.

The flip side of completion is, of course, a state of *in*completion. When we are feeling incomplete about something, a part of our focus and energy is preoccupied, digging and scratching at whatever the concern might be. We approach present matters and future possibilities with limited awareness because our attention is divided. As so many of the disembodied spirits in this book have demonstrated, we may even turn our back on the Light as we occupy ourselves with whatever feels left undone.

Perhaps the greatest irony about completion is that it is never finished! There is no end. Being the interactive, interconnected bundles of energy that we are, experiencing life means bumping into, communicating with, and sometimes emotionally prodding or pushing each other. Being in a state of completion, therefore, becomes an *ongoing* process. It is an approach to life, a commitment to clearing up our communications and following through on what we feel are our responsibilities.

By constantly and consciously moving *toward* completion, we declare our willingness to be more aware of our thoughts, feelings and behaviors. With more awareness, we notice those situations about which we feel incomplete: the anger or guilt we haven't acknowledged, the forgiveness we've refused to offer or accept, the resentment and blame we are holding onto. As incomplete interactions rise to the forefront, we are then faced with choices about whether, when, and how to complete them to free ourselves of responsibility. Completing past and present interactions, we clear the path for greater choices about our future.

Maintaining Healthy Boundaries

We all have varying traumas in our life. We all feel anger, loss, and an abundance of strong emotions. We are all, at different times and throughout different circumstances in our lives, potentially vulnerable to spirits paying us a visit. Fortunately, however, most of us do not leave the door open and indiscriminately invite them in. We do not hold onto a thought that our space is not our own, that violation is the norm, that we are victims of others who are more powerful.

Instead, we heal our wounds and close the door to any unwanted energies. We claim our space by:

- being committed to movement and growth
- connecting with our emotions and shedding our anger and guilt
- examining the patterns of our life within relationships and changing those patterns which don't work
- caring about our physical health and paying attention when our body is trying to tell us something
- noticing the limitations in our thoughts, the times we think we are unloving or unloved, and intentionally working to change those thoughts
- acknowledging that WE are the authority in our lives

As we consciously strive to maintain healthy boundaries and to honor our own space, we close the door to other people who do not support us on our journey. This we do out of love and respect for ourselves, realizing that we deserve to be surrounded by those who accept and nourish our healing. No longer do we spend time with people who strive to discourage us, belittle us, or control us. No longer do we share our space with those who seek to meet their needs at our expense.

When we are committed to ending some of the deep patterns of trauma and pain, intrusive energies are no longer drawn toward us. When we are ready to heal, we, instead, attract the right helpers to support us along the way. Help takes many forms and is equally available to everyone. For one person, a book he reads may give him the motivation or insight needed. For another it may be a prayer she hears in church, a vivid dream, or the whisper of guiding spirits in a sweat lodge. For yet another, help may come in the form of a psychologist, rabbi or friend. Spirit guides us, patiently awaiting our willingness and our faith.

Our space is our own. We can decide to love it, cherish it, maintain it. With respect toward ourselves and others, we gently but firmly attract only those energies that support us in our healing.

Communication

With a willingness to honor our thoughts and feelings for purposes of healing, we can communicate as honestly, lovingly, and openly as possible. We can share our own personal truths, our own perceptions. Because they are based upon our uniquely individual experience of the world, they are *always* valid. We are all enriched when our understanding is broadened by another's sharing from the heart.

One simple guideline in staying complete with communications is to express ourselves with honesty *and* compassion. Both are necessary, for honesty without compassion is cruelty, and compassion without honesty is pity. To communicate only one or the other is disrespectful and inhibits growth. Difficult truths are more easily accepted when they are expressed with kindness and genuine caring. Although simple in concept, we often struggle to do this in our daily lives. At times, since we are all just learning our lessons, we do say things vehemently out of fear, anger, and pain. Likewise, we may speak with gentleness but hold back on candor. Neither approach allows us to express our truth fully, with respect and understanding. Nor does it allow the other person the greatest chance of hearing us. A state of incompletion ensues. It is then in our best interest to further our communications, with honesty and compassion, reattaining the state of completion.

Forgiveness of Self and Others

If we are truly seeking a state of completion, then we must also have the willingness to release our hurt, anger, and resentment toward others for whatever they have done, or for whatever we *think* they have done. This is the process of forgiveness. When we acknowledge the fear and the feeling of powerlessness behind others' purposeful or inadvertent acts of cruelty, it is much easier to muster compassion. It is this compassion that moves us into the grace of forgiveness.

No one can *make* us feel a certain way. People say and do things, some of which may be hurtful. Yet, they are responsible for what they choose to do, and they will experience the consequences of their behavior. Our reaction, however, is our choice. We may feel angry because of misinterpreting another's intent or because of our own personal sensitivities. But we have our own choices about what to do with those feelings: hold onto them or get past them, letting them go.

Owning our own feelings is one of the most personally empowering things we can do. Honoring and respecting our feelings helps us choose healthier relationships with ourselves and others. Being honest with ourselves, we can decide to move away from an uncomfortable circumstance, redefine a relationship, leave a dissatisfying job, and so on. We are in charge! When we blame another person, institution, organization or circumstance for our feelings, we have given away our personal power and have become victims. Letting go of blaming others for how we feel and acknowledging our ability to make new choices are surefire ways to reclaim the power that is rightfully ours. Therefore, we forgive others not because *they* deserve it but because *we* deserve it! We deserve to be free of pain! We deserve to be empowered! We deserve to be in a state of completion!

Additionally, blaming ourselves for our feelings is equally powerless and leads to self-pity. Self-deprecation is a sign that we have not yet fully embraced our power, responsibility, and love. Accepting responsibility without blaming ourselves or others keeps our communications open, clear, and healing. We can acknowledge the hurt, pain, and suffering we *think* we have caused others, whether accidentally or intentionally, and then step forward to communicate or do whatever is within our power to rectify the situation. In this way we avoid the self-induced stupor of guilt, accept and forgive ourselves, and move on.

Let Go and Let God

Not everything that happens to us, that touches us, that interacts with us is within our control. We are, however, in charge of how we react. How we choose to interpret and feel about an event, what we resolve to express to others, and what we decide to do to take care of ourselves are all within our power. Thus, we can forgive ourselves even when someone else decides not to forgive us. We can communicate even when others choose not to. We can be honest and compassionate even if someone else wants to be dishonest and vengeful. We can heal ourselves even if those around us choose not to heal. Simply put, we can complete with others whether or not they complete with us. We can be in a state of completion even if others are not. Once we have given one hundred percent in trying to communicate clearly and honestly, realizing we neither control others nor their feelings, we can then let go. We can relax in a state of completion because we have done our best. We are then complete within ourselves. The outcome we leave up to God.

Keeping in mind the above components of communication and forgiveness, we are now ready to commit to moving toward completion. We can begin by reviewing our past to see if there are any situations begging for attention. "Who am I still feeling badly about hurting? Is there anything I have not communicated to loved ones which, if they died today, I would regret having held back? Is there anyone I have wanted to acknowledge, thank, confront, or be honest with? Is there something about which I am feeling guilt, regret or shame?"

We can then take action to complete our communications. A person can call, write, email, send a fax, or do whatever he needs to do to express himself with honesty, compassion, and responsibility. If we don't know where to reach someone, we can write a letter and burn it or rip it up and throw it out, trusting that the energy will reach the other person. If we don't want to reopen a relationship, we can send a letter without a return address. We can be as creative as we want to as long as we hold in our mind, the entire time, our intent to communicate with honesty and compassion for the purpose of healing. How the other person responds is, again, not within our control. We have let go, reclaiming our power. Everything else we put up to the Light. WE are choosing to be complete whether anyone else wants to or not.

Although it is more tangible to communicate with someone who is still embodied, it is never too late to complete on the past. Throughout this book we have shared communications with souls who are in transition or who have already passed on. Intent is everything, and if we speak from our heart to another spirit, he or she will get the message even if his/her awareness is outside the body.

When we have finished our communications from the past (taking days, weeks or months to be thorough), we can thank ourselves. On a daily basis, we then find it unnerving to let communications slide by, possibly creating new, unresolved issues with others. With determination, we can start each day with a clean slate, affirming our commitment to continually remain in a state of completion. What a wonderful gift we have just given ourselves!

Chapter 19

Together in Spirit

Spirit journeys. We each embark upon our own adventure, stepping into this physical realm to create, experience, and remember who we are. Our interactions and relationships with one another provide continual lessons along the way, giving us opportunities to choose and rechoose who we want to be. As we reach out to forgive and complete upon our responsibilities toward others, we discover, in the process, that we have helped *ourselves* become more loving. As we strive to forgive ourselves and respect our own needs, feelings, and worthiness, we discover, in the process, that we have helped *others* become more loving. The destination is the same for all of us.

No matter where we are in our journey, Spirit brings us together and provides for us whatever our soul needs to experience. Each of us is exactly where we need to be, encountering exactly what we are ready to confront, exercising our free will to choose our behavior. Whether still in the body, just moving beyond the body, or long disembodied, our souls crave the same permission to forgive and to let go, moving forward with greater love and awareness.

And so it is upon this journey that we, the authors, have been brought face-to-face with disembodied spirits. These souls are our teachers, our healers, a gift to us from Spirit. They continue to awaken us to compassion and forgiveness, responsibility and completion. We have chosen to approach them with an open heart, allowing them to inspire our trust in each other, in life, and in Spirit. Sharing their stories is our gift to you.

We are in this life together, and together we can reach the state of completion. If we or others we know become earthbound, lost or confused during transition, we trust that someone like you has the courage and loving intent to help us complete the journey.

Goodbye and God bless. We love you. We bless you. We release you.

Appendices

Appendix A

An Overview: Elements of Completion

When helping souls make the transition from earthly existence into the Light, there are several important pieces of information we can share with these spirits. Although we have highlighted these throughout different stories in previous chapters, we reiterate them here for easy reference. Should you ever encounter an earthbound spirit or find yourself participating in a ghost clearing, these simple ideas are a good reminder of what you can convey to aid in the healing.

By having the willingness and intent to heal, and the certainty that Spirit is guiding you, your contribution can help create a greater atmosphere of love and acceptance for everyone involved.

House Ghosts

Clear statements directed toward spirits can help clearings proceed.

You're dead.   Let the spirit know that he or she no longer exists in a body. You may need to point out that many years have passed and that time has gone by on the earth plane while he or she was occupied with personal concerns. Life in that body, that lifetime, is over. "Loved ones have also died. The people in this house are NOT your family. They are not people you knew before. They are not your concern!"

Your responsibilities here are over.   Remind souls that they no longer have any earthly obligations. Not only are they free to go, but it is time for them to go. There is nothing else for them to do here. If a spirit still wants to stick around, wanting to be helpful to others, urge him or her to go to the Light first to learn better ways of helping. "Those people still embodied on earth need to access their own inner resources. They may need to accept support from those people still on the earth."

You're forgiven for what you did or didn't do. No matter what a spirit thinks he did or didn't do that hurt others, let him know that those people have long forgiven him. "Others have passed on. They now understand your choices and forgive you for your actions. They want you to know you are not being blamed. The people living here forgive you as well."

Loved ones (or ancestors) are waiting for you in the Light. Everyone who has come into a life on Earth has known love from someone. Remind an earthbound spirit that love awaits him or her upon reuniting with others in Spirit. Even if a soul thinks he is undeserving of love, remind him that others are anxious for reconciliation. We can also increase the entity's trust by being culturally sensitive and using terms familiar to him or her whenever possible. Not all spirits go to the Light, but there is ALWAYS a welcoming, loving energy eager to embrace departing souls. Guidance on the journey may be recognized as the Light, ancestors and loved ones, angels or other Spirit teachers, the Creator, or another form which may be dictated by the departing soul's belief system.

We love you, bless you, and release you to the Light (or to your ancestors). Finally, let go! Affirm to the spirit that he continues his journey with our love and blessings. "We have no hold on you here. We do not wish to delay your transition any longer." Say goodbye and urge him toward the Light.

In the name of Spirit. For stubborn ghosts who refuse to move on, do a bit more counseling. If necessary assert your self more aggressively, "In the name of Spirit (God, Jesus, The Highest Good, The Light, The Great Spirit) we command you (any entities that do not belong here) to be gone! I call on the Love and Protection of Spirit..." This is usually not necessary, but may work as a last resort.

Trust yourself. Be creative! Use whatever it takes to get a ghost to agree to move on. "You deserve peace… You are needed in the Light… We understand your dilemma… Further healing awaits…" Know that Spirit will take care of the rest.

Personal Ghosts

When working with someone who has attracted a personal ghost, have the living person communicate all of the preceding points, even silently. Additionally, try the following statements:

- ✧ "You now have a different path than I do."
- ✧ "I need to learn my lessons on my own, and turn to others around me for support."
- ✧ "I forgive myself for holding onto you since you passed on."
- ✧ "I want you to go."

For those people who have lost a loved one, have them take a few minutes completing any unfinished communications.

- ✧ Anything that was left unsaid can be expressed now.
- ✧ Anything that was said in anger can now be communicated with love, acceptance, and understanding.
- ✧ "I love you. I bless you. I release you."

The bereaved person may experience the grief anew, as if the loved one passed on yesterday instead of years ago. The bereaved may experience sadness, pain, anger, and hurt. For the next several days those feelings may surface, seemingly out of nowhere, and be gone within seconds. This is a healthy release of pent-up energy and is usually temporary. If it does not diminish, further grief work can be done.

There is always a personal connection between the living and the personal ghost that has attached itself to that person, whether the entity is a loved one or a total stranger. Exploring and completing that relationship is imperative to the healing.

The Dying

People in the last stages of a terminal illness, or those who are comatose, may be treated like personal ghosts. We communicate directly to the soul, helping him or her feel more complete with lessons in the present. However, since the person is still connected to the physical body, his choices need to be affirmed. He may either learn the lessons and move on to Spirit, or learn the lessons and come back, seating himself more firmly in the body.

The object here is not to help someone die but, rather, to assist the person in letting go of pain and suffering. Reevaluating responsibilities, forgiving himself and others, and moving forward on unfinished communications all clarify the person's choices. "I promise to relay any messages to other loved ones still here, so that they too may feel complete." Reaching a deeper state of completion, the loved ones will let go of the ill person. Reaching a state of completion and being willing to move out of stasis, the ill person will go on to more life…either in Spirit or in this lifetime.

Points to Remember…

- ✧ Always ask a loved one for permission to help. "Are you ready to say goodbye?"

- ✧ Ask the soul of the ill person if you may help. It is at this time especially that they need love, understanding, and acceptance. Their choices need to be honored.

- ✧ Accept the outcome, affirming the wisdom of Spirit.

Appendix B

The Healer and Client in Trance

The trance state is necessary—whether you are a healer, counselor, or layperson—in order to move your focus beyond the body and communicate effectively with disembodied souls.

The Healer in Trance

Healers can achieve the trance state through the following techniques:

- Self-hypnosis
- Drumming or listening to drumming
- Prayer, meditation, and deep breathing

Drugs are used in some cultures. They are NOT recommended because they force the trance state, are harsh and potentially addictive, and can easily get out of control.

The Client in Trance

Clients need to keep the following points in mind regarding trances:

House Ghosts. It is not always necessary for the homeowner or those present to be in trance. It is, however, desirable that everyone present participates in creating the sacred space and communicating their support for the spirit to move onward.

Personal Ghosts. Clients with personal ghosts almost always need to attain the trance state. This facilitates communication, not only with the spirit entity, but also with the client's deeper levels of awareness—subconscious and Spiritual.

Approaches to Trance

The metaphysician may use a variety of methods to induce trance. This can be done through hands-on work with the client, self-hypnosis, drumming or listening to drumming, or prayer with meditation and deep breathing.

The counselor may bring the client through hypnosis, taking him or her through the steps of the clearing: invocation, protection, communication, and releasement.

Before proceeding with a trance, ensure that

- ✧ The client gets in touch with his or her safe place, the power spot, first.
- ✧ Conversation with the entity happens at the edge of that place with the client inside and the entity outside.
- ✧ The client is "okay" with setting boundaries. This process can take a minute or, in some cases, several counseling sessions.

Points to Remember…

- ✧ The White Heart Meditation and channeling Love and Light can aid in the process of making the forgiveness more tangible.
- ✧ Some Spiritual healers prefer to interact with only the spirit entity who is attached to the person. The client merely needs to be receptive and to hold the intent of receiving the healing and releasing any spirits.

Appendix C

Guidelines for Clearings

 Following is a condensed listing of reminders for healers and metaphysicians who perform clearings.

1. **Create the Sacred Space**

    A. The Invocation
    Always call on the protection and Guidance of Spirit.

    B. The Circle
    Hold hands to create one powerful unit with the people involved. Envision a white screen or filter surrounding each participant and the group.

    C. Center
    Breathe deeply to build your personal power, increase energy, and focus your thoughts.

    D. Affirmation
    Affirm the power and certainty of the healer and client throughout the work.

    Additional methods include

    - ✧ "warding" the space with crystals pointing in the four directions
    - ✧ cleansing the space with holy water, frankincense and myrrh, or smudge

2. **Induce the Trance State**

3. **Maintain Boundaries**
   - Keep channeling Love and Light.
   - Stay focused on the intent of releasing the spirit(s).
   - Call on Guidance whenever necessary.

4. **Continue with the Steps to Completion**
   - You're dead.
   - Your responsibilities here are over.
   - You are forgiven for what you did or didn't do.
   - Loved ones (ancestors) are waiting for you (in the Light).
   - We love you, bless you, and release you to the Light (or to your ancestors).

5. **Accept Support**
   - Power in numbers

     If someone has been hurt by the entity, do NOT do the clearing alone.

   - Refer out

     If the work becomes too scary or complicated, apologize to the entity, tell the spirit that he needs to keep his distance, and affirm the continued safety and boundaries of both the client and healer. Call in a practitioner who is more experienced and certain.

   - Network

     A metaphysical bookstore usually has a referral list where practitioners may be found. Get references. The metaphysician, counselor, and client CAN work together for the good of all concerned.

APPENDIX D

Questions and Answers

Are there evil spirits who do not deserve to go to the Light?

If you call someone "evil," you have already judged him or her. There are spirits who are selfish, greedy, angry, and inconsiderate of others. However, it is not up to us to judge how much suffering they should endure. Everyone is deserving of peace and forgiveness.

Are there demons?

I have run across lower level astral entities, beings with little or no awareness. Their sole function seems to be that of draining a person's energy. But I personally would not classify them as demons because, once again, this may lead to labeling them as "evil." They are also called poltergeists and may be sent to the Light or, with love and forgiveness, back from whence they came.

What is the difference between earthbound spirits, guardian angels and Spirit Guides?

An earthbound spirit is still emotionally tied to the Earth, often with limited awareness, and tends to drain us of energy. Spirit Guides get their energy from Spirit and pass it along. Having risen above earthly concerns, they have greatly expanded awareness and approach us with only unconditional love.

Some people consider guardian angels as personal guides, here to help protect us. In this context, many guardian angels may be loved ones who have passed on, but with expanded awareness. Angels, on the other hand, can be considered to be more like Spirit Guides, but with even higher energy, awareness, and intent. I consider them to be the Spirit Guides' Guide.

Can a disembodied spirit make you do something against your will?

No! A spirit may influence your thoughts and feelings, but it can only effect those thoughts and feelings already present within you. Free will is the gift, and the responsibility, of every individual.

Is a "mentally ill" person possessed? What if he hears voices?

Many mentally ill people do attract ghosts to "haunt" them. The voices may be hallucinations, or they could point to the presence of an entity. Getting rid of any earthbound spirit would help the person, but the open doorway that attracted the spirit must also be closed to prevent any further intrusions. Counseling and therapy may be helpful in many situations.

My brother committed suicide. Can he still go to the Light?

Those people who approach transition with love and forgiveness, in a state of completion, move on peacefully. Those who make the transition with anger, resentment, and unresolved issues may get lost and confused. They may become earthbound or trapped in a state of existence "between worlds"—what some may refer to as purgatory. It is not a question of whether the Light turns them away, but whether they turn away from the Light.

Can you help entities who speak a different language?

Verbal language is but one means of communication. Much more information is often conveyed visually and emotionally. Pictures and feelings are universal in meaning, making it possible for two souls to communicate beyond words.

What will happen to earthbound spirits who do not receive help completing their journey?

Eventually, something in the spirit's environment will change, awakening the spirit to a higher level of understanding, awareness, and choices.

If someone thinks he has a ghost around him but doesn't, how do you treat that situation?

When the presence of a house ghost is questionable, we first cleanse the area of any past psychic impressions, replacing them with Love and Light. A ghost clearing may follow if necessary. In regards to a nonexistent personal ghost, we help the person complete any important unresolved issues from the past. We may, however, do the clearing anyway, acting as if there is actually a ghost present. This would make the work more tangible, helping him clear any intrusive thoughts and release any limiting parts of himself. Whether dealing with a house or personal ghost, the person is encouraged and taught to set boundaries and claim his space, closing the door to possible intrusions.

I used both smudge AND holy water to get rid of my house ghost. Why didn't that work?

With prayer, these techniques sometimes do work. However, you need to help the ghost feel complete and understand that there is somewhere else to go. Otherwise, he may come back days or weeks later, even more determined to let his presence be known.

Can the phenomena often connected with a ghost's presence be attributed to a person's kinetic ability—moving or affecting objects with one's own mind?

In rare cases, some people do exhibit an ability to affect objects with their mind. This is usually done unconsciously and happens due to an internal build-up of one's own psychic, emotional, and electrical energy. The overflowing energy may sporadically "leak out" and most commonly interrupts surrounding electrical currents. In the majority of cases where this phenomenon is demonstrated, the person does not have a ghost present. However, helping the person resolve emotional conflict and consciously release excess energy usually takes care of the problem.

My daughter has an imaginary friend. Could this be a ghost? Should I be concerned?

Many children have imaginary friends, some of whom may be ghosts. There is no cause for concern unless the child uses this situation to escape responsibility for her own actions and feelings. If it becomes a problem, the parent and child need to explore what needs are being fulfilled by the presence of that "friend." Seek to meet those needs in healthier, more tangible ways.

Can a baby or young child with no concept of guilt and forgiveness attract a ghost?

There are spirits around us much of the time, and babies, being especially connected to the world of Spirit, see those entities. Yet, rarely will the baby have a ghost attach itself to him or her. It is up to us as parents to provide a loving, nonintrusive environment for the child. Any ghost who may be attracted to the child is considered to be attached to the parent and family as well, and it must be dealt with accordingly.

I've heard of energy vortexes. What are they?

An energy vortex is a geographical location where energy is attracted and collects. There are different types of vortexes, some of which may be considered "gateways" to Spirit. Earthbound spirits may be attracted to the increased energy and can be helped from there to complete the journey toward the Light.

I'm neither a psychic nor a therapist, but I'd like to help. Can anybody do this type of work?

You can always bless others, surrounding them with Love and Light. With simple cases and cooperative spirits, this work can be done with minimal training. Yet, any healing must still be for the Highest Good of all concerned. For more complicated cases, call a professional. Perhaps you can sit in on the session. Your energy will help, especially if the client is someone with whom you are close.

About the Authors

Steven & Marcia Rogat

Steven's work as a healer, counselor, and metaphysical consultant has brought messages of awareness and hope to thousands of people throughout the years. A gifted clairvoyant, popular radio personality, and burgeoning author, he is well known for helping others look at themselves and their relationships with love, Light, and humor. He continues to offer seminars, lectures, and private appointments to those in search of personal insight and physical and emotional healing.

In addition to working alongside her husband, Marcia is a teacher, counselor, and educational consultant. She regards her keen intuition and sense of humor as survival skills honed during a quarter century of working with teenagers, teachers, and parents. A national trainer in healthy sexuality education, diversity awareness, and conflict resolution, she enjoys writing, speaking, and offering seminars to promote healing and inspire personal growth.

Also available by Steven Rogat

Healing Thoughts:
Applying Therapeutic Shamanism in Your Daily Life
Creative Thought Press, 2002
www.CreativeThought.org